Inside :

INSIDE

Voices from Death Row

Michael J. Braxton
Tessie Castillo
Lyle C. May
Terry Robinson
George T. Wilkerson

Edited by Tessie Castillo

Greensboro 2022
Scuppernong Editions

Inside: Voices from Death Row

Foreword

I had the pleasure of meeting two *Inside: Voices from Death Row* coauthors, Tessie Castillo and Lyle May, at a virtual event hosted by the Greensboro Bound Literary Festival in June 2020. Lyle, who has served twenty-two years on North Carolina's Death Row, called into the meeting from prison with an unforgettable message.

"We are human beings," he reminded the audience. "People on Death Row who have been essentially thrown away by society, we are human beings—many of whom have made mistakes, some of whom are innocent, but we are all human beings far beyond what we used to be."

The audience listened in pin-drop silence as he continued.

"Prison is a place, an experience, a period of time in which to continue to grow, to develop, to age, to die. It is a very different place than any other, but it is still just a place where people continue to be people."

His words encapsulate the heart of what makes this book one of the most important literary treasures of our time. Rarely do we find such a gem in which insight, storytelling prowess, and decades of first-hand experience combine to offer a unique glimpse into life on Death Row. With accountability, reflection, and grace, the coauthors recount the searing stories of their lives before prison and where things went wrong. They reveal their extraordinary efforts to grow and to build meaningful lives, even under a death sentence. The transparency of their honesty draws us to their stories.

Most of us are privileged enough not to think about Death Row. The thousands of men and women who languish there are perhaps a vague concept in our minds. Perhaps we feel anger towards them or pity. But every day, throughout the country, human beings are sentenced to death by our government, in our names, and we don't even know who they are.

The coauthors of *Inside* have set out to bridge that disconnect, to foster closeness and relationship between people on Death Row and people outside. When we see the humanity of our incarcerated brothers and sisters, our assumptions and stereotypes are challenged. We too start to grow.

During our call, Lyle explained, "The stories in *Inside* help describe our influences, but some describe the present. They are about learning, finding out what it means to be human."

All of us, inside prison and out, participate in the extraordinary process of change throughout our lives. For many, change begins with a spark. In my earlier life, I never dreamed that I would get involved with people on Death Row or that I would write three books about those experiences. But in 1984, I witnessed the execution of Elmo Patrick Sonnier in Louisiana. I came out of the execution chamber in the middle of the night and threw up in the parking lot outside Angola prison. I remember thinking, *The American people are good people. If I can bring them close to what I have experienced, we can change society's consciousness.*

That moment outside Angola prison was my spark. Tessie's spark came when she taught a writing class on North Carolina's Death Row. *Inside: Voices from Death Row* lights a cascade of sparks by offering people the unique opportunity to connect with someone on Death Row—and not just through reading this book. The coauthors call into events from prison to converse with audiences about what brought them to Death Row, as well as their aspirations, inspirations, regrets, and hopes. Also, the free *Inside: Voices from Death Row* book club invites readers into virtual conversations with the coauthors and, often, into lasting friendships. When we engage with real people, the work becomes personal. Relationships light the path forward.

The stories in this book bring the trials and triumphs of people on Death Row into our homes and hearts. They help illuminate important truths and answer important questions: Who are the people on Death Row? What brought them there? Whom have they hurt? Who hurt them? How does one find hope and purpose under a death sentence?

Inside: Voices from Death Row, both the book and the speaker series, invites readers and audiences to explore these questions through conversations with real people on Death Row. I encourage you to join these important discussions by visiting tessiecastillo.com, where you can sign up for the book club or invite the coauthors to speak to your students, congregations, conferences, and audiences of all kinds. Perhaps you, too, will find your spark and discover the dignity and intrinsic worth of all human beings.

SISTER HELEN PREJEAN
Author of *Dead Man Walking: The Eyewitness Account of the Death Penalty That Sparked a National Debate*

Introduction

> If you are willing to get closer to people who are suffering,
> you will find the power to change the world.
>
> BRYAN STEVENSON

In 2013, an unexpected meeting at a Super Bowl party led to the opportunity of a lifetime—a chance to teach a writing class on Death Row. There I met my four coauthors, who are currently serving death sentences at Central Prison in Raleigh, North Carolina and we embarked on a mission to uplift the voices of incarcerated people.

Our first book, *Crimson Letters: Voices from Death Row*, hit shelves in March 2020. The book recounts my coauthors paths to prison and their search for hope and purpose under a death sentence. Within a week, the North Carolina Department of Public Safety banned the book from state prisons and confiscated copies from my coauthors' cells, but readers stepped forward in a show of enthusiasm that has surprised us all.

Locked down by a prison and a pandemic, we promoted *Crimson Letters* through virtual events at schools, conferences, churches, book clubs, and community groups. At each presentation, my coauthors called from prison for moving Q&A sessions with audience members. With deep vulnerability and insight, they spoke about what led them to prison and how they found and continue to find meaning on Death Row. Many who attended later joined our online book club for small-group conversations with each man, and they became regular volunteers, even friends.

Through these public conversations, we realized we had left out pieces of the story, parts we'd been afraid of confronting or exposing. Thoughtful questions from audience members teased out these tender or prickly stories. Eventually, my coauthors and I decided to write *Inside: Voices from Death Row* to fill in those missing pieces.

We want to acknowledge how these men came to Death Row and to honor the pain and loss suffered by victims and their families. All royalties from the sale of this book are donated to support crime victims and their families.

George Wilkerson was convicted of homicide in 2006 in Asheboro, North Carolina. He has been imprisoned for 17 years, since the age of 25.

Terry "Chanton" Robinson was convicted of homicide in 2000 in Wilson, North Carolina. He has been imprisoned for 23 years, since the age of 26.

Lyle May was convicted of homicide in 1999 in Asheville, North Carolina. He has been imprisoned for 25 years, since the age of 19.

Michael "Alim" Braxton was convicted of homicide in 1993 in Raleigh, North Carolina, and in 1997 in Tillery, North Carolina. He has been imprisoned for 29 years, since the age of 19.

We also want to acknowledge the harm that the criminal justice system causes to all those impacted by it, including those charged and convicted of crimes, victims, and the loved ones and communities of both. May we all work towards a system that is just.

Inside: Voices from Death Row expands upon our efforts to lift up incarcerated voices by combining the most moving and popular writings from *Crimson Letters* with over a dozen new, powerful essays and poems from the coauthors. Each new essay I contributed to this book presents a challenge or ethical dilemma I faced when working with men on Death Row. Whereas in *Crimson Letters* I often chose to avoid controversial issues by omission, *Inside* leans into these discomforts.

In addition to their work on *Crimson Letters* and *Inside*, my coauthors have accomplished remarkable feats. In the seven years we've been working together, they've written award-winning poetry books, recorded albums, and obtained degrees in higher education despite efforts of some prison officials to thwart them. More importantly, these men have overcome the scourges of poverty, racism, domestic violence, abuse, neglect, mental illness, and the ever-present specter of violence—and have grown into the accountable and introspective men they are today.

What motivated me to work with my coauthors? Witnessing their daily struggle to make positive choices, their constant self-reflection and recalculation, and their striving not just to realize dreams and talents but to become better people despite a death sentence. I wanted to honor these men's struggle toward betterment by making it visible, by making *them* visible.

The death penalty might not impact most people, but most people impact the death penalty—through silence, action or inaction, voting or not voting. This book, our speaking engagements, and book clubs allow my coauthors and I to rightfully represent the residents of Death Row as people with voices, opinions, and interests, rather than a shadowy, abstract population. We recognize that apathy, not malice, is the greatest menace to change and seek to foster emotional proximity and authentic relationships so people outside prison who can look away might choose not to.

Reading this book is a step toward overcoming the stereotypes that allow myth and caricature to flourish over truth and reckoning. Yet, the journey doesn't end here. When you've finished reading, George, Chanton, Alim, Lyle, and I invite you to join us for intimate conversation on justice, redemption, and humanity behind bars.

With gratitude,
TESSIE
May 2022

GEORGE T. WILKERSON

Court Kings and Flight Lessons

fifty or sixty of the back doors in the projects opened
onto the unwooded sides of a mini-park that doubled
as our broken playground: layers of gang graffiti
decorated our basketball court; our geodesic set
of monkey bars was missing many of its climbing limbs;
and one of our three swings was just two chains.
but, though bullet-dented, our slide was intact. in '93
my neighborhood crew lay claim to what we saw
as our inheritance: we owned that park. i first got
pukey-drunk there, swaying on those chains and stumbling
as i ran from cops into bordering woods where
cops stopped, unwilling to get lost in the darkness that swallowed me—
all on the same night, initiated in moonlight
into our 'hood the day i graduated
fifth grade. i was twelve.

that summer we judged our basketball goals
too high for us to dunk so we shinnied up
one of the poles and rocked it forward till it bent.
for months we got to be like Mike,
but that goal kept bowing
until it kissed the concrete at our feet.

that year the afterschool program
came outside to stage a strange activity.
a small team assembled a chicken wire cage,
eight feet per side, on our playground, in a grassy area free
of liquor bottles, Coke can crack pipes, and wadded condoms.

within it they erected a gnarly grayish slab of driftwood
they draped with plastic milkweed,
like a fake Christmas tree,
and stacked perforated brown boxes around its base.
high on real weed, i sat on a squeaky swing, idly
swaying and chain-smoking cigarettes i'd stolen
from Food Lion. from the program's apartment poured
about twenty excited elementary school kids and their mentors,
who straightaway opened the boxes. suddenly, the cage bloomed
with large, deep orange–winged butterflies. *Monarchs.*
above the lecture on larvae, pupae, imagoes,
and long-distance migrations on the scale of miracles
i could hear the hypnotic whispers of a thousand wings
beating against their neighbors and chicken wire
cage until they settled like tiger fur on their perches.

following the talk, using fat tongue depressors,
the mentors buttered sugar water onto bare
arms and legs of eager kids, then grabbed their wrists
and walked them two by two into "The Butterfly Room."
perhaps smelling the sweetness
of naïveté and innocence, those regal creatures
lit on them by the dozens, sipping
at caramel and chocolate skin. most stood there trembling
with giggles, though others spread wide their arms, crucified
by awe, and spun in slow, silent circles. a couple cried
in terror. but still
for a few moments
they all got to wear an otherworldly cloth that I could imagine
felt soft as silk and light
as the filaments God used
to weave my dreams with.

for hours afterward, when butterflies, cage, everything
was gone, kids pranced around like juvenile court jesters
harlequinned with patches of crusted sugar water glittering
on their skin.
i stood there smoking
cigarettes and pushing children
on the swings, squeaking them as high as i could
while daring them to launch their bodies into open air,
flapping and shouting, "I AM A MONARCH I AM
A MONARCH!" before they hit the earth,
tucked, rolled, got up, and ran
to the back of the line.

The Places In-Between

By the time I was six, my dad, Ronald, a soldier in the U.S. Army, had decided that he had chafed under the military's restrictive lifestyle long enough. He wanted to relax, settle down, own a business, and be a family man to his wife and four sons.

Against my mother's pleas and protests, he resigned from the Army just six years short of its lifelong retirement check and bought a Laundromat that soon paid half as much as a military stub. Then, it paid nothing; rather, it took everything. My mom has told me that money was the root of all their fights. I can almost hear her thinking, "I left Korea for *this*?"

Looking back, I agree with my mom that the Laundromat was a bad investment. It utilized aged machines that would soon need replacing. Neither was it self-sustaining or able to generate a profit to support a large, hungry family. On the plus side, it conflated home and work, generating a different type of currency in the form of quality family time.

In the lobby, where the machines wheezed and chugged and rattled as they spun, were several arcade games. Since we owned the games, pumping quarters into them was only a formality. The snick-snicking sounds a quarter made upon entering the skinny slot, the secret clicks and subsequent chink-chink of quarters dropping, enchanted me not only for their sound, but also because when the game sprang to life, so did my parents' faces.

As children, our moods depended on theirs. I was snicking quarters into the heart of my family.

Although we kids weren't any good at the games, my parents competed good-naturedly, talked trash to each other, swatted flirtatiously, and tickled whoever was playing. Winning was beside the point. Eventually, showing a respectable ability to win despite distraction, my mom became unbeatable. Or maybe my dad was happy letting her win.

I was too short to see the screen. When I wanted to play, my parents would slide a chair in front of the game for me to stand on. One of them would stand behind me, cradling my body with theirs. Their warm hands rode my own, guiding the joystick, letting me be a part of their competition. As my loyalties were divided, I won as much as I lost.

They laughed a lot back then. Even as our world began to crumble, they laughed, and we boys laughed with them.

It was the last period of our lives when I'd see them smile at each other.

One evening, when I was still six years old, my mother entered the family room after an argument with my dad. A purse dangled from a spaghetti strap on her shoulder.

"I go to store," she said in her Korean accent. "Boys want go with mamma?"

Shameless in our eagerness, we hopped off the sofa. We seldom got to go to the store. My dad glowered at us like we had betrayed him for siding with her. I avoided his eyes. Smug and defiant, my mom stood by the door as we hurried to put on our shoes and run out to the car.

At the store, while my mom shopped, we boys chased each other gleefully, playing tag in the aisles—until my younger brother Daniel stumbled and cracked his head open on a shelf.

Blood and screams poured out of him. He needed stitches.

As soon as we got home from the hospital, our parents sent us to bed. They argued for hours afterwards. Bleary-eyed at breakfast the next morning, our mom gently set bowls of cereal in front of us, repeatedly shushing us. A couple of minutes later our dad stepped into the room.

"Get up and come here," he ordered us.

"But dad, we're eating—"

"Now."

We sulked, but obeyed, clustering in front of him. He looked down at us cryptically, then peered past us at our mom. He unbuckled his belt, paused, then whispered it free of his jeans in one smooth pull. He folded it in half, then half again. He grabbed my older brother Mike's left arm, yanked him up on tiptoes, and swatted his butt a few times.

With the first hit, pandemonium erupted. Mike shrieked and we three younger brothers shrieked with him. My mom yelled for my dad to stop but made no move toward him. My dad's only response was to drop Mike and reach for me. I spun to run, and he caught my arm. I felt three thwaps. I cried more from fear than pain because it was the first time he had used a weapon on us.

Once he'd spanked all four of us, he said, "That's for going to the store. And playing. You play here at home, not at the store."

While I couldn't explain it then, I intuited new dimensions to his spankings. A subtext. Reasons in addition to, or disconnected from, obvious causes. His gaze had never left our mother, as if it were really her he had been spanking. And she cried as if it were true.

On a night shortly after that incident, my dad called me onto the front porch where he was smoking a cigarette. Everyone else was inside.

"C'mere, son," he said softly, motioning me close beside him. "Son, I have something to tell you..."

We sat hip to hip. He laid a heavy arm across my slender shoulders.

"I'm dying, son."

I stared up at his face, my six-year-old mind struggling to process what he'd said. I started crying. He pulled me to him.

"No, daddy, please, I don't want you to die." I sobbed into his hairy chest, my pleas muffled by it.

"Shh, shh, now, don't worry," he said. "I've still got some time."

Once he comforted me with numerous assurances, he made me swear not to tell my mom or brothers.

In the years that followed, he'd repeat this scene: gravely inform me of his impending death while I cried and begged him not to die, then he'd make me promise never to tell. And I didn't—until years later.

When, as a teenager, I finally broached the subject with my mom, she made a guttural sound and scrunched her brow in exasperation.

"You father is a lie," she said. "He not die. He only feel like he die because I divorce him."

She seemed sort of pleased by this.

Divorce was a declaration of war between my parents, turning them into generals of opposing armies that ripped our world apart. They fought over the hearts and minds of us kids—our loyalty—and like any war-torn and ravaged land, we bore the ugly marks of conflict. They had dual custody, so we were marched left and right between them, leaving bits and pieces of ourselves behind each time.

Eventually, it was clear that we kids loved our parents equally despite their efforts to make us choose a favorite, so my mom proposed a peace treaty: she wanted to take the younger two and go her separate way, leaving my older brother and me with my dad. He flat out refused, telling her she was fucking crazy to split up the boys like that. Rather, he wrote in stone that we four boys were to always remain together, either with her or with him.

That was when their war took on a new dimension. When Dad heard that Mom made us go to bed by nine, he'd let us stay up late until we fell over from exhaustion. Then, he'd just pick us up and carry his sad sack of shit to the nearest couch or bed, chuckling low to himself about how we were too weak to keep up with his insomnia.

As soon as she found out he let us eat all the junk food we wanted, she began pointing a sharp finger at us while saying in her broken English, "You be just like you fahdah—fat bum if you no stop eating junkkk."

She turned the last word into a disgusting sound as if trying to get the thought of it hocked up and spat out. Then, she forced us to eat every vegetable grown in the secret garden behind her house.

We kids were about the only thing our parents kept in common besides their hatred of each other. She hated him because he was a "fucking pig," a perpetual offense to her sensibilities. He hated her for not loving him forever no matter what, as she'd promised, and because he suspected she'd only married a soldier boy to escape the oppression in Korea.

She started putting on airs as if they were jackets, and he sunk into his savagery like it was a tar pit. They were two time-elapsed movies of evolution moving in opposite directions. He seemed to grow hairier and more slovenly. He went shirtless in winter and barefoot over gravel and broken glass, putting his cigarettes out with his bare heel. She raised her nose higher and stood up straighter. She dug dust from every corner of her polished floors on her hands and knees, accompanied by a bucket of suds and rags.

His violence grew in proportion to his gut—more overt, brutal, and volatile—as hers became more sophisticated. He'd ground and pound the living shit out of us in sudden explosions of rage while her artful criticisms, contemptuous looks, and snorts could be so sharp and slick, I'd barely register a thing at the time. Later, I'd feel an emptiness gathering within and a sensitive spot where insecurity was festering.

We were constant reminders of the absentee parent, whipped back and forth between them like sandpaper rubbing old wounds raw.

When I was six years old, my mom went to live in Minnesota with her sister.

After she left, dirty laundry, dishes, and dust in our dilapidated house piled up. Rather than elaborate Korean meals, our dinners consisted of baloney sandwiches, hot dogs, Ramen soup, and anything "instant." The spankings intensified, becoming more frequent and less predictable as my dad's ability to control himself frayed along with his mind.

My mom flew in to visit once a month. My dad kept begging her to come home, but she refused. Though their romance had failed, she was determined to be a good mother, which to her meant being a provider.

She'd visit, bearing baskets of clothes, groceries, toys, and an envelope of cash to help with bills.

She gave Mike, the oldest at eight, tutorials on how to cook and clean. This mirrored her own childhood: When her mom left her dad, she took over the role of caregiver for her three younger siblings while her dad descended into drunkenness and violence.

However, her own mother had brought no child support. Instead, my mom sometimes sang on Korean street corners for money—or went hungry.

After delivering her care packages, hugs, and kisses to us kids and weathering a thunderous argument with my dad, she would light out again. Her presence was as fleeting and enchanting as a fairy godmother.

In 1989, when I was eight, my mother remarried another soldier. That fall, we boys went to live with her in Fayetteville, North Carolina. Within months, her new husband was stationed in the Middle East, but not before he impregnated her.

My mother refused to tell my dad our address although legally they shared custody. My dad searched for us by coming to Fayetteville and driving everywhere around the city. Then, one day, he popped up at our school. He'd found us. We boys were excited to see him; our mom was not. She offered him a deal: if he promised not to take us out of school without her permission, if he promised not to show up at the house unannounced or fight her husband, she would bring us to see him regularly.

She had two more conditions. First, he could not live in Fayetteville, but could move to an adjoining town. Second, he had to beat us when she brought us to him. She claimed that she didn't want to strain herself while pregnant.

My dad readily agreed. He was willing to hurt us to love us.

Being rambunctious, quarrelsome, and clumsy enough to break things on accident, we boys merited frequent trips to dad's trailer for beatings. At least once a week, mom drove us there. Without a word, dad lined us up on the couch and beat us—all four of us, no matter who had committed the initial infraction. He claimed the shared pain would help keep us together. Our mother never told him what we'd done to provoke her anger, and he never asked. He'd stare at her while beating us and she'd stare back smugly.

After those beatings, she would leave us there for a few hours. After she'd left, he'd transform. Instead of telling us not to cry, he'd gather us in a hug and cry with us. He'd entertain us with raunchy jokes.

"What do you get when you cross an onion with a donkey? A piece of ass that brings tears to your eyes."

I was both drawn to my father and scared of him, like cocaine—or anything I've ever loved, for that matter.

Although we lived with our mom, we didn't spend much time with her. She was always busy cooking or cleaning or sleeping. However, in the evenings after dinner, she'd stretch out on the couch and watch TV, asking me to massage her warm, socked feet that smelled like baby powder.

My fingers would tire and ache, but I'd persist until her eyes closed and she drifted off to sleep. How many of those brief periods would it take to equal the hours we spent with our dad each week?

I lived in a perpetual state of homesickness, hungry for my mom's attention even though she was right there.

In 1991, when I was ten years old, my stepdad gave my mom an ultimatum: she either got rid of her sons or lost him.

He said we drove him nuts, and he couldn't afford to maintain their middle-class lifestyle and feed us too. I'd gotten used to living in a house and eating my mom's delicious cooking. But that year, we boys moved back to the projects to live with my dad.

When we arrived, I noticed things I hadn't before. The atmosphere was bleak. Clumps of dying grass floated in a sea of red dirt that sprouted strange flowers—bullet shells, used condoms, crack pipes made of medicine bottles or Coke cans, broken glass. To run and play was dangerous. The first gun I ever owned I found just lying on the ground.

Giant, rusted, bullet-dented dumpsters stood like sentinels around the complex while pungent threads of marijuana smoke, the burnt rubber smell of crack, and the sickly sweet scent of beer flowed together to create a neon exit sign that promised a quick escape.

Many of the neighborhood kids were bony with distended bellies. Some held empty soda cans, absently sipping water from them, though the dents and faded paint gave away the can's age.

As neighbors, we all shared the same broken playground, swing set, and rusty slide; played on the same graffiti-covered basketball court; and cut our feet on the same shards of glass. We cringed at night from the same staccato sounds of gunshots, smashed windows, and rattling hedges as crackheads roamed. We crowded happily around the same boxy aluminum community mailboxes the first of every month, waiting for our welfare checks and food stamps. Our family was blessed compared to most other families living in the projects: our other parent actually paid child support.

That time of month would be like Christmas. We'd go grocery shopping and buy things our food stamps didn't cover, cramming our freezer with hot dogs, bread, and baloney—our staples. We bought cakes and pies, potato chips, and tons of generic soda.

Most importantly, we shopped with a level of dignity that allowed us to look cashiers in the eyes as we paid them.

When I complained about receiving a pitiful allowance, my dad pounded a lecture into me: "Be satisfied and go ride yer bike—at least ya fuckin' have one, you ungrateful little shit. We may be poor, but yer sure as goddamn hell the richest fuckin' poor kids around!"

I knew it was true although I didn't like the way the truth was hand-delivered. All I had to do was look around; poverty would spit in my eye.

Being poor presented obstacles to going out. We tended to use mom's child support to help defray the costs. For the times between child support deliveries, dad devised a plan to get all five of us to the movie theater as inexpensively as possible.

Before driving to the theater, we'd fill our pockets with dollar store candy—only some of it paid for. At the theater, dad would purchase one movie ticket. Then, he'd tell me, "Goddammit son, you need to pay attention. You know what to do, but don't fuck around once you get inside."

He'd tick points off on his thick fingers.

"Don't go to the bathroom to piss, don't go to the fucking arcade. Keep your grubby little dick-beaters to yourself, and get your skinny ass in there before everyone starts showing up. We'll be at that door in two minutes. You'd better be too."

With a quick shove from my dad, I'd be in the theater, easing past the gatekeeper, holding my ticket ahead of me like a magic key. Once past him, I'd creep ninja-style to the Emergency Exit (without an alarm) and open the door to my father and brothers waiting outside.

They'd come slinking in as I held the door open and made a sweeping gesture as if I owned the place. My dad, bringing up the rear, would smash past me, sweating, wheezing, and growling.

"Stop acting like a goddam idiot and shut the fucking door before you get us all caught." He clubbed me in the head. "Remind me to beat yer ass when we get home."

In addition to movies, my dad made sure we had cable TV, plus HBO and Cinemax. A couple times, we had to sell some food stamps for the going rate of fifty cents on the dollar to pay the bill, but it was worth it. We had TVs in the bedrooms, to which we ran extensions, and he let neighbors in adjoining apartments bore holes through the walls so they could thread extension wires through too.

One neighbor even climbed into the crawl space above the apartments, where the itchy insulation was home to billions of roaches, to run a second wire. His foot and knee slipped off the slender beam and landed on the drywall ceiling, creating a crack running the length of our apartment. Our hookups looked like a nest of skinny black snakes slithering in every direction but down.

My dad wasn't a drinker though he talked like he was drunk. Many thought he had a speech impediment. In reality, the sheer excitement of speaking to someone other than his sons caused his words to tumble out of his mouth like an overturned box of wrestling kittens.

Sagely, he'd share his smokes and his opinions—the two came as a package deal—with anyone willing to listen to a burly, grizzled man who seasoned his speech with handfuls of mangled foreign language phrases. Between his gruff appearance and garbled speech, Dad was seldom able to interact with other adults unless he was giving them something. He knew it too, and it hurt.

Another strange thing about my dad was that he was both narcoleptic and an insomniac. Sleep danced away when he tried to catch it but would turn around and pounce on him at the oddest times. At night, he'd wedge himself into a corner of the couch, propped up by the back and arm in case he passed out. Sitting in absolute dark, he was but a disembodied voice and a pulsating red-tinged face lit for seconds at a time by the ever-present cigarette.

Thanks to his tendency to fall asleep while smoking, every seat and armchair in our house looked as if an army of melted caterpillars had burrowed into it, and there were gaps in his mustache, beard, and chest hair. His narcolepsy never stole him more than an hour's rest, seldom more than fifteen or twenty minutes, so he was never really able to relax.

"All I fuckin' want is some goddamned peace and fucking quiet—is that too much to ask?" he'd say while looking up toward heaven.

I considered his narcolepsy a unique blessing since it gave us so many good laughs and brief respite from his abuses. Sometimes, we boys would be gathered in the living room, listening to one of his verbal tirades, when mid-sentence, a switch would be thrown: his chins would pillow the fall of his heavy head as it hit the carpet of his chest hair.

We'd heave a concurrent sigh of relief and remove his dwindling cigarette before it burned his fingers. Sometimes, we'd change the channel on the TV or switch seating positions. If we were feeling brave, we might even change our clothes.

Wilkerson family from left Albert, mom, Michael, George, Daniel, Dad, 1985.

Eventually, he'd awaken and continue his rant exactly where he'd left off. He'd stop when his empty fingers reached his lips, already formed around the memory of a cigarette. Noting the altered seating arrangements, the change of clothes, and our faces fighting giggles, epiphany would blossom bright pink in his cheeks.

With a huff, he'd condemn our goddamn disrespect and ask why we hadn't fucking woken him up. Nevertheless, I'm convinced he saw the humor in it.

With my dad's progressing schizophrenia came an extreme paranoia, a belief that everyone was out to get him, use him, play him, treat him like he was stupid. (He was anything but stupid—he had savant-like total recall.)

Thus, he no longer limited his fights to my mom. When I was seven, I watched him beat a man almost to death, breaking both fists and caving in the man's forehead. My dad was arrested several times for assault, which contributed to his difficulty getting a decent job.

When I was eleven, my dad began enlisting me for missions. He'd be feuding with someone in the neighborhood. Our apartment complex sprawled across a quarter-mile block of land and consisted of hundreds of units, each housing between one and twelve occupants.

Whether you were looking for trouble or not, there was no shortage of enemies. I was sent to slice tires, shatter windows, and sabotage central-air systems. I flung multicolored smoke bombs through open windows and set booby traps on doors using gallon-sized resealable bags swollen with our shit and piss.

Dad also ordered me to combat kids within my age or size bracket. The neighbors did the same to us. My dad wanted our family to give as good as we got. I had several assault charges on my record by the age of twelve. As my strength and ability developed, the charges escalated in severity, and people were more severely injured.

Dad shoved me into the forge of life and hammered at me until I was sharp. Trapped between his world and my mother's clean and orderly existence, I swam through a shadow realm where nothing and no one was solid or dependable. All that mattered was survival. I learned to always carry a weapon. And then, as years went by, I learned to become the weapon.

Missed Amends

During the summer of 1996, when I was fifteen, my three brothers and I were split between our parents.

I was in court for various charges, including violation of the probation for habitual larceny and assault I'd been on since age twelve. The judge told me I could either leave Asheboro and go live with my mom in Fayetteville until I turned eighteen, or go to a juvenile detention facility for eighteen months.

I chose to live with my mom and so did my older brother Mike. By then, my mother had remarried yet again and owned a Korean restaurant, where I was put to work washing dishes. My younger brothers, Daniel and Albert, joined us right before school started in the fall.

I soon learned that my mom and I were no less prone to fights than my dad and I. I asked her to buy me a car for my sixteenth birthday since I'd been working in her restaurant without getting paid. In January of 1997, two months before I turned sixteen, she made me a deal: if I found a job and worked all year, saving my money, she'd help me buy a car in time for Christmas. I happily agreed and found a job at Taco Bell.

All year, I envisioned how my new car would look packed to capacity, my friends' arms akimbo out the window. The music system would pound as I rolled around corners, announcing my arrival as if a red carpet had been laid out. My popularity would explode as I graciously granted rides to whoever kissed my . . . ring.

When the year was up, two weeks before Christmas, my mom took me to a car lot and helped me pick out a car. But when it came time to pay, she refused to co-sign although I couldn't get credit to finance a car at sixteen years old, nor did I have ten thousand dollars in cash to buy the car outright.

I threw a fit, demanding she explain how she was "helping" me buy a car if she'd neither co-sign nor pay the difference. (I'd saved up only fifteen hundred dollars.) She never did answer except to say, "I no co-sign." I raged at the humiliation I'd face in front of my friends, to whom I'd bragged all year about getting a car.

In retaliation, I withdrew all my savings from the bank and blew it on revenge.

Christmas morning, everyone gathered in the family room. The gifts had been distributed, and we were about to open them—but everyone stared at me. I sat amid a mountain of fancy packaging while they had smaller mounds around their knees.

"Okay, I'll go first," I chirped, carefully selecting a present. I shook it by my ear, wondering aloud what it was. I unwrapped an expensive Nautica jacket and feigned surprise.

"Oh, thank you, Santa—I've been wanting one of these all year!" I said sarcastically before tossing it aside and snatching up another present.

I looked my mother dead in the eye the whole time. Her lips were a tight line. When her face twitched, I felt I'd glimpsed a shark fin. I ignored it, along with the looks on my siblings' faces. They didn't know yet that I'd bought fifteen hundred dollars worth of gifts, mostly for myself, and padded the base of the tree with them. They thought our mom was showing favoritism.

After that, my mother went into attack mode. Whenever she took the family out to eat or to the golf course or on mini shopping sprees, I wasn't invited. I might go up to my room for a few minutes, come out, and everyone would be gone. I felt alienated and invisible. I was sorry, but clueless as to how to make amends.

The following summer, my mom took the family on vacation to Niagara Falls—all, of course, except for me. It occurred to me to throw a house party partly to repair my social status, which was still damaged over the car incident.

The party was great, but things did get messy. I'd planned to fish out the beer bottles, trash, and cigarette butts from our pool before my family returned. I had honestly intended to mend the blunt burns on the carpet, scrub the floors clean, and air out the house. I never considered that mom might ask a neighbor to spy for just such a party.

Abbreviating their vacation in Canada, she rushed home to discover her squeaky-clean home defiled. Worse, I'd forgotten my parents kept a gallon-sized Tupperware container crammed with stacks of bank-banded hundreds, fifties, and twenties—our college funds—in their bedroom. During the party, somebody had stolen it.

When my mom arrived home, she leapt on me, her hands encircling my throat. She was crying and screaming. I did not resist though I easily could have broken her grip. I knew I deserved whatever I got.

Mike walked over and pried her fingers loose, draped an arm across her heaving shoulders, and guided her back to her car. He told me to stay.

All I could say was "Mom, I'm sorry" to their backs. Mike just shook his head. When he returned, he told me our mom had banished me from her home. She never wanted to see me again.

I went numb.

In 1998, Mike and I moved back in with our dad. One afternoon, Mike and I were finishing up an exercise routine on our weight equipment in the spare bedroom when dad barreled into the room and dove right into a verbal assault.

Mike groaned. "Dad, please, not now."

At that, Dad came at Mike swinging. Mike caught his arm and stood. Dad punched him in the stomach with his free fist and it was on.

I jumped out of the way to evade wayward elbows and more than five hundred pounds of thrashing flesh. The bench toppled; bars and plates clattered. All of us were screaming obscenities. I was mushed into drywall.

I tried to break it up but got swatted aside. I seemed to be the only one taking hits while they grappled with each other.

For four or five minutes, they roared and cursed. Steel objects clanged around the floor, getting kicked this way and that. I got sideswiped into walls and knocked to my knees. They would not stop.

Mike pinned our dad against a wall, trying to control his arms and screaming for him to calm down. Dad frothed, his face reddened with exertion. Mike looked back at me, pleading.

I stood there crying in frustration, shaking, keening. My ears buzzed as blood flooded my brain. Like many things in life, I didn't know when I'd had enough until I had.

I snapped. Something like a war cry, wordless and guttural, erupted from my throat. It was a sound I'd never heard before. Without thinking, I snatched up a five-pound chrome bar a foot long, stepped forward, took our dad's right arm from Mike and shoved it out to the side. Mike did the same with the other arm. Our dad looked crucified.

"Stooooooooop! Stop! Stop!" I howled.

Aside from our ragged breath, all was quiet. Mike and Dad eyed the shiny bar I held high overhead.

I screamed so hard, white flecks of foam speckled Dad's cheek. "Dad, this stops today! Right fucking now! Do you understand me?"

Joining in, Mike roared, "Dad, we are your sons, not your fucking punching bags. Your *sons*. You had a bad day? So what? It ain't our fault, so don't take it out on us. We are your sons, and we love you—"

"—but we will kill you," I interrupted. "We will beat you to death and get away with it, and you know it. If you don't swear right now to stop trying to hurt us."

Dad quit struggling and looked back and forth between us. Tears brimmed in his eyes.

"Finally...my boys have become men," he said with pride.

Speechless, Mike and I looked askance at each other, then back at our dad.

"Alright, goddammit!" Dad said. "I promise! Now, let me go, you crazy sons of bitches!"

And that was that. He never attacked us again.

After that incident, I moved out. I was seventeen. I started making a living as a full-time drug and fence (buying and selling stolen goods) dealer.

By 2004, when I was twenty-three, I had become the production manager for a furniture manufacturer in Asheboro. I yearned for peace with my family, especially my mom. She had moved into a new house and allowed me to visit for a few hours at a time. She didn't know about my illegal side ventures.

That year, around Christmas, I decided to win back my family. At the furniture manufacturer, I handmade a plush, red recliner for my mom. It looked like a throne.

Remembering my selfish Christmas years before, I stuffed my pickup truck with gifts for everyone before driving to mom's home. My truck was a blur of wrapping paper streaming down the highway toward my family. I couldn't wait to tell them about my new plans. I wanted to go to college. They'd be pleased and proud.

On Christmas morning, with most of us still crusty-eyed and slightly hungover, we slumped around on couches. My sister Sara, from my mother's second marriage, distributed the presents. Mom's throne sat in the center of the TV room downstairs. She'd been stunned and thrilled by my generous gift, which she took as a sign I had changed.

Soon, everyone had a pyramid of presents in front of them.

Except me. I had a shirt box. And a card.

From their looks, this was not a conspiracy. They were as surprised as I. They tried to downplay it.

"...no big deal, bruh..."

Wilkerson boys from left Daniel, George, Dad, Michael, Albert, 2000.

"...really didn't know what you liked..."

"...had a *ton* of people to shop for..."

"George, honey, it's not about how much you get," my mom offered. "It's the thought that counts."

"I know. You're right, Mom. It's the thought that counts," I replied. "And it's pretty clear what everyone thinks about me."

I could sense their collective cringe. I felt ashamed and defeated, wondering if I'd ever get beyond my past. How could I fit back into my family? I wanted to laugh at the inside jokes too. I wanted to be safe and dependable. I wanted them to smile when they saw me, not greet me with the look of caution and suspicion one gives a rickety ladder.

Fuck this, I thought. Somehow, I would break the cycle.

I put on a plastic smile and said, "Hey, I get it. It's no big deal. Look, I've got to work in the morning, so I'd better be heading out. Got a long drive ahead."

I went around the room, hugging and kissing everyone. I didn't know then that it would be the last time I'd ever touch them.

Their sympathetic looks were almost too much. I couldn't take it. I had to get the hell out of there. In my haste, I forgot to tell them about my college plans.

Two weeks later, I was arrested for a double homicide.

She Thought She Could Hug Me

it's the first time she's visited me since I caught my death
sentences, a garden-variety maximum security prison

visitation booth that a floor-to-ceiling cinder block wall chops
in half. at waist level, a window: shoulder-width, a child's-

face-tall; five iron bars then plexiglass then chicken wire then
plexiglass then, hopes crumpling, my tiny Korean mom, her downcast eyes

pinching into flat wet lines, melting mascara. beneath the window:
a perforated steel plate then corrugated steel filter then

perforated steel plate—a contraband trap to speak through. inside,
its holes grow fuzzy with dark mold from moist words, decades'

and decades' worth, a hundred thousand prisoners' worth. we fold
and tuck ourselves, bend our chambered souls toward this

inhuman interface. silence rains

for the first few minutes—well, mostly,
except for my mom's full-body sobbing,

which the sound trap muffles some, even as it
autotunes her suffering, lending her sobs its metallic,

mechanical echo like crying
into a soup can. what can I say? what can

I do to comfort her? how can I wrap her in my
discredited sentiments whose waves break

their foamy words against my teeth, then recede? my lips
tremble. I look away. I study this cramped

and musty space, notice the fluorescent
light flickering with a sizzle sound, pressing it down—caking

light like white icing across the black iron bars. the bars
throw inch-thick shadows like scorch marks through the window

and onto mama's pretty face. she shoves palms
into eyes, scrubs, scrubs, mutters

I'm sorry I'm sorry, scrubbing at the pain and disappointment
stains. *I'm sorry I'm sorry my baby*

my baby—though subaudible now, i can see
her heart wailing across her lips, quivering. i see

her temper igniting there. i see *my baby my baby*   leap
and fire the air like yellow-white embers that turn

orange then red then black as they ash
into my eyes. inside i feel myself rasping

and ashing as fury beats her jungle drums, pounds her
hands against plexiglas *my baby my baby*

                                             as if to reach beyond
the coming years <<<*give me back my baby*>>>

and I can't even tell her
it'll be okay, can't tell her

I'm okay mama I'm okay
because it won't be

and I'm not.
it was through her

eyes that i finally saw
the past, myself, her son, *her baby*—and the wretched

thing her baby had become
and I wept.

The Huggy Boys

Laughter can be something sturdy, dependable as a leg, thick as a tree trunk. In my pre-prison days, I remember when my mischievous fiancée, Kim, discovered I was ticklish. During our intense arguments, she'd get this squinty, impish look on her face. I'd stop mid-rant, lift my hands in a defensive position and pat the air while trying to mollify her.

"No...stay the hell away from me, you damned animal!"

Then, I'd take off running.

Kim would roar like a warrior princess and stalk after me, giggling gleefully, her light brown hair flying everywhere as I dodged tables and televisions, hurdled over sofas, flung threats, pleas, and couch cushions at her. Always, eventually, she'd anticipate my direction and dive to intercept me. Despite weighing 100 pounds to my 175, when she got a hand on me, it was over. She'd climb my wind-milling body, tying her legs around my waist as she stabbed brutal, French-manicured fingers into my ribs—and I would lose my motherfucking mind.

I'd scream incoherently, my body bucking with spasms, and try to dislodge her by throwing myself back first into walls and kitchen counters; I'd slam sideways into door jambs, back-drop onto the floor to roll around and put out the fire. Nothing ever worked. She cackled, clung tightly, and punished me until tears and piss leaked out of us.

I'd loved Kim from the moment she hugged my dad. My dad was obese and rather hairy. Even in winter, he went shirtless, his rotund torso sheened in sweat. He was a hugger, and his hugs were a type of litmus test: our shirts came away damp and dark where they'd pressed against his soggy body, giving him a visual of our devotion. When I'd introduced him to Kim, she had unhesitatingly slid into his meaty arms and post-hug had peeled her sweat-wetted shirt from her breasts without flinching. She'd beamed.

I'd asked her to marry me soon afterward.

But three months after my arrest, Kim left me. I huddled on the floor of my pretrial jail pod, wrapping my body around the wall-mounted stainless-steel payphone as she took back half of our soul. It was the first of many relationships to disintegrate in the acid bath of prison life.

Weeks later, I was begging my mom not to abandon me. In her adorable broken English, she disowned me for breaking her heart and dishonoring the family. She told me I was self-centered because I couldn't see how much they were suffering for me. At the time, I was too blinded by fear and anger to understand. *I* needed to grow up? *I* was too blind to others' suffering? *They* weren't the ones facing the friggin' death penalty. *They* weren't the ones listening to seventy crackheads, drunks, thieves, rapists, and dope dealers fart and snore on bunk beds as hard as concrete all night long.

I tried sending everyone letters to keep from fading into a ghostly afterimage. Nobody responded aside from periodic "updates" and obligatory birthday and Christmas cards. My siblings and friends, all in their twenties and thirties, were moving too fast for me: starting families, building careers, living life—too busy to stop and write a letter. I could hear them saying, "Who has time for that shit?"

In those early days of incarceration, I hadn't come to terms with a possible death sentence. Perhaps one day I'd be forcibly strapped to a gurney, wearing a diaper, as a salt-based poison flooded my bloodstream like liquid napalm. A dozen witnesses would watch me writhing—some gladly, some sadly—and the audience would include family members from both sides of the crime.

Would my family come witness my final moments? Would I want them to?

I knew I deserved worse than being forgotten. By nobody's standard, not even my own self-indulgent one, had I been a good friend, brother, or son. And now, by the time I started to recognize it, it made little difference; it was too late. My relationships were too weak to overcome the obstacles presented by prison.

Ironically, my dad, the nightmare of my youth, was the one person who stayed by my side when I became incarcerated. When I was at the jail, he visited every week. He couldn't legally drive because of his narcolepsy, so he walked thirteen miles from home, against my tearful protests. Jail visits were only fifteen minutes. He said simply, "You're my son. I love you. Plus, I have nothing better to do."

Evidently, love truly does cover a multitude of sins because he was blind to mine.

Then one night during my trial, after court was out for the day, my three brothers came to visit. As soon as I stepped into the visitation booth and spotted the look on my older brother's face, I knew our dad had died.

After his death, self-pity was irresistible. Who would tell me they were proud of me when I was nothing to be proud of? Who would wrap their heavy words around my doubts? I'm not sure whether I wept because he was gone or because I no longer had him to prop me up. The distinction makes all the difference because the first focuses on his loss, the other on mine.

Once I arrived on Death Row in 2006, the last form of connection I'd had—the phone—was also stripped away. I had become so dependent on and attuned to the voices on the other end that I could detect the subtlest emotional shifts, like dipping fingers into water to test its heat. But when I was escorted through the red-rimmed entrance of Death Row, I learned we had no phone access except a monitored ten-minute call each December. A couple of years into my sentence, a smirking officer who sat across the desk, timing and listening, began making faces to ridicule my tearful conversation. I ended my call early and didn't make one the next December, or the next. Or ever again.

I felt like an untethered astronaut lost in space, trying to resist giving in to panicky madness in the face of too much black and empty time, an endless dial tone squalling in the ether. I began romanticizing my past, distorting, omitting.

I rarely received visits as everyone I knew lived scattered across the state, hours away. No contact, no visits, no phones. My relationships were disintegrating. I became resigned to dying alone and withdrew into myself. My world diminished to the size of my cell.

Several organizations provide pen pals for Death Row prisoners, and everyone here had at least one. Having met their girlfriends via pen pal service, some guys bragged about their paper sexcapades. They wrote erotic letters, got paper cuts on their penises while tracing their silhouettes on the page (miraculously acquiring the extra length and girth they'd always wanted), and sniffed and licked at crusted vagina-butterfly prints.

I didn't get the appeal of trying to initiate a romantic letter relationship. I was having a hard enough time trying to hang on to friends without complicating it with sexual frustration. For some, a pen pal was less about romance and more about a chance to redefine ourselves, to sketch a larger-than-life outline—or a brand-new one with a little help. Most of us had things about ourselves we knew needed changing, but to see it clearly, we needed fresh perspectives on parts of ourselves we couldn't (or wouldn't) reveal to fellow prisoners, or even family. It's amazing how often the people who love us most refuse to let us change, always skeptical of our sincerity, bringing up past mistakes. It's like personalized stereotyping where one's positive efforts sit in the viewer's blind spot.

In 2012, I received a letter from a young college student who goes by Gigi. She was studying to be a nurse, but college's pervasive drug, alcohol, and sex culture overwhelmed her. She was self-destructing. She couldn't talk to her parents and had no older siblings; she asked if I would help her learn from my mistakes. She'd read about my case—how I had been immersed in a parallel culture as a drug dealer—and decided I would understand the temptations. I was curious and flattered to receive her letter.

My first impulse was to write back immediately, but something pulled me up short. What type of person would ask a guy on Death Row for help? What if she was one of those women infatuated with true crime stories, or a writer posing as a student so she could write her own story, or an agent for my prosecutor trying to gather evidence against me, or a lonely woman looking for erotic letters?

I wondered about myself. *Why am I so eager to write her?* Part of me argued that I was a Christian now and it was my duty to help deter others from my criminal path. Another part of me noticed how attractive she was in her photo and wondered if I was inadvertently aiming for romance. I struggled to reconcile how I could seek intimacy without the sexual element. I had long ago accepted the hard reality that sex was beyond my reach, but I knew I could still benefit from friendship with a woman.

The thought of being open and honest with Gigi about personal things excited and scared me. Prison is a hypermasculine environment where the dominant consensus defines the only acceptable emotion as rage. Generally, we discuss safe topics: sports, food, sex. We talk about the world around us, ignoring the one within. We avoid touching one another emotionally the same way we avoid seeing each other naked, and almost for the same reasons.

In my nearly eight years of incarceration, I had learned to be *alone*, convincing myself I needed no friends. I associated with people around me daily, yet felt something noticeably missing in these interactions. The men around me appeared to me as empty husks, animated mannequins. Like my family and friends, they had shrunk to the two-dimensionality of a flat photograph—no heavier, no sturdier. In my mind, starved of human contact, their personalities had taken on the exaggerated, oversimplified quality of cartoon characters.

Or, perhaps, I was projecting how I perceived myself.

We were like goldfish that stop growing if they're kept in a small bowl: Death Row's physical, alienating structure combined with negative self-perceptions to create our fishbowl. It was mine, at least.

As my appeals arguing for my life crawled along in court, I began a battle against a more imminent death sentence: I started fighting to stay human. I would have to relearn how to feel in order to connect with others, for apathy is not only an enemy of humanity but also of community itself, which is a sacred communion in God's eyes. At the time, these thoughts were more intuited than articulated. But how to soften and re-sensitize what I'd spent the last eight years hardening and deadening? I wondered whether it was too late.

Once Gigi and I began corresponding, reading her letters was like touching a live wire; they were so emotionally charged. Anger, defiance, anxiety, envy, vindication, petulance, enthusiasm, gratification, indignation— this was the language with which she described her world. For a long time, my emotional range had remained stunted between anger and fear.

Gigi taught me to speak. She became my Rosetta Stone. When I shared my stories with her, she challenged me to shove aside my idea of masculine dispassion and grab my throbbing, wriggling, burning feelings—take possession of them.

Whereas before, my story was the bare outline of a picture, the casual silhouette cast by a rational accounting, she helped me to color it in, thicken it, breathe life into it. Gigi led with her heart and dragged her mind behind it, forcing it into line. Between the pages of our correspondence lay a judgement-free zone where we tolerated no bullshit from each other. We could be idiots, contradict ourselves, make highly biased comments, rant—anything but lie. We accepted each other as-is, and the safer and more secure we felt, the more open and forthright we became. We attacked each other's crap, but we never attacked each other.

Perhaps providentially, a short while after Gigi and I began our correspondence, Death Row got its first-ever creative writing class. The Mental Health department touted the class as therapy. About half of Death Row was taking medication for "serious or persistent mental disorders," and the promise of therapy was that naming one's demons might deprive them of their power over us.

Though I was not on medication, my inner life was definitely disorderly. Confusion plagued my thought-life, stole my peace.

Picture a sentence stretched across the page. Each word represents an idea in itself; by linking with the others in a specific order, they form a higher-order concept, a coherent thought.

Now, disassemble that sentence and dump the words into a Scrabble pouch. Shake vigorously. Technically, the components are there, but the thought is disjointed or discursive. When I tried to express myself, my coherence tended to crumble into that jumbled mass. When it came to complex thoughts, I literally couldn't think straight.

Flannery O'Connor famously said, "I don't know what I think until I read what I say." Writing let me empty out the pouch on paper and arrange the word tiles into sentences, imposing order on my inner chaos. I began to explore my past and to see how many of my decisions lacked the rationality I'd thought I based them on. To my surprise, I was more like Gigi in that my intellect was enslaved by my emotions. I couldn't believe how blind I'd been. I shared this insight with her, and together, we navigated our lives. When one of us acted on emotional impulse, the other would point out how those emotions recruited our rational mind to justify and implement the impulse. In this way, we expanded our choice catalogs. If we made bad decisions, we now did it with eyes wide open—which made it more difficult to do bad things in good conscience, which led to fewer bad decisions.

As my self-awareness grew, so too did my feeling of space—my fishbowl ballooned in volume—and my sense of others. People's personalities gained weight, density, significance. Words opened a new world to me. I was able to redirect my self-attention onto Gigi, stressing over her decisions and well-being. It was a bootlegged form of redemption, as I could only advise her against making the same bad decisions I'd made. I hoped it was an expression of my repentance. Words on paper provided us with the raw material we needed for empathy. She became a safe place to direct my affection, as if toward my baby sister. Gigi's triumphs were my own; we rejoiced together. Her failures were mine, too; I blamed myself.

I saw my mother had been right: my family must be suffering because of my death sentence. *No wonder nobody visits or writes*, I thought.

Despite the depth of my correspondence with Gigi, a letter can't capture the squint and cackle of a mischievous woman or the low, slow tone of reason creeping into a heated conversation. It can't transmit the telepathic glance or my sarcastic wit. It can't replicate the raspy frog in my throat as I fumble to figure out what to say; it can't show I care enough to get choked up when I apologize to my family for the pain I've caused, though I mailed those letters anyway.

In 2016, Death Row's fishbowl opened up in a whole new way. For decades, social justice activists, friends, families, and Death Row prisoners had hounded the prison administration to allow us regular phone access. We were the only Death Row unit in the country without phones. The administrators routinely gave the same responses: "No," "Maybe next year," or "Soon."

Then, in March 2016, maintenance workers came and installed a rectangular, stainless steel box to a wall in the dayroom of each pod. We tried to act nonchalant but our eyes kept straying toward what appeared to be a payphone.

Some of us surreptitiously picked up the receiver to check for a dial tone. Nothing. It was cruel to give us a phone without the wiring. *Soon*, we hoped.

Someone asked me who I was going to call first. I said, "Eh, I don't know. I haven't given it any thought." Truth is, I was scared and embarrassed I'd have no one to call. I wrote to everyone I knew, asking them to send me their numbers.

After a month, only Gigi had responded. After two months, only Gigi had responded.

The first time I used the phone from Death Row, I felt like a virgin on his wedding night—eager to put this thing to use, not sure if it'd hurt, scared I'd screw something up.

My first call was, of course, to Gigi. When I heard little sister's Valley girl accent, I shivered with pleasure. When she realized it was me on the line, she almost peed her pants, she said.

Later on, one of my younger brothers sent me his number, and we started talking. We were hardly recognizable to each other. We had been boys when I got arrested. Similar to prison, we mostly discussed food, sports, sex. Now closer to middle age, we had opinions and experiences to discuss. To my relief, the love was still there.

I thought this might be my chance to be seen as I was now, that perhaps we could see each other rather than the superimposed images that had kept us blind-spotted. I was no longer trapped in a family fishbowl. I was anxious to find a new role, to build a new reputation in real time.

It was the most alive I'd felt since being sentenced to death.

All at once, I received letters from my other relatives—my mom, my sister, my other brothers—with their phone numbers. Each wrote some version of "I'm not good at writing, but I'd love to speak to you."

It felt a little like coming home.

Death Row's culture has a strange trait: We shake hands a lot. Since we are mostly stuck on our pods, our social interactions are limited throughout the day except when we go to meals, religious services, recreation, etc. During these periods of movement, we might briefly interact with men from other pods, which is when all the handshaking takes place. In church services, it has assumed the quality of a spiritual

ritual. As our members stream in, everyone shakes hands with everyone else, weaving in and out. It must seem from above like an elaborate choreography accompanied by murmurs of "Peace and blessings," "God bless you," or "Peace, Brother." It's the same in greeting and in leaving. To call it excessive is an understatement.

If my pod is lined up in the hall for commissary and someone from another pod happens by on the way back from an appointment, he might nod to one person, fist bump another, shake hands with the next, pull the hand clasp into a half hug with another—each gesture signifying degrees of intimacy. Seeing one such scene as our pods split after a meal, an officer dubbed Death Row as "The Huggy Boys."

When I first got here, having been around gangs most of my life, I read the handshakes and hugs as a feature of social hierarchy. I still think that's an element, but it doesn't explain how widespread it is and how excessively we do it. Perhaps it speaks to something deeper: that we aren't as disinterested in human contact as we pretend.

I have become one of the most incorrigible greeters. I've helped evolve the handshake to new levels, creating one that's nuanced and involves bone-cracking tensions when thumb presses to thumb as our four fingers pull against each other and release one by one in an audible snap. It's akin to my dad's hugging, I suppose—a next-gen litmus test. To the discerning, grip tightness, force of snaps, and fluidity of transitions speak volumes. To do it properly, in sync, says *we are one*. To see it done from an outside perspective is to witness a five-second hand dance that engages the entire body as it transitions through its stages, from initial clasp to half hug to handshake to finger popping to full release.

Despite the emotional indifference that often fogs Death Row, reality solidifies around our senses: if I can scrape against it, if it can burst my eardrums, crack my knuckles, or cool my tongue, it's real.

Limp Gray Fur

I need a break, I thought as I sat amid a pile of papers, loose pages, and scraps, each holding a fragment of a thought, a paragraph, or a quote. I had accumulated bits and pieces of an idea like someone saving up to buy something, and I figured I might finally have enough for an essay. Or at least a poem.

I got off my bunk and stepped out of my corner cell on the tier. Stretching my aching back and standing at the railing, I peered down into the boxy rectangular dayroom and noticed the two terminally ill men on my pod sitting catty-cornered in their wheelchairs.

I wondered what they were speaking about. I couldn't remember ever seeing them interact at length before. Neither thought much of the other. I noted the way one gestured to a fresh surgical scar on his chest near his right armpit, where a doctor had carved out a thick slab of malignant muscle. The other nodded, then pantomimed something being threaded down his throat and into his lungs. He pressed a hand to his chest and breathed in a deep, exaggerated fashion. The other's head cocked, half listening, half resting, then gave a slant nod.

I heard nothing; nonetheless, it made sense to me. Who of the twenty other men on our pod could commiserate with cancer besides them? Gary and Davy had been wrestling with mysterious health issues for a year, and recently both had been diagnosed with Stage Four cancer.

Gary lives in a cell on the first floor near the dayroom. All day, he sits in his wheelchair in his doorway with a standard-issue navy blue woolen blanket draped across his shoulders like a riding hood. He slouches so low, his back is folding into an "n," and his pale face is almost resting on his own lap. It's difficult for me to witness this slowing, sinking, thinning, balding, wheezing process. Despite being on Death Row these past ten years, I've not been around anyone I knew was dying. Of the 150 or so men here when I arrived, twelve have died of natural causes or suicide, but none on my pod. The last North Carolina execution occurred in 2006, right before I arrived.

When I came to Death Row, Gary was the second person to speak to me. At first, he came across as sort of creepy—like the old man in *Family Guy* who keeps inviting his neighbor's teenage son to his basement for popsicles. Big, blue-black bruises and ugly black moles riddle his flesh and grow across his arms, chest, and stomach. He has a greasy demeanor combined with a soft voice and effeminate mannerisms.

Before Gary was formally diagnosed, he kept trying to get medical attention. Sometimes, he would fake or exaggerate symptoms like walking down the hall, appearing ready to pass out, then sinking to the floor when he knew an officer was looking. They'd panic and rush him to the prison ER, a way for Gary to get the attention he craved. Now that he is legitimately diagnosed with cancer, Gary flaunts a vindicated attitude that says, "I *told* you I was dying, but you wouldn't listen."

As for his apparent degeneration, I'm unsure how much is contrived. Several weeks ago, he "fell" in his cell and was carted to the hospital, where he was isolated in a room without TV access, people to talk with, or commissary items. He begged to come back to Death Row. Before he fell, he'd become a nearly unresponsive recluse, convincing us he could drop dead any second. But upon his return, he said, "Man, it was empty up there. Even though I don't talk much, I at least like being on the edge of things where I can watch and hear people."

He has hardly shut up since. His bleak but brief hospital stint secured him a snack bag to supplement his trays, more pain meds, and an extra mattress.

Now that he is energetic and engaging, lively even, it makes me hesitate to empathize because I feel I'm being played, at least to some degree. If he stays with it, I can work at forgetting he's probably faking some symptoms—and who can blame him? For most of his life, he's been unpopular and kept from entering the inner circle, yet now, several guys are doting on him, asking how they can help. His snack bag items (peanut butter, Ensure, cheese, saltines) provide bartering currency since we don't typically have access to them. He slurps up the attention like dirty nectar, an unwitting—or clever—social butterfly with skull-patterned wings who decided he loved people after all. For Gary, pain meds, attention, and donations of coffee, cookies, and candy seem enough to bring comfort to the dying.

I'm still trying to figure out what comfort looks like to Davy.

Davy is one of those people you either love or hate the moment you meet him. He has a no-holds-barred, middle-fingers-in-the-air attitude that is authentic and abrasive. He's five feet tall but carries himself as if twice that. If you can look past his perpetual asshole persona, you'd find an asshole still. If he doesn't like you, he'll tell you plainly, "I don't like you. Get the hell away from me" in a gravelly voice that cigarettes shredded long ago.

From sickness, Davy's skin has turned cartoonish, a Bart Simpson yellow, and his right leg has ballooned in proportion. He resembles a drawing by a first-grader, a barely recognizable sketch in thick, waxy primary colors.

To some, Gary and Davy are walking corpses slowing up traffic in the hallways with their wheelchairs. Others are opportunistic and offer to get their trays for them in the chow hall. Davy told me how one guy would walk to the table carrying a food tray in each hand, obviously measuring and weighing each. Davy always got handed the one with the smaller piece of cake.

I saw another guy bend down at the serving window and holler to the guard, "I need to grab a tray for the guy in the wheelchair too," then take both trays to his own table and combine them quickly so he could ditch the empty one into the dishpit window before a guard entered our side to monitor the line.

Most guys on our pod try to stay out of Davy's way so as not to make things worse for him, which is the best they can do to help him—and themselves by avoiding his scorching tongue. At least Gary is approachable and will accept a token of compassion—a honey bun, a packet of Kool-Aid, conversation—to help ease our collective discomfort at being useless to stop him from shriveling into a raisin.

I feel that as a Christian, I ought to know how to handle someone dying. But I don't. It's like I'm staring at a complicated math problem, and my answer will determine whether I pass or fail. So, I asked someone who does know the answer: I prayed.

Recently, seated in a chair in his doorway, Davy was watching our pod's TV, which is mounted high on a wall across our dayroom. I stepped out of my cell to stretch my back, just in time to see a woman on TV spit in a man's face.

Davy cringed and barked, "That's fucking disgusting!"

I looked back at him, and he twisted towards me.

"Did you see that?" he said. "I can't stand someone spitting on someone else. It's nasty. I'd rather you slap me than spit on me.

"I was on a date one time with this girl whose ex-boyfriend popped up," he continued. "They started arguing, and she spit in his face like that. I ended it right there." His bony finger jabbed toward the TV.

I told him about an abusive ex-girlfriend I had. She was a slapper. Knowing I wouldn't hit her back, she liked to slap me when she got angry—and sometimes when horny. Smitten in lust with her, I tolerated it.

This led Davy to share a story about a girlfriend who got mad at him because he didn't get mad at her when she told him she'd cheated on him—which led me to describe the time I got slit from wrist to elbow with a rusty steak knife and had to escape the hospital because my girlfriend jokingly remarked to the intake nurse that I had tried to kill myself for her, prompting the doctor to have guards posted outside my room while a shrink tried to have me committed.

Davy and I chuckled over the stupid things we did for women and ribbed each other's idiocy. For half an hour, cancer left the room so two guys could have a pissing contest, trying to one-up each other with the most dramatic story inspired by true events.

Was this the answer to my prayer? I wondered. *A way to comfort Davy?* I could spend time with him, laugh with him, let him be just one of the guys.

For weeks after, I tried to stage another "unplanned" interaction. But something about it struck me as a tender, affectionate gesture—and I winced. I admit that emotional sensitivity has never been my strong point. Intellectually, I'm aware of others' emotional states, but it takes vulnerability to allow oneself to connect to others. I've only ever really connected with women on an emotional level because I see men as threats. Not to mention, I'm in prison, where any sort of tenderness is viewed as weakness or homosexual in nature.

Back in 2002, when I was twenty-one, my cat got hit by a car. Though it had no visible injuries, clearly it was broken and dead, its carcass nothing but a lump of limp gray fur.

My girlfriend sobbed as I walked over to pick up our beloved pet. As soon as my fingers touched the cold fur, they recoiled. Some atavistic trait activated within me. When I tried again to touch it, my fingers bounced off an invisible force field. It was almost comical how I repeatedly reached my hand out only to have it ricochet to the side before reaching my dead cat.

I cursed under my breath, "Man the fuck up!" It didn't help.

My girlfriend whined, "Baby, we have to get him out of the road!"

No shit. But what I said was, "I know, I know, but I can't touch him! I don't know why. Why don't you try?"

"You're supposed to be the man, not me," she shot back.

I was willing to leave him lying right there. She nearly slapped me when I suggested it. Eventually, I had to poke at Smoky with a stick to maneuver him onto an old blanket, which would become his burial shroud.

I don't want to merely poke at Davy to maneuver him to a well-worn area in which I can wrap him to make myself more comfortable. I want to be able to touch death with him, help him carry it with bare hands. I want to at least show, "Hey, I'm with you, bruh. This shit stinks and it's messy and repulsive, but I'm with you." I don't know if it actually matters to him. We don't speak about our feelings.

I don't know whether it's Davy I'm trying to help or if I'm using Davy as a pretext to convince myself I can be selfless, that I'm more compassionate now, that I've changed. I want to feel I'm no longer the scared little boy who entered prison quick to fight battles with fists; that I am now the man of God I claim to be—a man who is quicker to forgive than to fight, though no less scared sometimes. Maybe I'm scared to find out I haven't changed that much.

Perhaps my discomfort comes from knowing that one day I'll die too. Cancer? Heart attack? Execution? Shank? If so, then this is training; a way for me to face my own demise and tell myself with confidence and courage, "Okay, George, man up. You've already been through this. It stinks. It's messy and gross. But quit crying and grab this thing with your bare hands."

There is a certain dignity in that, I think.

Vacant Lots and Aviaries

On a dewy morning in 2013, I saw something bizarre covering the grass near the perimeter wall beyond our volleyball court. It sat in the shadow of the wall but stained it darker. That swath of uncanny blackness was thicker somehow. It had heft.

About thirty of us had just come outside for our daily hour of recreation. Since the ground was still moist enough for the red dirt to muddy our white shoes, nobody ventured onto the patchy grass. Instead, we kept to the paved half of our yard. As I stood near the gate absentmindedly deciding whether to exercise or play basketball, I yawned and squinted toward the bewildering stain. It was a puddle of darkness the size of a school bus. *What is that?* I asked myself, drifting forward. My skin prickled.

I stepped into the grass, then stopped. Off to my left, from the weight pile, came the thud of a heavy medicine ball plopping onto concrete, and suddenly the stain, only twenty yards away now, disintegrated into the lighted sky with tremendous popping sounds like an exploding string of firecrackers. I recoiled and heard somebody scream, "What the hell!"

Birds! Dark gray or brown lemon-sized birds. Hundreds of them! They flew so close together that each one's wings slapped against their neighbors' with loud *clap-clap-claps*. The birds didn't scatter but stayed knit together as a gigantic magic carpet that shot straight up. Its middle billowed higher (*clap-clap-clap*) before it arched forward, swooping toward us. I felt a moment of terror, but the group S-curved to my right only feet above my head (*clap-clap-clap*) toward the side wall. At the last second, that fantastic avian blanket bent up the wall, curled over it, then dropped down and out of sight.

That was the day I started paying attention to the birds. My heart beat hard as I stared after them, trying to process the poetry of how a dark stain in empty space could hide so much life. I wondered what they had been doing—sleeping? Had we startled each other awake?

I'm not sure how the feeding began, but I doubt it started with honey buns and Doritos—food that cost us money. Unlike other prisoners, Death Row residents have little access to prison jobs. There are perhaps fifteen jobs to divide among the roughly 140 of us here. Each job pays only between forty cents and a dollar per day; that's eight daily hours of work for, at best, seven dollars per week. Most of us are utterly reliant on the kindness of family and friends to send us money. It's too scarce and precious to throw at birds.

It is also against prison rules to bring food to the rec yard, where the birds are, and to catch an infraction is to pay a ten-dollar fine and spend weeks in solitary confinement, called the hole. The prison staff assumes if we are toting around store-bought snacks, then we must be looking to barter for some debauchery: pills, handjob, cigarette, bottle of hooch.

Thus, the feeding had to begin with something worthless, like dry cereal or biscuit remnants. But I was too proud to ask other prisoners, "Hey, uh...you gonna eat them biscuits?" Only the poorest among us would be desperate enough to walk around snacking on a pocketful of stale bran flakes or shitty prison biscuits.

Considering it was late summer, I suspect that feeding the birds wasn't incidental. It wasn't a matter of a guy turning out his faded red jumpsuit's pockets to empty them of crumby contraband that the birds gobbled off the dirt. And it wasn't something guys had *always* done, given the consequences. Since Death Row's relocation twelve years prior, we'd been using this rec yard and had seen only a smattering of birds. Something new was calling them to congregate *en masse*. It was almost Biblical.

Death Row was going through changes both outwardly and inwardly. A couple months prior, for the first time, we were granted access to a creative writing class. Before then, whenever we requested educational opportunities, the prison's administrators responded with a curt, "You are not here to be rehabilitated." The unspoken subtext: *You are here to be executed.*

There was neither hope to regain our freedom nor hope to become healthier, better people. Even among us prisoners, the prevalent attitude was *What's the point of self-improvement? It won't help me get out.*

Dr. Kuhns was a new psychologist appointed earlier in 2016 to oversee Death Row's mental health treatments. In his mid-thirties and lanky, he always wore slacks and a sweater-vest-over-button-down combo that had a laid-back, New Age patchouli vibe.

One of the first ideas he injected into us was this: five out of every seven people sentenced to die ultimately get their sentences reduced or overturned altogether—that is, two-thirds of us could leave Death Row alive.

Armed with the unshakable faith of a sandblasted prophet and braced with the knowledge that one hundred of us could walk off Death Row, some to go home, Dr. Kuhns wanted to prepare us for reintegration. First, though, he needed to convince us we could, to help us see with blinding sight.

Skinny statistics are hard to hang onto when one is caught in the cosmic supergravity of endless, empty time, concrete and concertina wire, and a culture of despair. Spending decades on Death Row while convinced you'll be executed is traumatic, especially if one is innocent. About half our population has been diagnosed with chronic, severe, or persistent mental illness.

So widespread are the psychological disorders that Death Row is considered a "residential treatment area," an extension of Central Prison's

Mental Health Unit. As head of outpatient treatment, Dr. Kuhns was able to set up his office on Death Row, making himself available daily. As part of our individualized treatment plans, he prescribed therapeutic activities along with, or instead of, medication—activities like anger management groups, literacy pursuits, yoga or meditation therapy, and depression management.

Dr. Kuhns believed in holistic treatment and that medication should be a last resort or, at most, a small part of a well-rounded plan. Before he arrived, patients saw a therapist once a month and received a cocktail of psych meds daily; that was the total extent of their treatment. In fact, the monthly "therapy" sessions weren't geared toward actually healing the patients but were simply opportunities for the shrink to convince guys to accept their fate—which would tighten the mental and chemical straitjackets he or she had wrapped the patients in. The aim had been sedation. It was a one-size-fits-all approach that fit no one.

Though in 2013 we prisoners were just awakening to the growing bird population on Death Row, I wondered whether they'd staked out their claim to our rec yard before our presence there.

In North Carolina, the Death Row unit is a hastily built wing hidden within Central Prison's sprawling compound. The rec yard is wedged into a corner of the prison's thirty-foot-high inner perimeter wall, which consists of humongous, brown two-ton bricks. Originally, the wall was much lower because it had been built using prison labor—prisoners were forced to imprison themselves—hence the eventual rebuilding by government workers.

The rec yard is boxed in on its other two sides by the compound's gray, four-story buildings. Spiky spirals of concertina wire guard the fence tops that trim concentric squares within an area that was repurposed (again) in 2001, after the old sector had been demolished to make way for Death Row.

Beyond layers of walls and chain link fences, what remains is our rinky-dink rec yard. Above it is a crisp slice of blue-white, apple-pie sky, fifty paces per side.

In the yard, birds and humans each hold clearly defined territories. The section of the yard where brick fragments of the old sector still protrude from the building—that part belongs to the pigeons, wrens, and sparrows. A fifteen-foot-high fence splits it from the main yard. Pigeons line the rooftop's ledges. Smaller birds roost in broken crevices up and down the building's side. Our well-worn footpath traces the edges of the yard, skimming right past their fence like a foot-wide muddy ribbon. On the other side of the dirt track is our volleyball court.

Like dark-humored mockers, the crows dance and laugh (*ha-HA! ha-HA!*) amidst the coils of barbed wire bolted five feet from the top of the adjacent perimeter wall. Above them, on the wall's walkway, rifle-toting guards pace back and forth between gun towers overlooking our yard.

The hawks swim lazy figure eights half a mile up or alight on a spotlight that swivels on the gun tower roofs, all while stalking our yard. Sometimes we emerge for rec and discover remnants of hawk suppers: platter-sized rings of bloody feathers lying on the grass.

Back then, one Death Row resident, New York, usually stayed in the exercise area doing pull-ups, push-ups, dips, and squats, but one day I noticed him on the footpath, making a lap. Pushing fifty, New York was a lifelong convict, short and thickly muscled, and his free world contacts kept his inmate trust fund account stacked with store credits. Altogether then, it surprised me to witness the next few minutes.

New York pulled out a gallon-sized resealable bag from beneath his shirt, fat as a throw pillow and filled with wadded-up white bread and biscuits. When he approached along the footpath, the birds sprang to life. Unhinged, they made enchanting chirping noises as they flocked toward him.

From the roof, pigeons leapt over the fence, free-falling from the sky, flapping a couple of times before they plopped into the dusty grass. At ground level, wrens and sparrows hopped and skipped through gaps in the chain link fence. Their delighted twitters sparkled in the air. For sixty seconds, New York stood nodding, sowing fistfuls of bread and biscuits in broad sweeps. He made it rain. Chunks thunked off bird heads and bellies, prompting them to turn towards the touch. They snatched their dusty manna fragments, flew home to drop them off, and came back for more.

After feeding the masses, New York folded the empty bag and slid it in his pocket, then waded through the birds, gently shooing them out of the way to continue his lap. For a minute, dozens of birds went back and forth. Then, the pigeons posted up on the roof again, cooing and preening and splatting their crap on the ground below. The wrens and sparrows tweeted merrily from within their hidey-holes.

Walking casually, New York took a few minutes to complete his lap. Like most of us in prison, he was typically secretive with his feelings, his features inscrutable. He spoke in whispers as if his very words were contraband. When he circled back, saw the bread gone, and heard the happy bird chatter that greeted him, his blank face split into an unrestrained grin (I never knew he had so many teeth!), and I saw the guileless little boy he must've been before the streets had hardened his lips, before the prison had hidden him. This was the *real* New York. His gold tooth glimmered in the sun.

He sidled to the fence, leaned his palms and forehead on it, and spoke tenderly to the birds. "How you doin' today? Your bellies full? Yeah, yeah, I always make sure you straight, don't I?"

As he spoke, his right hand stroked the fence. After a moment, he continued to exercise, still grinning and gleaming. Later, when I passed him in the hall, his veneer of indifference was fitted into place, his gold-flecked grin tucked away with his bread bag.

According to Dr. Kuhns, a dying man has more to lose than his life.

Although statistically most of us would probably leave Death Row alive, Dr. Kuhns preached that even if our deaths were certain, we had something to hang onto: our identity and dignity as men. We didn't have to let prison define us; we didn't have to live by anyone's definition of us.

Our identity is an empty lot onto which we can build anything we wish, but if we don't fill it ourselves, somebody will fill it for us. Indeed, we realized that by default, many somebodies had already filled it while we stood by in ignorance. Knowledge empowered us to clear out our accumulated junk, to demolish the prison structures others had erected to contain us, and to redefine ourselves with ideas and boundaries as we saw fit.

Later on, to illustrate the power of storytelling, another doctor introduced us to a psychological principle called the self-fulfilling prophecy: what we believe about others determines our attitudes and actions toward them, which subsequently influences their attitudes and actions. For example, many people, both free and imprisoned, believe "once a criminal always a criminal" and define all prisoners, whether guilty or not, as subhuman, moral reprobates. Therefore, they shun and vilify the new prisoner; prison staff mistreat him and expose him to inhumane conditions of confinement; fellow prisoners victimize him and/or try to force him to conform to the brutal, criminal culture dominating prison life.

As a result, the prisoner starts believing it is hopeless and pointless to resist or change for the better. The prisoner succumbs to prison's rhythms, attitudes, and behaviors—characterized by crime, violence, and moral decay—making the prisoner worse than when he arrived. This confirms the preconceived notion of prisoners as irredeemable and perpetuates the cycle.

However, it is possible to break this destructive cycle and to replace it with a cycle of growth and positive reinforcement. While it would be years before we learned to consciously recognize this principle in our own lives, this is exactly what Dr. Kuhns empowered us to do. Instead of being puppets to prison culture and public perception, instead of letting circumstances and other people determine our attitudes and behaviors, many of us would choose to take control of our lives, to plot our own stories, to birth some lightning.

As a Christian, I would decide to just be me: undefined, unlimited except by God's physics and morality. I wanted to grow into man as God had created man to be.

Dr. Kuhns called this process "changing the narrative." His aim was nothing less than to transform the Death Row zeitgeist. To expedite this, he recruited teachers from Duke University to lead classes on Death Row, beginning with writing therapy.

The first semester's theme was "Writing from Captivity," an overt inoculation against the idea that imprisonment equates to powerlessness. The class featured texts such as Viktor Frankl's *Man's Search for Meaning*, written from captivity in a Nazi concentration camp; Dr. Martin Luther King's letters from jail; and the Apostle Paul's New Testament letters, written from dungeons.

One of the first memoirs we studied was by a man who'd been a science teacher before his incarceration. He viewed prison life as a man-made wilderness that induced men to behave in unnatural and dehumanizing ways, guards and prisoners alike. The very architecture of confinement reinforces the culture caged within. The endless layers of walls and fences not only estrange bodies from their former activities, but also divorce psyches from their former selves. Many people define themselves by where they are (or are from), what they do (or did), and who they interact(ed) with. The prisoner finds himself in an ostensibly civilized structure inhabited by wildness, like a zoo that works to devolve men into monkeys.

In an effort to maintain his humanity, dignity, and identity, the author began studying the nonhuman creatures that shared his prison habitat. He spent time journaling about plants, animals, and insects he observed, especially in his rec yard, many of which he recognized from his pre-prison days. They consistently behaved the same in prison as out of it. Wildlife, he concluded, stayed true to itself. It respected no arbitrary boundaries or social constructions. *Why not man?* he asked himself. *Why not me?* The writer made us ask ourselves too.

To us twenty-plus participants, Dr. Kuhns distributed journals and asked us to engage with and write about the wildlife here. Although some birds had always inhabited our rec yard, I think it was because of this assignment that the feeding truly began—for the birds and for us.

By spring 2014, a handful of guys were feeding the birds, including me. That year, two geese appeared near the far wall, where I had seen the eerie puddle of birds the summer before. The base of that wall was the original prisoner-built wall, seven feet deep and tall, like a huge step. Its top was overgrown with lush grass.

One day, a goose was atop it, sitting on a pile of eggs. On the ground below, another goose started marching back and forth when it saw us coming. We assumed they were mates. Though we gave them no names because we didn't want to get attached, I see them now as Adam and Eve—symbols of new beginnings.

As we approached, Adam became visibly agitated. When we got about five yards away, he established a boundary with a cacophony of threats; he flapped his broad white wings, charged, hissed, honked at anyone who came nearer. He was quite intimidating. Most of us had never seen such large birds in person before. Their bodies were as big as basketballs, their wingspan between three and four feet, their thick necks at least a foot long.

None of us wanted the geese to turn us into shrieking, flailing little boys, so we stayed where we were, as men, well beyond the noise-bubble Adam had made. They ignored the bread we tossed them. Adam seemed dignified, too proud to accept our charity. I could relate to that. We stood in clusters around them, wondering where they had come from and why, of all places, they'd chosen to lay their eggs on Death Row's rec yard, right out in the open.

The next day when we tossed bread to the geese, Adam waddled over to it. Eve didn't move. Her world had shrunk to one activity: sitting on the eggs. She was so still and picturesque, she could've been a trophy on a mantle. Adam would pluck up pieces of bread and hop-flap onto the seven-foot step, laying it gently on the grass before Eve, and she'd bend her neck, almost daintily, and gobble it in one gulp. Then, she'd return to trophy-mom pose. Adam would eat a piece for himself and bring his wife a bite, then repeat until the table was empty.

Though Adam was usually hypervigilant, tracking the forty or so men milling around the rec yard, one day I noticed he was less aggressive. He kept his beak open, his tongue lolling around, and he was audibly huffing. It occurred to me he must be hot and thirsty. On and around our footpath were shallow depressions, and into one of these I poured out my water bottle, making sure Adam saw me. Immediately, he loped over and lapped at the water, shoving his beak and face under the cool stream flowing from my bottle.

I was moved to compassion at his evident relief and desperately wanted to pet him, but I restrained myself and tried to verbally soothe him. "See, we're not trying to hurt you. We only want to make sure y'all are okay."

Adam cocked his head, eyeing me steadily, and seemed to understand my tone, if not my words. Then, he resumed slurping the water. I was pleased he didn't bite me or swat me with a wing for my undue familiarity. When another guy poured water into a divot atop the step for Eve, Adam merely hissed half-heartedly.

Over the next few weeks, the topic of geese built a nest in our mouths. Our eyes lit up and our breath expanded gleefully at the thought of Adam and Eve trusting us with their most precious possessions—their lives and lineage. Pale men who hadn't gone outside in years went to visit our new neighbors. The guards pretended not to see the bags of biscuits bulging under our shirts as we went to rec. We even set out bowls of water for the geese, and an officer supplied a large tinfoil pan—the kind you roast turkeys in—that we filled with water and placed in the wall's shade. It was the geese's personal pond, just big enough for two.

After a time, the geese were getting heavy, which was dangerous on several levels. They looked scrumptious to predators. Adam seemed slower, and I imagined he'd get winded easily if he had to fly evasive maneuvers or fistfight one of the foxes that found a way into our yard. I was so concerned about their encroaching obesity and diabetes (both had killed my dad) that I started bringing Adam and Eve a more balanced diet. Figuring we weren't doing them any favors with all the carbs we fed them, I smuggled sandwich baggies full of green beans, corn, lima beans, and bran flakes from the cafeteria. Though they devoured the meals I brought them, they nevertheless found bread irresistible.

I was certain we'd so spoiled them that they could no longer forage for themselves. Admittedly, I had no idea what geese eat in the wild. When the rain barred us from going outside, I worried our geese would go hungry all day or might think we had abandoned them. I had tasted hunger for days on end before, and I still bore a stretch-marked heart, distended by abandonment.

Though I fretted about our neighbors' welfare, beneath my apprehension lay an undercurrent of joy. It felt good to care for the needs of other creatures, to be needed by them and prove dependable—prove to myself, that is. I had hurt a lot of people in my life by letting them down, by putting my needs and wants above theirs. These geese offered me a sip of homebrewed atonement.

The geese didn't care about my past reputation; they judged me by our present interactions. They didn't shield themselves from us with impenetrable walls and razor-wire attitudes, but demanded we scoot over in our already cramped rec yard to share our grass and dirt and slice of sky.

As the time approached for the goslings to hatch, I sensed a corresponding stir of new life within me. To Adam and Eve, this wasn't a prison for the condemned, but a paradise for those with wings. To them, and to me now too, our rec yard was a secret garden in which to grow together with unchecked luxuriance.

Even now, two decades after Death Row's relocation, fragments of moldy red brick stick out like broken ribs from the prison and lurk beneath the surface of our rec yard's hard-packed orange dirt. Whereas before the old processing dorm stood welcoming new prisoners, now fist-sized chunks of it lay just beneath the surface of our ramshackle volleyball court—beneath our sense of fun and community—poking up to break complacent hopes and toes.

The solid boundaries enclosing the yard are designed to restrict our movements; the shabby castaway appearance meant to dampen our enthusiasm for nature and activity. I find that such pressures tend to magnify what's inside a man. Rather than dampening our morale, the walls create a perfect echo chamber that amplifies life.

Everything on Death Row is full contact, including our communion. Our volleyball net is more ironic than hard-and-fast rule. With eyes that blaze like meteors, we crash against it, throwing ourselves into each other. We've torn shoulder sockets, herniated discs, and chipped vertebrae. We've bruised whole sides of our bodies during these friendly empathetic collisions to demonstrate our devotion to the game, to each other, to life.

We share the bread and wine within us: our hope, the gorgeous sky-wafers, our mutual bruising.

From the dirt of Earth, God made man, then filled him with the breath of life. And it's true: the ground calls us all to return its dust to it, but some of us resist. For kinetic spirits, there is grass and sky and wildlife. We emerge from the side of Central Prison to play in earth, replenish our God-given humanity, and cling to its sweet breath by the sweat of our brow. The walls press us into each other and toward the only space left open to us: up—the place from which that thing with feathers descends. We go to catch and sing the sun in flight.

§

Voices from Death Row

TESSIE CASTILLO

"Don't shake the inmates' hands," said the beefy prison guard, who towered at least a foot over my head. "The men won't wash their hands for a week, and they'll use them to masturbate. I don't want to be cleaning jizz off the walls."

I glanced at the floor while Dr. Kuhns, the soft-spoken prison psychiatrist standing next to me, told the officer I was a volunteer who'd come to teach a journaling class to the men on Death Row.

The guard curled his lip and waved us into an adjacent classroom.

"Can't believe I have to put extra guys on the shift for this shit," he grumbled as we walked past him.

When we were out of earshot, Dr. Kuhns apologized. "Sorry about him. We just started offering classes to prisoners a few weeks ago. Some of the staff are supportive, but others..." He shrugged.

"It's okay," I said, looking around the "classroom," which was nothing more than a concrete room with a whiteboard on one wall and a few chairs stacked in a corner. Dr. Kuhns and I arranged the chairs in a circle.

"I'll stick around for your first class to help with introductions," he said.

I nodded. I'd been in the prison barely fifteen minutes and already the tension of the place clawed at me. The walk to the classroom seemed endless: corridor after concrete corridor interrupted by heavy automatic doors that grew louder as we got deeper into the belly of the prison. Operated by an unseen controller, the doors opened without warning and shut behind us with ominous clangs. We saw lines of prisoners trudge past. They glanced at us, hunched and hollow-eyed like coal miners wasted from lack of sun. But it was the air that added the final touch—basement air. Too still. Too stale.

As we sat down to await the men, nervousness skittered through me like tiny spiders. I'd never imagined that a chance meeting with Kuhns would lead to this day. What would it be like to be in a room full of men convicted of murder? How would they react to a woman among them? Adding to my general unease, Dr. Kuhns had asked me to keep these meetings a secret.

"The prison doesn't want news about the classes getting out to the public," he'd explained, adding with a sad smile, "People want us to punish these men, not teach them anything."

After several minutes, a line of men in blood-red jumpsuits shuffled into the classroom. I jumped up and offered my hand (damn the guard) which some of them took, though few smiled in return. The correctional officer remained outside in the corridor. As the last man sat down, I took a deep breath.

"Welcome to the first day of journaling class," I said. "My name is Tessie, and I'm here to teach you how to share your stories."

I described my teaching background and expressed a desire to help them write about their lives. Then, I asked the men to introduce themselves. As they went around the room, I tried to remember their names. Most of them looked at the floor when speaking although some perked up when it was their turn to explain why they'd signed up for the writing class.

"I didn't get much schooling, so this is an opportunity to learn" was a common theme, as was "I have a story to tell." A couple admitted signing up out of boredom or curiosity.

After introductions, Dr. Kuhns passed out journals and I asked the men to write for ten minutes about anything they wanted to share. They hunched over their notebooks, the room filling with the soft sound of scribbling.

As they wrote, I had a better opportunity to look at them. The dozen or so men represented all ages, heights, and girths, and were about eighty percent Black and twenty percent white.

Before my first day of class, Dr. Kuhns had sent me a class roster. Overcome by curiosity, I had used it to research their crimes. I assumed that the death sentence was reserved for the most heinous crimes, those involving children, rape, torture, or serial killing. After all, many murders are committed each year, but not many people wind up on Death Row.

To my surprise, I discovered very few men in my class had been convicted of exceptionally grisly murders. The vast majority of their crimes involved drug deal skirmishes or robberies gone wrong. In fact, one man in my class had not killed anyone at all. He had been the getaway driver for a robbery during which an accomplice had shot someone, and while he received the death penalty for his crime, the actual murderer did not.

When the ten minutes were up, I asked the men to put down their pencils.

"Who would like to share what they wrote?" Everyone looked at each other, but no one said a word.

"Come on," I coaxed. "Anyone?"

A short man with a round face raised a tentative hand.

"Go ahead, Chanton," I said, pleased that I remembered his name.

He began reading with a cadence that revealed a long life in the streets and little formal education. He had written a scene from his childhood about a bird that escaped a trap he had set.

"The day I watched that bird escape, not once did I consider what the ordeal must have been like for it," he wrote. "I didn't consider how afraid it must have been, swallowed up in the darkness. The loneliness and confusion it must have felt...would its family miss it? Were there young that depended on its safe return for survival? Today, on Death Row, I am that bird. Yet here, there are no cracks to breach, no slits from which to escape, and the only air to breathe holds the aroma of death."

His story earned appreciative claps and words of encouragement from the rest of the men. After Chanton's story, a couple of others volunteered to share. Some had written about simple things like their dislike of prison food, or "chow," but others dug deep and shared personal stories. A tall man named Paul with graying dreadlocks shared an essay about a visit from his granddaughter and how much it pained him to be separated from her by thick Plexiglas walls. Another wrote of the loneliness of prison since none of his family members would write to him. Each recitation was met with claps and murmurs of support. By the time our two hours were up, the shyness in the room had eased and the men were eager to share.

After the first class, I continued to visit every two weeks. Sometimes, a correctional officer sat in a corner of the classroom as I taught, but usually the guard on duty patrolled an outside corridor and I was left alone with the men. Not once did any of them give me a reason to feel afraid.

Most of the classes followed a similar format. At the end of our two hours together, the group voted on writing prompts, which they completed before the next class. During class, the men read their excerpts aloud and offered each other feedback. Most of the prompts they chose were about yearning for freedom and family. Another consistent theme was regret that they couldn't see their children grow up.

For one exercise, the men selected the prompt "women." I braced myself, fully expecting an onslaught of porn-inspired fantasies.

But when we gathered to read their pieces aloud, not one person had written about women in the context of sex. Most wrote tributes to the strong mothers, grandmothers, aunts, and sisters who'd raised them. Others wrote tender stories of first kisses and grade-school crushes.

After a few weeks, Dr. Kuhns suggested we divide into two groups for an hour each. The smaller size would be more conducive to a critique-style class. In this intimate setting, I got a closer look at each of the men. There was Alim, a large bear of a man with a booming voice that would have been perfect for radio. I loved to hear him read because he injected dynamics and theatricality into his readings, which were fraught with regret and remorse. Alim was the only man in my class who ever admitted he was guilty of murder. The majority remained silent on the topic of guilt or innocence, and I never asked.

Chanton, the soft-spoken man who had shared his story of the escaped bird, encouraged the other men to share more and never held back on his own stories. He laughed often and radiated a warmth that filled the bland, cement room.

Lyle, tall and gangly, spoke rarely and smiled even less, but when he did speak, his words revealed a raw intelligence and insight that could silence the group. He was a good writer and had already written a memoir of his life leading up to his death sentence, but his pieces lacked emotion. I encouraged him to open up more. He seemed reserved and a bit standoffish, yet I later discovered he harbored a deep desire to help others.

Most of the men suffered from some form of mental illness, anxiety, or depression. Often when someone was absent from class, I was told he had been too despondent to get out of bed that morning. Several admitted that our class was the only reason they got out of bed. Some men drifted into the classroom like zombies, then slowly came alive, massaged awake by the sharing of stories. They grinned shyly when it was their turn to read, nodded at constructive criticism, and encouraged each other. I was careful with my critiques because I saw that under their tough exteriors, the men were sensitive and anxious to please their teacher.

After months of listening to their stories, it was clear that, with few exceptions, the men had followed similar paths to Death Row. They wrote about growing up in poor neighborhoods and witnessing violence as young as three or four years old. They recounted the recklessness and adrenaline of adolescence in a frustrated culture where street cred was everything and you earned it by being tougher and meaner than the guy next to you. In a world where compassion was perceived as weakness, the men were conditioned to show a reptilian coolness, trip-wire responses to perceived disrespect, and loyalty to crew even if it meant taking a life or losing one's own.

Paul, the man with dreadlocks who'd written about his granddaughter the first day of class, wrote in one of his pieces, "My stepdad left when I was nine, telling me I was the man of the house. It was a brutal environment. People had to know they couldn't fuck with me. That's where my focus had to be. But I didn't do a good job. I was not a good big brother or 'man of the house.' I was afraid. I was a kid. I was conflicted. My spirit is gentle, yet I had to compete and contend with killers."

Six months into the journaling program, another man was sentenced to Death Row. The newspapers described the events leading to his trial in vivid detail, and most of the public comments were of the "Off with his head!" variety. Though I cringed reading the description of his crime, I couldn't label him a monster, given the experience I'd had with my students. I wanted to share my story about the men on Death Row, but I recalled Dr. Kuhn's warning about not letting the public know about our classes. For weeks, I grappled with the decision, in the end deciding to publish an editorial in the local paper.

It's hard to describe what compelled me to write about the class despite the possible consequences—it was probably the same motive that drove me to volunteer on Death Row in the first place. My heart beats for society's rebels and misfits. Perhaps the rulebreaker in me senses kinship. There's authenticity to people who have suffered a lot. The more time I spend with people discarded by the rest of society, the more those experiences convince me that most people, even the rulebreakers, are not dangerous, immoral, or unredeemable. Everyone is broken in some way, only some of us are broken in ways that are easier to hide.

I published the editorial in May 2014, in part to convey a more accurate and humane picture of people on Death Row and in part as an act of defiance. An excerpt reads:

> I have been meeting twice a month with about fifteen men on Death Row, and the experience has been both edifying and moving. I don't see heartless killers, though they might have killed in a moment of heartlessness. I see anger

problems, stubbornness, lack of self-control, immaturity, and miseducation. I see those qualities in people outside prison too. I see them in myself sometimes. But in these men, I also see pain, regret, a capacity for kindness, and self-reflection—and a desire to be seen for what they are: flawed and very human...After spending time with these men and listening to their stories, I don't claim to know them thoroughly or to fully comprehend why they did what they did. Nor do I defend the crimes of any man on Death Row...But I will defend their humanity because I see it every time I walk through those prison doors. I would challenge those who support the death penalty to spend time getting to know a Death Row inmate on a personal level. In each of these men, there are many things worth understanding, worth supporting, and worth saving.

Two weeks later, I received a letter from the prison warden:

Dear Ms. Castillo,

It is in the best interest of all parties concerned that you be dismissed as a Community Volunteer. Therefore, effective immediately, you will not be allowed to enter the facility as a Community Volunteer. I thank you for your service to Central Prison.

As I read the letter, my hands shook and guilt pooled in the pit of my stomach. In publishing the editorial, I had risked the consequence of dismissal. For that, my students had lost one of the only things that broke the relentless monotony of life in prison. I had risked something important to them without asking their permission.

I appealed my dismissal but it was denied, so I began writing to the men. The first round of letters I sent out received a flurry of responses from Chanton, Lyle, Alim, Paul, and later, a man who was not in my class, George. The men graciously accepted my apology for the editorial and over the ensuing weeks, months, and, eventually, years, we developed a steady correspondence. The men wrote about life in prison, family, books, spirituality, personal growth, and coming to terms with their sentences. At times, the letters were cheerful. On other occasions, they seemed half mad from emasculation and grief.

Paul once wrote, "Living in this environment is to experience death in the form of life. There is the anguish of living day to day knowing the suffering you have caused and not being able to make amends. Watching your family deteriorate as you drift further apart, not being able to comfort, console, or even wipe away the tears, you die a little every day."

Lyle, the tall, quiet student, confessed, "Over the years, I continue to lean on prayer and try to live my life as it should have been from the beginning. And as I go along, discovering all these wonderful things about life that I can no longer touch, taste, smell, see, and feel, I beg God for mercy. I plead with him to give my time here purpose beyond punishment."

I imagined Alim's booming voice as I read his words about Death Row: "I'm accustomed to being the 'exhibit' with my life experiences, thoughts, and feelings on display. But rarely is there an opportunity for meaningful exchange. It's like everybody wants to look at the monster, but everybody is afraid to let the monster see them. People on Death Row are vulnerable because they want to be known, they want to be understood, and that is usually because people have already seen the worst of who they can be... it is easy for me to tell you about the worst thing I have ever done in my life... I wear a uniform that says it: 'There is the killer, the one in the red jumpsuit.' But how easy would it be for you to tell me the worst thing you have ever done—and then, what if you had to wear a uniform or some symbol to let everyone know your sin?"

Over months and years, the letters piled up. Secrets spilled from the folders where I kept our correspondence. Voices cried out to be heard. In 2016, I proposed the idea of a book to four of my correspondents— Alim, Lyle, Chanton, and George. The men agreed to work with me, and over the ensuing years, sent me dozens of essays about their paths to conviction and their struggles not only to cope with a death sentence, but to thrive in spite of it, proving that grace and self-reflection can grow even in the most unlikely of places.

In writing this book, I have come to believe there's little that separates people inside Death Row from those outside. We are all a complex jumble of hopes, dreams, virtues, and mistakes. We all strive to be better people. We all fail often in that endeavor. Yet, part of being human is learning to rise again—as these men do, despite all odds—to prove that we are all more than our worst crime.

TERRY ROBINSON, A.K.A. CHANTON

Plumland

One summer, my older brother Ray and I dropped in to visit family after recently moving away from the neighborhood. I was excited to be back at my old stomping grounds, especially since my cousin Chris lived nearby. Chris was adventurous. Everything from tree climbing for pecans to combing ditches for crawfish was a theme offered in his storybook.

Today, when Chris came by, he said, "Hey, Duck, ya wanna go to Plumland?"

Doggone right I wanted to go to Plumland. My nodding head was more a reaction than a reply. At seven years old, anything with the word "land" in it sounded good to me. Ice creamland. Cakeland. To me, a place called Plumland held the potential for something biblical, like Eden.

Before I knew it, our journey had begun. As I slipped into my role as devout sidekick, Chris led me across a railway and through a wooded area. Once we came to a busy freeway, I knew I was venturing into forbidden waters. *My momma would kill me if she knew I was way out here,* I thought. But I could already taste the sweet plum nectar exploding in my mouth. I decided that what my mom didn't know wouldn't hurt her.

Before long, we were squeezing under the tight crawlspace of a fence and navigating through insect-infested weeds as tall as our heads.

And then... Plumland. Rows upon rows of pillowy treetops draped with succulent red ornaments. Even the ground, with its speckled ensemble of heavenly droppings, gave an offering.

I went plum crazy. The rest of the afternoon passed in a blur. Drunk off rapture, I vaguely remember that the subject of swimming goggles came

Ray (brother) and Chanton, 1980.

up. A department store called Nichols just so happened to be across the roadway. Chris said we were going to get some goggles. Still munching fruit, I shrugged and followed along. Chris was eight. He called the shots.

We dashed across the freeway, maneuvered through a maze of parked cars, and breezed through the main entrance as though we belonged. Chris said we had to pretend we were with our parents so no one would notice us.

Once inside, we beelined for the toy department. I was still hyped on plum juice and couldn't keep my hands to myself. I was troubleshooting every toy I could but was careful to put each one back. At one point, when I was holding a Tonka truck, Chris said, "You like that truck? Put it in your pocket!"

I didn't put it in my pocket, but Chris did. He took it from my hands and shoved it in my pocket. And nothing happened. We moved onto the next toy, another Tonka truck. Chris said we could have it because this big store didn't care about little stuff like that, so I put it in my pocket. Along with another Tonka truck. And another. Next, we saw some wristbands. I didn't know what they were used for, but Chris took a pair, so I did too.

Eventually, we found some goggles. By that point, I was a thieving mirror of Chris's mischief, cramming the swimwear down my trousers in likeness. Next, there was the cap gun. And the caps. Then, more Tonka trucks.

After a while, it was time to go, and man, was I loaded. Tonka trucks looped around my waistband like a Batman utility belt. Wristbands packed into my socks, and goggles jiggled in my drawers. Head high, I walked like it was the greatest day of my life.

I hadn't noticed the scattered trail of Tonka trucks rolling down my pants leg and causing havoc in the aisles as patrons maneuvered their shopping carts to avoid collision. Chris was a few paces ahead with the exit door in sight. Then, out of nowhere, a burly Black dude with a navy-blue uniform and badge swooped in and grabbed Chris by the arm and me at the shoulder.

"Y'all bring y'all ass wit' me!"

I almost yelled, "Help! Stranger danger!" but then I looked into Chris's face and knew. He hadn't told me about this part. I could already feel the belt whacking across my butt when my momma found out.

Watching the playback, the security guard seemed pissed—but not just because of lost property value. He chastised us with his silence and disciplined us with his glare. By the time our parents arrived, I knew what jail was like. Even a butt whooping paled in comparison to the disappointment in my mother's eyes at the thought of me taking something that wasn't mine. In one failure of judgment, I had undermined everything she worked for. How I wish I could say it was the last time my actions wouldn't match the man she had raised me to be.

A Letter to My Son

Dear Dyquante,

Hi, son. Thank you for the letter. It couldn't have come at a better time. After twenty years in a place where joy is scarce, it's nice to hear from my family. Your letter is the most meaningful thing that has happened to me on Death Row. It's not every day a man here receives words of encouragement from a son he hardly knows. Also, you spared me the resentment I know you must feel towards me for not being there when you were growing up. That couldn't have been easy. It's very thoughtful of you, son, but your own wellness should come first. Sometimes anger is medicine.

I know I haven't earned the right to call you my son since I haven't been much of a father. I could come up with a million excuses, but the truth is that I didn't try. I wanted to be there for you. I even promised myself that I would be a better father than mine was to me. As it turned out, breaking promises runs in the family. And now, here we are: a father who has passed nothing to his son but the consequences of my poor choices. Yet being able to call you my son means that no matter how bad things get, we will always have the chance to make it right.

I must've read your letter a hundred times—okay, maybe not that many, but more than normal or necessary. Each time I read it, my spirits were lifted beyond these prison walls and taken through an imagined period of your childhood: the first steps you took, wobbly yet determined to stand in life on your own two feet; watching your face beam proudly because your report card was marked with good grades; your courage mounting in the face of failure as your first bicycle ride ends in a fall; and that first crush on a girl whose bubbly smile and dimples enticed you to share your schoolyard candy. I read and reread your letter, turning the words into fictitious memories, forging a relationship with you from a sheet of scribbled letters. It pains me beyond words to admit that none of the memories are real—I was not actually there for these important milestones in your life.

I'm sorry. I know it doesn't matter much now, but I can't go on with this letter without saying it. I've got regrets for days, and though I'm filled with apologies, they do little to change the past. Still, son, I'm sorry because with all the dirt I've done and the trail of hurt I've left behind, I failed you the most. I'm sorry that my letter will have to pass from one prison officer to another before it reaches you. I was nine when my dad wrote a letter to me from prison and I did nothing to break the cycle. I'm sorry I wasn't there to dispel the ugly rumors about my misdeeds or to confirm the ugly truths. But now, I've come too far towards accepting myself to hide who I am from my son. And that shitty relationship between you and your mom...yeah, that's on me too. You can't dog someone out the way I did to her and not expect their love to bite. I'm sorry that while you were being delivered to the world, I was on the corner delivering crack. I'm sorry that your late-night crying fits to be held or changed did not bring me running. The neglect and abandonment and the fact that I've yet to teach you a single thing—please, son, know that I am sorry. And though I couldn't be prouder to have you for a son, the thing I'm probably most sorry for is that you ended up with a man like me for a father.

In your letter, you asked me a question, a resounding one at that: What did I do to your mother to make her look at you with such hatred? Your question took me back to a time when I didn't much like myself, and I cared about hurting others even less. It was a time of shame and shamelessness that I've put far behind me, but your letter brought it roaring back. That one question is the measure of all my indecency and the sum of all my failures.

You want to know what I did to your mother to make her look at you the way she does? Everything. It might help to understand how Shatima and I met. Every child should know the coming together of their parents. Given our smeared past, I can only assume your mother was too sore with me to tell your origin story, or maybe she did and twisted it up until I'm just some horrible guy in the story. If so, then I should be horrible by my own account and no one else's.

In 1990, Shatima left Brooklyn, New York, to visit relatives in my hometown in North Carolina. In those days, much of the social influences were out of New York—hip hop, fashion, drugs. I was sixteen and impressionable as fuck. I'd dreamed of someday going to New York. Shatima was the first New Yorker I had ever met, and that made her interesting to be around. She was tall for her age with legs that looked primed for dancing. Her style of dress was right out of a *Right On* magazine—bell-bottoms, hoop earrings, fly sneakers, and a fresh 'do. That's how we talked in the '80s and '90s, Dy—"fresh" this and "fly" that. It meant your mom was cool. She had smooth, copper toned skin and unwavering brown eyes that toppled the confidence of boys. But to me, the most interesting thing about Shatima was her accent. Her pronunciation was so proper; she could've been an orator. I was used to the fast talkers in the dope game, always working an angle, or that hospitable Southern drawl heard across every countertop. The way Shatima strung words together was lyrical. A few times, she thought I was mocking when actually I was mimicking her to practice my New York accent.

At the time, I had a girlfriend, Renee, who was best friends with Shatima's cousin. The two friends were neighbors, which meant I didn't have to go far to see Shatima—she was always sitting on the porch. Sometimes, she came over to borrow sugar and we talked. Other times, I just watched her without saying much. It's like that when there's a jealous girlfriend. I couldn't be caught looking too long or smiling too much at

Shatima, which made me want to interact with her even more. We men can be that way, Dy, always wanting what we can't have. I didn't have eyes for your mom at first. I was mostly interested because she was off limits. Even so, my interest wasn't romantic. I was in love with Renee. I simply admired Shatima because she was different.

At the end of the summer, Shatima went home to Brooklyn. I focused on the relationship with Renee, which was veering downhill. The dreaminess for me in her eyes had begun to fade and I grew desperate for attention and affection. I decided I needed money. I was flopping out as a drug dealer, which is the case when you're hustling backwards—making one dollar but spending two. Then, one day, an older guy offered me money to be a lookout for him. I didn't know what for until I saw him snatch a woman's purse and run for his life. I was exhilarated just watching the crime unfold. I rooted for him to get away even as I swore off such a despicable offense—that woman could've been my momma. But a week later, I was hard up for cash and struck out on my own. It would be the first time I snatched a woman's purse—and the last.

I'll never forget that woman's scream as she dashed wildly behind me, yelling for me to bring back her purse. I felt scared and horrible—all her valuables were being carried off in my hands. That's fucked up. I almost feel like I'm perpetuating the violation against her by admiring someone whom I victimized, but that woman refused to give up the chase. I still think about her today. Thanks to her yells and pursuit, I was caught and shipped off to prison at seventeen years old.

What was it like for you, Dyquante, being on Rikers Island in New York for the first time? Could you smell the dread of prison in the air? Feel the walls closing in on you? Did your chest harden with fear of prison? Did your eyes blur with regrets? That's how it was for me. I had to adopt the behavior of guys I despised because their very existence put a daily strain on my courage. I acted like I didn't care about hurting people so that no one would want to hurt me. It was a long while before I realized that my fears were self-imposed. It's the belief that prisons are dangerous that makes the people in prison act poorly to protect themselves. I got into a fistfight or two that likely could've been avoided, but in prison, I learned that a good fistfight today was prevention for tomorrow.

After two years, as my release date approached, my worries began to shift. I was less concerned about the threat inside prison and more about the betrayal outside. Renee had written to me only once. I wondered how she could do that to me. I grew angrier by the day.

About one month before my scheduled release, I called around our hometown reconnecting with friends. Guess who I talked to—Shatima. It had been three years since I had last seen her, but her raspy voice was a clear indication of her maturity. Our conversation flowed like we were old friends. Shatima let me know that Renee had been fooling around with other guys while I was locked up. These secrets forged a friendship between us that left me feeling obligated. Shatima was jeopardizing her own relationship as "one of the girls" to give me a heads up. The least I could do was be a great friend. I swore I would pay back Renee for her betrayal, and I didn't care who I used to do it.

In those first couple of weeks after my release from prison, I dropped by a few times to see Shatima and her relatives. Their house was the hangout spot for all the neighborhood kids, so sometimes, I was there the entire day. Shatima had changed so much that I found myself noticing her a lot. She still had that refined dialect, but now it was a Southern blend. She towered over other teens her age and her slender legs moved with grace as she swished her hips side to side, exuding confidence. We talked idly for a week or so—no emotional spark, no romantic flare. Seriously, son, that's how close it came to you not being born. I'm not saying that as a good thing, just a factual one; sex was never in the plans.

Then, Renee came over one day and saw Shatima and me together. Her look was a razor's edge. I saw an opportunity for revenge. So, I started coming around more, and I acted as though Shatima was the best friend I had in the world. The ploy made Renee hot with jealousy, but I didn't consider how it would affect Shatima.

A few nights later, while Shatima and I were watching a movie, our moods took over, and you, my son, were conceived. I know because she whispered to me that night, "What are we gonna do about the baby?"

At the time, I thought she was crazy as hell, but in the spirit of the moment, I answered, "I'm gonna be there for you."

It turned out she wasn't talking crazy. She was being hopeful because she had real feelings for me. Call it wishful thinking, but she was convinced from our first time together that she was pregnant. I didn't believe it, but I played along until an ultrasound confirmed it. Shatima and I were having a baby. I was excited, Dy, but I was also scared. Most of all, I was conflicted. I tried to love your mom the way she deserved to be loved—which wasn't that hard since no woman had ever treated me as good as Shatima—but while Shatima was giving her heart to me, mine still belonged to Renee.

One day, a fistfight broke out between them, which got them both expelled from high school. I was faced with a dilemma: I was having a baby with one girl and in love with the other.

Son, I hope you know that I'm not telling you this because I was proud. It might've been a boost to my ego back then to have two women fight over me, but I was a teenager myself and dealing with insecurities. I figured the best way to face my problems was to turn my back on them. Apparently, that went for babies too—out of sight, out of mind.

I wish I could recount a nobler ending between your mother and me, one worthy of two people who were once friends. However, the truth is that things turned bad real quick and most of the hurt was my doing.

First, I falsely accused Shatima of cheating, which gave me the excuse to break it off with her. Then, I ignored her phone calls and rejected her attempts at reconciling. Shatima swore she had been faithful to me, but I pretended not to believe her. Damn, that was low. I watched her cry and plead her case for some shit I made up.

Even worse, I got back with Renee and flaunted our relationship in public. I still remember the look from Shatima when she saw me and

Renee holding hands; it was a cutting glare that made me drop my head. I was guilt-ridden all the time, but too selfish to consider her happiness when my own seemed dependent on pushing her away. I turned up my depravity by cussing her out and putting her down all while you, my son, were showing in her belly.

And when things went south between me and Renee for the final time, instead of patching it up with Shatima, I dealt the most despicable blow yet: I slept with her best friend. That was it right there, Dyquante— the one offense that made your mom despise me. You ever went too far to make a point then realize too late that the point was not worth the person lost? I hope you never know what it's like to lose someone like your mom. Then again, because of me, maybe you already do.

There's not much left to tell after that. You were born and shipped off to your grandparents in Brooklyn. I had thought it was just me that Shatima wanted nothing to do with. For all my negligence during the pregnancy, my attitude changed once you were born. I figured if I could be half the parent to you that my mom was to me, then we had a shot at making it in life together. I did at one point make a wholehearted pitch at custody of you. I had to try because otherwise, I would never be able to look you in the face after everything I put your mother through.

Unfortunately, Death Row was in my immediate future before we had much of a chance. I was on the fast track to nowhere for so long that anything good in my life felt wrong, like I was unworthy. I learned to sabotage the good in my life by treating people like shit. I needed to push people away before they were around long enough to hurt me. What I didn't account for was the collateral damage to you.

You want to know why your mother looks at you the way she does? It's because of the way I made her look at me. I brought discontent and disorder between you and your mother because I left her with a reminder of the hurt that I'd caused. I'm not excusing any lapse of parental judgment on her part; she'll have to answer for that. But as for the role I played, my sincerest apology, son, because I never meant for you to suffer for my failures. It was never about choosing between Shatima or Renee. The person I should have chosen was you.

I love you, son,

CHANTON

Salvation

The day I walked onto Death Row, I felt like an alien. My mind was a haze of confusion and disbelief. I wore sadness on my shoulders and disaster behind my eyes. The thud in my chest was of condemnation.

With leaden steps, I entered a warped capsule that was desolate though filled with men. Men with empty gazes and dejected postures, like forgotten relics tarnished by the cruelties of incarceration. I had never seen a walking dead man before, but I was now cast among the lot of them.

I dragged what was left of my mother's son and my state-issued property into a dim six by ten single cell, collapsed onto the folds of a mattress, and cried. As sleep reached up to cradle me, I prayed that I would not wake up again.

The next morning was better than expected. Some guys woke me to see if I wanted breakfast. A part of me viewed the gesture as thoughtful, another part, suspicious.

I arose, stiff and exhausted yet feeling more like myself. My survival instincts kicked in. I had to get it together. I studied the cell which was to become my permanent residence. Along the back wall was a vertical window of thick Plexiglas, shielded by a steel plate. Each wall was scarred with graffiti and chipped paint, with globs of toilet paper plastered over a cooling vent. The toilet was crude, steel, indecent.

Worst of all was the place upon which I was to lay each night: a thin metal slab bolted to the wall beneath a tatty mattress darkened with stains. I inhaled deeply, filling my lungs with the putrid smell of my reality, and found acceptance.

Later that day, the staff told me to pack up my property and move to another block. There were two co-defendants expected to arrive who had to be housed separately.

I walked onto another pod, identical to the one I'd left, except this one seemed smaller and even more cramped. Metal-framed bunks furnished a dayroom area that resembled a military barracks more than a prison block. Stashed away in the far reaches of a darkened corner was a tiny cavity—the shower.

Single-man cells spanned an upper and lower tier as prisoners meandered from room to room. Some men loitered around the dayroom tables while others sat wide-eyed before a blurred TV screen. There was one particular table designated as the gambling spot, where several men smoked stogies and drank coffee over a card game. The entire dorm was veiled in clouds of tobacco smoke. The air was stale and suffocating.

I received several glances though no one paid me much attention. They carried on as if to make me feel less uncomfortable. A tall, lanky guy sauntered over and indicated which bunk was mine. His accent was West Indian. I felt obliged though I couldn't help but wonder what he was up to.

We made brief introductions as I put my things away. He said we'd chat later when I was done.

Suddenly, a balding, middle-aged white guy launched himself up from the card game, his face twisted and steaming. He slammed his palm down on the table, puffed his chest, and roared, "This muthafucka ain't got a goddamn thang! He's just calling to be calling! I'll tell ya what. Call me one more time, sum-bitch, I'mma give you sumptin' to call about!"

The threat permeated the room in search of its victim. I froze. The West Indian guy assured me that everything was fine, that the uproar was deliberate and quite common. I asked what they were playing and he answered, "Penny poker."

Penny poker? I had never seen anyone make such a ruckus over pennies. Apparently, neither had the pudgy, blond-haired guy being yelled at. With his fingers interlaced and shoulders scrunched, his eyes roamed as low as the floor would allow. I felt sorry for him. I made a promise to myself not to gamble.

Several minutes passed before another guy approached and introduced himself. His face was mostly hidden under the bill of a cap and tinted shades, and he grinned as though he knew something no one else did. I was immediately suspicious—and nervous. His upper teeth were crowned with gold fronts, and he talked with the exaggerated swagger of an old-school pimp. He was strange and mysterious, the type of guy who whispers for no reason.

In no time at all, he was whispering to me.

"Aye, yo. I've got a way outta here. You wanna get outta here, don't cha?"

Hell yeah, I wanted out of there, more than anything. A longing for my family erupted inside me and bubbled over like fizzled cola. I didn't know the guy, nor trust him, but if he had a way to break out of Death Row, I wasn't going to pass it up.

He turned and headed for his room as I followed closely on his heels, cautious yet optimistic. The guy entered first. I checked behind me to be sure no one followed. From the doorway, I observed a room that was well-kept, with books lined neatly inside a wall locker and cosmetics situated atop a steel countertop. In the middle of the floor was an Islamic prayer rug. I was scared as shit when I entered.

The guy reached for a book, opened it, and began speaking to me about something he called the Pan-African movement. He said that we needed to elevate the consciousness of Black people to break loose the mental shackles of our oppressors.

What the hell? I kept waiting for him to peel back the prayer rug to reveal an underground passage, one that he had tunneled with a spoon. He didn't. I was disappointed to learn that there would be no path back to my family. I began feeling smothered under the dense layers of captivity.

Later that night, while most men were locked in their cells, there were a few of us assigned to the dayroom bunks due to overcrowding. I considered this a privilege since we were allowed to move around after lights out, stay up all night, and talk. The arrangement was similar to the county jail, so the transition was smoother than I had imagined.

Around midnight, the door to the pod squealed open and in walked a clean-cut, baby-faced young'un. There were tattoos on his arms and a bob in his step, yet his eyes held a certain unexpectedness.

I was laid back on the bunk, thumbing through an African book for my freedom. The young guy put his things away, turned, and offered me a cigarette. His courtesy compelled me to open up to him. We talked the remainder of the night.

One day, Young'un was upset with a mutual friend of ours and he wanted me to decide between the two of them. When I didn't, Young'un was upset with me.

The situation carried on for weeks, in which time we both learned things about each other that we didn't like—Young'un was stubborn; I was frustrated. Our friendship became strained after that.

A few years passed, and I hardly recognized Young'un. He grew troubled. Even his smile seemed to ache. I know why he was hurting—the same as I. It was the difficulty of living without his family.

I reached out to Young'un several times, but he shut me out. The shadows of his transgressions were upon him and there would be no defeating his inner demons.

On August 5, 2007, he hung himself with a bed sheet. He was twenty-eight.

Afterwards, Death Row changed for me. Before, I had hoped for a reversal and acquittal. Suddenly, the chaos was real; the likelihood that I would not leave Death Row alive.

Anger inside me stirred for the executions. I thought about my legacy and how I'd be remembered. I didn't want the pain that I'd caused to be the end of my chapter. I didn't want my voice stifled away in a pine box. I didn't want my children to wonder what kind of father I would've been, nor my accusers to determine the man I was. I didn't want my life to be a blemish on history.

What I wanted was to have a say in how I'm remembered. I wanted the people I loved to know that I tried to be a better man. I'd seen how regrets could consume a man's spirit; I wanted my regrets to be a tool for a change. And if I should perish on Death Row, then I wanted nothing more than to be at peace with myself. That is why I write.

Chatty

Fridays on Death Row are good for one thing: visits from family and friends.

Today, when I arrived at Visitation, I found my mother waiting beyond the fortified glass. She smiled earnestly, unfazed by the officer who secured me in an isolated booth. After greeting each other, we talked momentarily before I noticed that she was squirming in her seat. Her effort to contain herself was evident although I still hadn't guessed why.

Then, out from beneath the steel counter crawled an adorable, yet furtive, tot. She wore a teddy bear t-shirt and fluffed trousers and her plaits were fastened with assorted hair bows.

She whirled around to study me with cinnamon eyes that held me in their gaze. A subtle smile crept along her face before she struggled to climb onto the seat, defiant of her pint-sized stature. There was a fearlessness—a result of her naïvetè—which left me feeling intimidated.

I searched my thoughts for an explanation, but they only gave way to guilt. Her confusion was marked by an arched brow as the discomforting silence increased.

She then rocked on her haunches, squared her shoulders, and declared, "Hi, I'm Caleiyah, and you're my granddaddy."

My tears betrayed me as I feigned a cough and risked wiping my eyes.

"That's right, baby," I affirmed with a joyous smile, then added, "I'm your granddaddy."

Gosh—there was so much I wanted to say, yet I didn't know where to begin. I wanted Caleiyah to know how much I needed to hold her and the agony I felt because I couldn't. I wanted to say how sorry I was for not being there and that I promised to make it up, though I knew I might never get that chance. I wanted to say, "Look, Caleiyah—I've made mistakes, but people can change."

So many things I wanted to say, yet they all felt like excuses. With a heavy sigh, words rolled off my tongue.

"So how're you doing, baby?"

It was all the encouragement the two-year-old needed to take charge of the situation.

Caleiyah chatted up the silence, providing the lowdown on everyone she knew. Her knack for storytelling left little room for opinions; still, I admired her outspoken personality.

She was making things easier for me as I tussled with past decisions that kept me away. I posed questions at random, then listened as she rambled on. We played games, sang, and did other activities that dismissed the divider between us. They were the first moments I'd spent with my granddaughter—while my death sentence meant they could be the last.

A knock from outside the door announced the time when visitors prepared to leave. Caleiyah seemed distracted by the sudden departure of others as she glanced back and forth. With tremendous effort, I buried my sadness though my voice yielded to the pain.

Caleiyah stood up on the stool, pressed her forehead to the glass, and said, "It's okay, granddaddy. I'll be back."

What a remarkable child to have taken my woefulness and molded it into comfort. Her interaction excused my failures with no apologies required.

They gathered their jackets and headed for the exit while Caleiyah blew kisses goodbye. Soon, the elevator arrived and took them away, and finally, I cried alone.

Mending Fences

One of the most difficult aspects of spending twenty three years on Death Row is being stowed away from the outside world. Unlike other facilities, Death Row implements a measure of isolation that wedges a gap in the mental evolution of its denizens. Though outlets are provided as a source of information—like TVs, newspapers, and visits—the basic cable viewing and local coverage lacks the ability to stave off the inevitable wasting away from lack of connection.

Then, in June of 2016, telephones were installed on Death Row. This avenue for communication was an enormous leap from the single ten-minute phone call we'd previously been allowed annually. The "holiday phone calls," as they were called, were administered under strict procedures, and oftentimes, our contacts were at work or unavailable. Not to undermine the value of those precious moments and the tender voices of our loved ones, but ten minutes a year is insufficient time to fully sense that you've spoken with someone.

Today, things are different. The atmosphere on Death Row is alive with the promise for potential amendment. With the installation of the telephone, I'm a notion and a few clicks away from reaching out to those I love.

The first call I made was to my mother, who had relocated to be near the prison after I was sentenced. My mother visits me weekly. She and I have sung, prayed, and cried together throughout the years to lessen the pain in each other's eyes. Just being able to talk with my mother by phone was an honor.

The second person I called was my Aunt Patsy. Much like my mom, Aunt Patsy has been essential to my endurance with her continuous faith and optimism. She has visited, written, and sent funds as if I were her own son. Aunt Patsy has been a friend I can confide in, and, right or wrong, she believes in supporting her family in every way she can—I admire that most about Aunt Patsy.

After those two calls, I got around to making my most anticipated call, one seventeen years in waiting—a call that came with hesitancy and doubt and would either offer an incredibly wonderful experience or sizzle with awkwardness and discomfort.

With jittery fingers, I punched in the digits. The phone rang once, then twice. Each clatter of the ringing that thrummed in my ear made the dissonance in my head more evident. On one hand, I desperately hoped someone would answer; on the other, I prayed to God no one would.

Suddenly, the automated recording sprang to life. I resisted the impulse to hang up. What was I to say? Where would I begin? I was completely unaware that my breathing had stalled until a sigh of relief escaped me.

"...Thank you for using Global Tel Link."

Then, I heard her voice. "Heyyy, Duck!"

Everything hit me at once: a plethora of memories and emotions from a life I once knew. A tear slipped out of my eye before words left my mouth as I realized why the moment was so endearing. It was because nothing will ever be more important than family. I've always stood by that philosophy, and I'll die by it. I smiled as my worries morphed into joy.

"Hey, Aunt Pudding. It's good to hear your voice."

Aunt Brenda, whom everyone in our family called Pudding, was my mother's older sister by one year. As kids, the two were best friends. My mom looked up to Aunt Pudding and wanted to be just like her.

Then, at sixteen years of age, Aunt Pudding married and moved away from home to start a family, which left my mom feeling abandoned. But their relationship hardly suffered; instead, it strengthened as they grew.

The dynamics of family closeness was similar with all my aunts and uncles. Whether a bill needed to be paid or someone needed a place to stay, they'd always provide for each other.

This closeness was the inheritance for the children of the family. Aunt Pudding was a mother of six, though my brother and I made seven and eight. I spent countless Saturday mornings on her living room sofa watching Bugs Bunny cartoons and *Soul Train*. In the backyard was an old pecan tree I'd climb while Aunt Pudding hung clothes out to dry. Her house was a staple in the community for many of the neighborhood kids, and the lesson that our closeness reinforced most was that nothing was more important than family.

All that changed on May 17, 1999. Aunt Pudding's eldest son learned of my inquiries into a murder and covertly alerted the authorities. After meeting with the detectives and detailing the crime, he was given an ultimatum: testify to my involvement in open court or be criminally charged himself.

This act caused a rift in my family from which there would be no healing.

I never blamed Aunt Pudding for standing by her son. It was indicative of how my grandmother raised her children. It's why my mom stood by me. Regardless of our children's shortcomings, they are our greatest responsibility.

Still, the ordeal took a toll on my mother and Aunt Pudding's relationship. The sisters spoke occasionally—though they were careful to avoid mentioning their two sons. Other family members differed in opinions and ultimately chose sides. Some doubted that the cousin would lie about something as serious as murder while others were persuaded by the testimony of DNA findings. It was an explosive circumstance that fragmented our family's closeness. I wondered if I'd ever hear from some of them again.

Then, about five years ago, while visiting with my mother, Aunt Pudding took ill and was hospitalized. Initially, the diagnosis looked bleak, but she slowly began to pull through. Many in our family gathered at her bedside to offer support and prayers. It was the closest they'd been in fifteen years.

Though I was unable to share in the experience, I agonized in seclusion. I'd lost my grandmother and an aunt already; I couldn't bear to lose Aunt Pudding. There is no greater pain than the hurt I've felt at not being able to say goodbye. If I ever had the chance, I'd find a way to make things right.

With the telephone installation on Death Row, I was given that chance. I expressed my eagerness to reconnect with Aunt Pudding and my mom made it happen. Aunt Pudding and I were in such high spirits that all the messiness seemed forgotten. Our conversation flowed like cool spring waters over the jagged stones of past controversy. It reminded me of more pleasant times—back in the days when Aunt Pudding's doors were open to me even in the wee hours of the night, or when I would raid her fridge to satiate my appetite while she encouraged me to eat more; back in the days when our love was unconditional, and the only sides to be chosen had long been determined by blood.

I will always love my Aunt Pudding although amidst the chaos, I'd forgotten what that felt like—until now. Nothing will ever be more important than family. The proof is in the pudding; just listen to her voice: "Heyyy, Duck!"

"Hey, Aunt Pudding."

What could be more important than that?

Boondocks Country: A Eulogy from Death Row

In memory of Joseph Earl Bates; born May 1, 1968;
died September 26, 2003 by execution

Joe Bates and I weren't the best of friends—the unlikeliest of friends, perhaps. But that's kind of how Death Row works. Here, a Black man from the projects and a white man from the country can find friendship in the sorrow and comfort of a shared fate.

The first time I met Joe, he sat scrunched behind a handful of poker cards at the dayroom gambling spot. It was my second day on Death Row, and I was still feeling out the place and its inhabitants. Like Joe, all the men seated at the table were white, their bodies covered in tattoos that were worth a second glance. I wasn't too alarmed since racial groups tend to stick together in prison, but the sight raised my suspicions and kept my nerves on edge.

Joe's brown eyes shifted between the deck and the dealer while his fingers fidgeted with poker chips. He had the makings of a skilled player (I'd seen enough of them to know) as he peeled back the cards with just enough light to keep his hand a secret. He wore scruffy leather boots, the kind good for scouring around in ditches—I knew because I'd had a pair just like them as a kid. Joe's boots tapping the floor reminded me of home.

Death Row would take some getting used to. The air was clammy; voices carried through the dorm, depriving any space of quiet; and the TV set was cased in steel. The men tread with cautious steps like they were playing a perilous game of Twister, careful not to incur another's anger. Fitting in meant keeping distracted, so before long, I was seated at the poker table too.

As it turned out, there were no racially motivated cliques—just a group of like-minded gamblers passing the time. Sometimes, I was the only Black guy at the table, but it didn't matter since the only color we were after was green. Joe and I soon faced off over poker pots without much need for words. Whenever we did speak, it was mostly sharp retorts as a clash of wills pitted us as rivals, neither of whom could stand to lose.

During one game, he said, "I bet ten on the end. I ain't got a damn thing." He flung his poker chips into the pot.

I pursed my lips. The last time he'd bet on what he claimed was a busted hand, he'd turned out a flush and snickered devilishly as he'd raked in a load of money. But with every player folding their cards in front of me, I was left with no options.

"I call," I responded, my challenge confirmed only when my chips joined the pot.

"Whatcha got?"

"Shit…whatchu got? I called to see your hand."

Joe hesitated, giving me a moment of hope before turning out his cards. "Here. See, I told ya I ain't got shit."

Sometimes, he really didn't have shit and still his cards were better than mine. A high pair to my low pair. Two pair to my one. I lost to Joe a lot.

"Keep on calling me with nothing, Young Buck. You better fold that shit sometimes," Joe offered sarcastically after his cards were laid out and he was declared the winner.

It was sound advice, which I probably would have heeded had it come from anyone but Joe. He had a tendency to be controversial. He couldn't just humbly take our money; he had to win with a snide comment. I felt that his remarks suggested he thought he was better than me, so I kept on trying to best him.

But one time, I won at poker and instead of the usual rhetoric, Joe said, "Good hand, Young Buck."

I looked up, startled. Maybe he wasn't such a sore loser after all. After that day, we continued to talk smack as the poker cards served us both wins and losses, but I began to look forward to our bantering.

One day, as teams were being selected for basketball, Joe was a captain with one spot left on his team. The game regulars had all been called— some gray-haired men, out of shape and with little athleticism. As Joe considered his final pick, he looked at me long and hard. My hope grew with each passing second; it was my chance to make an impression on the group.

Joe opened his mouth to call my name and said, "Um, gimme Tony."

I couldn't believe what I'd heard. Tony was a hundred years old (not really). He was a tall guy, in fact the tallest amongst us, but he suffered severe back spasms and walked with a cane. I trudged away with my head hung low. Later, I decided it wasn't personal. Joe had chosen his friend over me—I would've done the same.

Daily routines are essential to getting through long days on Death Row, and Joe's patterns differed from the rest of the men. He cleaned his cell obsessively with generous use of Pine-Sol, then scrubbed down the pod, then scoured his cell again later in the day.

"Just 'cause Death Row is a dirty word don't mean it's gotta be a dirty place," he'd say.

Every morning, Joe cranked up a brewer he'd cobbled together from Styrofoam, tinfoil, and wires, rousing us from our sleep with the aroma of coffee in the air. In the afternoons, he rolled cigarettes for anyone with fifty cents. Whenever Joe wasn't being useful to others, he dawdled between pastimes. He poured over radio parts, trying to figure out what went where. He built picture frames out of gum wrappers, shaped watch bands from boots, and mended clothes with a needle he had fashioned from a battery pole. He cut a slab out of the window and used a twisted bed sheet to feed peanut butter to the field rats at night. Sometimes, he handcrafted greeting cards; other times, he obsessed over daytime soaps—one dayroom table in front of the TV was practically reserved for him. And though it was considered contraband, he started a rock collection and rejoiced over every find.

He loved reading Westerns, especially Louis L'Amour. Joe narrated the scenes from the author's books in a highly animated state, as though drawing from his own experiences. At his recommendation, I tried my hand at a few Western books and decided I liked Joe's version better. He had a knack for escaping Death Row through the stories he read, and he took the rest of us with him. In no time at all, I came to understand Joe's value to the Death Row community. I knew little about his background, but his usefulness earned my respect.

Amongst all the services Joe provided, he was also a tattoo artist. Often, men disappeared into his cell for hours, returning with his artistry inked into their skin. I'd been tatted before, so I knew the pain to expect, but I was curious about the device he'd engineered. One day, I selected a pattern, gathered up some coin, and headed to Joe's room. He and I talked a lot that day as he tattooed my arm. The conversation started out much like our poker rivalry—though instead of chips, we traded stories of our pasts. Eventually, tired of the competitiveness, I stopped countering long enough to listen to Joe's experiences. I realized that he and I shared many of the same interests.

For one, we were both southerners who enjoyed the woodlands except I was from the projects, borderline country, and he was from the boondocks—two worlds apart. Joe wore his lengthy brown hair in a ponytail, which, according to him, symbolized his Native American heritage, while my kinky dreadlocks were Caribbean-inspired. He talked with a thick, twangy accent like strummed banjo strings and was quick to cock his brow at my muttered lingo. He gave me the run-down on the dream catchers that hung from the ceiling of his room while I pitched to him good old-fashioned prayer, yet we both believed there was something else to come. By the time I left his cell that day, I bore more than just his artistry—I'd gotten to know the story of Joe.

I awoke to a funk in the air—not an odor, but a sour mood. Men's shoulders drooped, and their eyes lacked luster. That night, a man was scheduled to be executed.

The condemned was a middle-aged Black man with local ties who was fairly popular on Death Row. I'd seen him once or twice without knowing the horrors he faced. I was still getting used to the daily torments of life on Death Row, and I hadn't much considered the part that was death.

A sweltering sadness replaced the day's usual banter, causing me to retreat to a comforting naïvetè in my head. Even Joe deviated from his daily norms. He was late to rise from bed and soon lost himself in front of the TV. The whispered conversations were barely private in the quietness; smiles weighed like lead.

The day after the man's execution, Death Row was quiet. Some men slept in, having spent the better portion of the night staring out the windows at the candlelight vigil held by the abolitionists across the street. Others spoke briefly about the deceased before their ire turned to petty grievances. I avoided conversation about the execution, but the reality of Death Row could not be so easily dismissed.

The rivalry between Joe and me continued, and before long, we were back at the poker table trying to best one another, only now we shared coffee and laughs afterwards. Joe would even pick me during basketball games over others like old man Tony. On a few occasions, we drank hooch together. One batch was so potent, I ended up on my knees, vomiting into the toilet, while Joe teased me playfully.

A few years passed, and the executions continued. The men lolled in the aftermath of each death until a state of rest returned. I pretended the executions weren't real and told myself that the men who marched off to the lethal injection chamber were really being isolated elsewhere. Since none of the men executed in those early years lived on the same pod as me, I didn't see them often, and it was easy to ignore their sudden absences. Although I tried to deny it, each execution penetrated more to my core. Truthfully, I was terrified as shit the same thing would happen to me.

As for Joe, he was the bounce-back type and hardly sulked for long, knowing that his chores and contributions to the pod were often the start of everyone else's day. I didn't always express my gratitude, but I appreciated waking up to the smell of Pine-Sol and steaming coffee, welcome pleasantries after long nights spent contemplating my fate.

One day, a man from our dorm received an execution date. Ed was rather meek, oddly quiet, and spent most days sheltered away in his darkened cell. He was a chronic loner, but that day well-wishers filed around his cell door offering their sympathy and prayers. I debated whether to visit Ed. I hadn't spoken more than three words to him in three years, and I worried anything I said would seem disingenuous. On the other hand, by not comforting Ed in his darkest times, I knew I was being insensitive, so I turned to Joe for advice.

I found him tucked away in his cell, fussing over a clash of watercolor paint in front of a coffee-straw easel. His tongue poked out the corner of his lips, a sign of his steadfast focus. His cell floor sparkled from a recent buffing performed on his hands and knees. The burning blend of scented oils made his quarters a sanctuary on Death Row. He never turned anyone away. I gratefully rapped on the door.

"C'mon in, cuz," he greeted without looking up from his paint-mixing dilemma, adding, "What's on your mind?"

"Nothing much. I was gon' holler at Ed, but I don't know what to say. You know he got a date…"

"Shit." Joe placed the paintbrush down and turned to me with a heavy sigh. "I got an execution date coming up too."

The words resounded in my head like the roar of thunder sweeping through a canyon. My body went slack with helplessness and confusion. My very blood seemed to still.

Not Joe. Why would anyone want to kill Joe? It was like I'd forgotten the business of Death Row or had assumed that only the worst men were executed. My naïveté rolled up into a ball of reality and crashed down on me, hard. Joe was one of the best of us. He devoted every minute to helping others. Where was the system that allowed the salvation of a man who'd proven changed?

I remembered a recent conversation between Joe and me that now began to make sense. Like me, Joe had often fantasized that the men we saw led away to execution weren't really killed.

"Maybe they take 'em to a penal colony in space," Joe had mused.

I toyed with the idea to avoid debate and did some wondering of my own. I was happy to know that Joe wasn't unhinged—he was just holding on to hope.

After Ed was put to death, the spirited, charitable Joe we all knew began to fade. The pod went untidied and the air was starved of the sweet smells of caffeinated mornings. Joe sold off his art supplies, bet loosely at poker, and barely watched TV.

Desperate to console him, I opted for rhetoric: "Don't give up, Joe."

Even then, I worried whether I was being inconsiderate of his struggles and more concerned for my own. My only emotional takeaway from the previous executions had been relief that it wasn't me. I was often cold and insensitive to condemned men in their hour of need because their lives weren't as important to me as staying distant from the nightmare we shared— though I realized that without compassion, I was as good as dead inside.

As Joe's date approached, he minimized his presence by secluding within his cell. I sat with him one day, attempting to sympathize with his utter dread.

"I'm scared," he admitted. "I don't wanna die. Did I ever tell you that I was innocent?"

No...he hadn't told me—and his failure to do so left me questioning the timely claim. Isn't that what he was supposed to say? Wouldn't I say the same if I were him?

Then, I decided that none of that mattered in determining whether he should live. I'd grown to trust and admire Joe, despite his past mistakes. Growing up, my momma taught me that through God we could all be redeemed. The wages of sin only last forever when we refuse to repent and evolve. I believe that people are inherently good and that even our worst mistakes can invoke positive change. Yet here was our own judicial system giving up on humanity under the guise of justice.

In the days before his execution date, Joe chatted lightheartedly and kept his composure by day, but at night he was sinking fast. I took to my room and cried all day for my friend whose life was ending.

When the day of reckoning arrived, I was at his door before the sun touched his window to get a jump on the time we had left together. He divvied his time amongst friends and donated his personal belongings as we spent the day reminiscing over laughs. When the white shirts came to collect Joe, I hoped they would meet his resistance. I swore to myself I would stand with him.

Joe cooperated without incident. With the officers watching like silent sentinels, we gathered around Joe and he hugged us for the last time. Then, without a word, he turned and walked away, flanked by guards.

The following morning, and every morning since, the absence of Pine-Sol and brewed coffee sets in like an ache.

Life over Law

As the body of a little boy lay sprawled on the ground before viewers across the nation, my eyes welled up. Adam Toledo was thirteen years old. He had been captured on police bodycam footage bolting down an alleyway in Chicago after police had responded to a complaint about gunfire. Although his oversized windbreaker broke his speed, young Adam had pushed ahead of his pursuers. An off-camera voice had commanded him to stop. Adam complied, tossing aside an object later determined to be a gun. Then, he turned around with his hands up—and he was shot and killed.

I didn't know the boy, but I understood his impulse to run. I too came up in the streets where the word "freeze" triggered the instinct to flee for those desperate to avoid jail. For a long while, I studied images of Adam's face on the TV screen. He had a tight-lipped smile, a cross between joyous and bashful. His eyes were deep-set and beaming with promise, too youthful and tender to be mistaken for menacing.

Along with several men on Death Row, I watched as a woman on-screen took to a podium. In a sea of flashing lights, she addressed the loss of her son while dabbing at the grief that streaked down her face. "Why did he have to be killed?" she asked. I was wondering the same thing—until a comment from someone next to me broke into my thoughts.

"He asked for that. His little ass shouldn't have had a gun."

My anger spoiled any chance at grasping words, so I responded with stony silence. Jeers of support for the commenter sounded around me. I felt helpless to pierce the mass desensitization that plagues our country when we see Black and brown lives gunned down again and again and again. Even some people on Death Row, who know firsthand our nation's disregard for lives on the barrel end of a police gun, believe that an unarmed child deserves quick execution.

As I watched footage of Adam's skinny body sprawled on the ground, as the jeers of my fellow prisoners echoed around me, I recalled a day when I too had felt that instinct to run.

I bolted across the yard as the clattering behind me warned of Deputy Taylor's pursuit. After ducking a clothesline, I hurdled a garden and bounded over a fence, fear of my pursuer's gun fueling my ill-planned escape attempt. When I touched down and rolled to my feet, I was so winded I could barely go on. I wondered if I should surrender.

Taylor, however, went airborne over the fence and crashed into the ground. His face pulled back in a grimace and I sensed he, too, was exhausted. With a glimmer of hope, I pushed back defeat, gulped down air, and gave fleeing one more try. Running from the police was scary as hell when escape wasn't guaranteed.

I pushed past the burning in my lungs and the throbbing in my chest. Another leap. A short burst. And the discordant sounds of pursuit faded.

I crossed the backyard until I reached the fence to my mother's yard, unhooked the latch and shouldered through the gate. Each step brought me closer to the thrill of escape.

"Freeze, motherfucker! Don't cha move!"

The voice, heavy as a wrecking ball, smashed all hope of escape as another deputy appeared in front of me and brought me to a sliding halt. A slender white man with pristine hair and a burning red face, his knuckles blanched from squeezing the pistol trained at my chest. My legs shut down and my hands pressed the sky as I waited on the judgment from his gun.

How had the day, which had started out sunny and full of promise, gone so wrong? The encounter with Deputy Taylor had begun only moments before, after his cruiser had snuck up on me as I was searching the trees for birds. In my hand, I'd held a Daisy air rifle—long, black, and menacing to anyone who hadn't guessed that the only threat it posed was to critters.

I knew Fred Taylor. He had been a correctional officer some years back when I was in the county jail. Back then, he was a soft-spoken, courteous young man, usually a stickler for rules, though some days he slipped me extra food trays.

But today's encounter was different. Taylor, a heavyset Black man even bulkier in his gear, had brought along his own gun to rival mine. The thick, angry steel had been tucked in his hip holster, ready to spring out at me like a jack-in-the-box with deadly intent. His wide-eyed look had been strained and foretelling. Deputy Taylor had been prepared to shoot me. Never before had I tried so hard to be still.

I had explained that the rifle was only a BB gun, though it felt more like a damned grenade—one I was anxious to put down before it ignited chaos. Slowly, I'd propped the air rifle against the wall, relieved not to incur a hail of bullets.

Taylor informed me there were warrants against me. I didn't doubt it, but the familiar instinct to evade capture kicked in. He undid his handcuffs and reached for my wrist. Too late. I jerked my arm free and turned on my heels. The spirit of all my previous dashes from the law had propelled my legs forward.

Now, facing the white deputy, a stranger, a chill overcame me that took my breath away. My body froze into a slab of ice about to be shattered into a billion pieces. My mind screamed *Wait!* but my voice burrowed deep within, to a place where bullets can't reach—too unreliable to have my back when I needed my words the most, too afraid to confront an officer with a gun.

Was I about to become a statistic, just another Black body gunned down? Just a month prior, a white officer in Wilson County had shot and killed my cousin Yule "Lil Tee" Reid on Christmas day. The officer had claimed Lil Tee was armed, but the shooting took place behind the cover of neighborhood row houses, where the only thing to survive was the officer's account. There would be no prosecution in the case, no justice for the Reid family. I had been with Lil Tee just moments before he was killed. I had heard the shots that took his life.

A glimmer of conflict flickered behind the deputy's eyes as he lowered his weapon, but the muzzle never descended below my torso.

"Turn around!" he ordered.

Near nauseous with relief, I complied, but suddenly Deputy Taylor, puffing up from behind, scooped me up and slammed my face into the ground.

"Git the fuck down!" Taylor yelled. His weight crushed my chest into the grass.

Instinctively, I struggled, then stopped at the thought of the other deputy with his weapon drawn. Hoping to ease the assault, I pulled my hands behind my back.

"C'mon, Freddie," I protested. "You ain't gotta do me like that."

"You shouldn't have tried to run," he grunted through clenched teeth.

I couldn't explain to this deputy the exhilaration of potential escape. It was the first lesson I'd learned from the older drug dealers, who'd said, "Don't be out here selling dope if you can't run." Running from the police yields power, invincibility, and, most of all, triumph—all of which must be earned by first getting away.

I listened for the clicking sounds of metal that would bind me to a stay of county regulations. Instead, I heard snapping and growling as my dog, Bear, pulled at Taylor's pants.

"Get back!" the armed deputy roared, jockeying for an aim.

"Wait!" I pleaded. "Don't kill my momma's dog!"

Sheriff Taylor slackened his grip enough for me to calm Bear. Then, he fastened me at the wrist, hoisted me to my feet, and shipped me off to jail on an old warrant for possession of stolen goods.

I was lucky to walk away from that incident with my life, considering the many less fortunate who've faced similar circumstances—though it's disheartening to think that not being killed by the police is a matter of luck.

The Adam Toledos of this country, the ones who leave police encounters in a body bag, are victims of a growing crisis where outdated policies and racial bias allow for radical policing that results in unjustifiable shootings—policies that allow for the choking of suspects after they're handcuffed and detained, policies that assign no culpability in shooting deaths when officers mistake cell phones for guns. Black and brown people, even children, are often gunned down not for violent crime—sometimes, not for any crime at all—but for exuding "typical suspect behavior." Then, the debate shifts to whether the officer's actions were "necessary."

Adam wasn't killed because he had a gun. He died because of a systemic imbalance that holds some people's lives with the highest regard while dismissing the humanity of others. Chicago police officer Eric Stillman had other options the night Adam was killed. He could've ordered the boy to the ground or waited to confirm a weapon before shooting. Instead, he instructed Adam to show his hands then killed him after he complied. There wasn't shit "necessary" about that—that was murder.

The carnage won't stop unless we, as a country, recognize that breaking a law or being suspected of breaking a law—or *looking* like a person who might break a law—does not justify public execution. Only then will kids like Tamir Rice be encouraged to play with toys without the threat of being gunned down. Nor will men like Eric Garner be choked to death for selling bootleg cigarettes on the sidewalk. When we insert common humanity into the element of policing, then people like Philando Castile won't be executed in front of their children for legally owning a gun, and people's bodies, like Mike Brown's, won't be left on a hot summer street for alleged petty theft. Only then can we ensure that being killed in a barrage of bullets like Andrew Brown will be ruled unjust, that mistaking a gun for a taser is still murder in the case of Daunte Wright, and that the heart-wrenching pleas of George Floyd will not be ignored.

As long as there are laws, there will be people who break them, and police tasked with enforcement. We cannot, however, tolerate a policing system with such high regard for the laws that the value of lives is lost. For what is law without regard for the lives it's meant to protect? It's just a repeat of history.

Humanity Undenied

Since coming to Death Row on April 10, 2000, I have ascended beyond its thresholds only twice; once in 2010 for a court session and once in December 2016 when I was scheduled to see a dermatologist at UNC Chapel Hill.

That day, I was escorted to an area known as Receiving. Officers from different units shuffled to and fro. Some sported faint smiles—their seniority was somewhat validated by proximity to Central Prison's most notorious.

Corralled in a holding cell that reeked of stale urine, I was put on display like weapons-grade cargo. Prisoners from various statewide facilities scrutinized me. A few nodded nervously as if ceding to a hierarchy of status. I sat, guarded, while their opinionated glares pricked holes at my dignity.

Soon, a jangling sound filled the air, announcing the arrival of chains and shackles. My waist was girdled in iron apparel; a steel box and padlock outfitted my wrists. Thus contained, I was ushered to a vehicle like toxic merchandise. Artillery joined our convoy as guns were collected at the gates.

But when the big gates folded outward, my spirits rose as I craned my neck for a glimpse of the outside world. The first thing to grab my attention was a traffic light. The sustainable relic from the last millennium was suspended high above earth, its illuminated orbs unbiased in providing safety for travelers. I'd imagined that with the advancement of everything else electronic, even traffic lights had gotten smarter. The familiar sight comforted me.

As we drove, I noted the assortment of parked cars side by side like dominos in their lots and the naturalness of the untempered environment. Brittled grass. Withering leaves. The vastness of the sky vaguely resembled the patch of blue outside my cell's window. The sight of trees along the highway took me back to when I was a kid taking refuge in the woods, scaling the colossal monuments with as much vigor as my inquisitiveness could muster. As I drank in these everyday sights through the window, the feeling of confinement began to gradually dissolve. I sat back to enjoy seventeen years of societal evolution unfold.

The first person of whom I took careful notice was a pedestrian of Asian descent.

The young, petite woman was swaddled in a trench coat and scarf, the silky black strands of her hair dancing in the morning breeze. Hands tucked away in her pockets, she walked with a determined pace as the steps of her sneakers pounded to a drum of freedom in my head. I guessed that she was an intelligent college student who was running late to class. Then, I chided myself for assuming that all Asians are intelligent. It could be that she hated school and was on her way to work. I quickly put my assessments in check. People were going to be judging me soon enough, yet with the chains and shackles it was unlikely their opinions would waiver.

As we moved on, the young woman faded from view and another pedestrian snagged my attention: a Caucasian male with cropped brown hair. Wearing baggy jeans and a hoodie, he strolled as if having no particular destination. I was moved. How nice it must be to have the liberty to head nowhere.

Other daily norms stood out: a guy pumping gas into a brown Chevy, a caravan of drivers spilling from a fast-food lane, a blond woman sitting at a bus stop reading a book. These simple acts of living filled me with inspiration and envy.

As we passed numerous homes, I imagined the warmth and comfort of finding rest inside. Lakes and rivers held mysteries to me. I observed the drivers along the freeway who kept pace with our detail. Strip malls and hotel chains looked like oases of renewed hope. I read roadway signs and billboards with the meticulousness of a good novel.

Our vehicle slowed and veered onto an adjoining roadway. A sign read "UNC Medical Facility." We had arrived at the regional mecca of medical treatment for society's rejects. An edginess crept over me as I prepared for the stigmatizing treatment to come.

Armed guards escorted me to an area marked "Outpatient." There, an orderly awaited. She was a petite woman with auburn hair and a tailored smile. Barely glancing my way, she greeted the officers and accompanied us inside. Admittedly, there was a politeness and professionalism in her disregard for me that did not seem spiteful.

As quickly as the thought entered my mind, I realized that my lesson in being dehumanized had already taken effect. As we moved about the corridors, watchful eyes landed on my crimson jumpsuit. I was overcome with shame. The contemptuous stares and cautious appraisals pierced me. I wasn't quite ready to go back to Death Row, but the idea seemed tempting.

We were shown to a waiting room and held there for some time. The officers from Central Prison, along with those from other facilities, flung chatter over my head as if my cuffed hands prevented me from understanding them.

Eventually, their attention turned my way. It began when the sergeant, who oversaw my transport detail, asked, "So Terry, when is Death Row going to perform another play?"

Grateful to be acknowledged, I replied that our performance of 12 *Angry Men* in front of guests from the Vera Institute for Justice had been exhilarating—not only due to nerves, but because it was the first time Death Row had been permitted to put on a play. The rehearsal process had been a grueling experience, but humbling, in that it formed bonds among many Death Row residents and staff.

The guards peppered me with questions and, before long, we were engaged in conversation about life, politics, and recent events. The officers seemed genuinely interested in the many productive ways in which men on Death Row were trying to reshape our image. I recounted some of the programs such as social psychology, houses of healing, speech and debate, and yoga. They could hardly believe it.

Some of my own generalizations about the guards began to unravel too. I still didn't doubt their course of action should I try to escape; I just concluded that it likely wouldn't be malicious.

A while later, a nurse came in who seemed experienced at working with incarcerated people. Her cordiality was refreshing; her eye contact, relaxing. I almost forgot that I was a prisoner. She spoke to me, rather than referring to me, and showed kindness and consideration. I was reminded of a time I once knew.

The entire process took an hour or so. Then, afterwards, we were back on the road to damnation. I sat in the backseat, miserable as I bid goodbye to all life's liberties I might never see again. I thought about all the chaos in the world: the forty-nine civilians gunned down in a nightclub in Orlando, Florida, for no other reason than their personal lifestyle; the nine church members in South Carolina executed while attending service for the capital offense of being Black; spectators bombed at an annual marathon; and the tiny bodies of innocent children littering the hallways of Sandy Hook elementary.

I thought of the heightened gang activity plaguing urban communities and politicians who pass laws that arm the mentally unstable. I thought of victims of sexual violence and random lives forfeited by inebriated drivers. Just the other day, someone had killed four people in my hometown of Wilson. I wondered if those lives would have been spared had the perpetrator known the trials and hardships of incarceration, the anguish of losing friends to the cruelty of lethal concoctions, the segregation from a world that has moved on without him. Prison can teach so much sorrow, but it can also grant a profound appreciation for the littlest things, like trees and traffic lights.

Death Row isn't a place that lacks humanity, like some people say. It is where humanity is rediscovered and restored. On Death Row, the meaningfulness of life tremendously exceeds the inevitability of death. We are all human beings, and as such, we're prone to make mistakes, but many incarcerated people are simply paradigms of the great fall before triumph. Our humanity is not beyond repair, and any judicial system that conceptualizes such nonsense is flawed.

To give up on a person's humanity says a lot about our own. We can never fully share in the humanity of others until we have recognized and repaired our own tendencies towards cruelty and unconscious bias. This means forgiveness, accountability, faith, and, in many cases, a second chance. No matter what our personal or collective opinions, no one will ever deserve to die.

§

Gifts

TESSIE CASTILLO

On a chilly evening in late 2015, I was settling into my couch with a steaming cup of tea and a letter from one of my prison pen pals. Over a year had passed since I had been banned from teaching on Death Row, but I had kept up a steady correspondence with several of my former students.

I enjoyed these nightly rituals—with tea to warm my body and a letter to warm my soul. Although my pen pals and I struggled through petty problems, our levels of self-awareness often subpar, the insights that shone through their letters and the tenuous inner peace they had achieved despite inhumane circumstances moved me. I'd laugh at their descriptions of childhood antics and grieve at the wrong track their lives had taken, at the incalculable suffering they had caused and endured, at the finality of a death sentence that implies one is unredeemable.

That night, after heaving the happy sigh of a parent whose child has finally gone to bed, I settled into a letter—I can't remember from whom—and was once again transported to the tangled jungle of hope and despair that is Death Row. As I read, a wisp of thought gathered: *I shouldn't be the only one to read this.* It wasn't the first time I'd yearned to share the gift of prison correspondence with other people. The letters offered glimpses into the inner worlds of men locked deep in the bowels of one of the nation's most notorious places—men who are known for the worst parts of themselves or, more often, not known at all. Yet, here in my hands lay evidence of decades of struggles each had endured to face the darkest parts of himself, to find meaning in suffering, and to feed the embers of hope that threatened to sputter out with each passing year in the dungeons. Was there a way to share these stories with a wider audience? Could we...write a book?

That night I dashed off a flurry of letters to my most frequent correspondents—Chanton, Lyle, Alim, and Paul—and proposed we create a book about their lives before and after their convictions. The book would serve as a testament to the humanity and resilience of incarcerated people and to the process of reflection and growth they often undergo. I mailed the letters with confidence that the men would share my enthusiasm to help the world see Death Row through the eyes of its residents.

The first hard lesson hit within days. While Paul and Chanton expressed support for the book idea, Lyle responded with caution. He explained that other writers and documentarians had reached out to men on Death Row for participation in projects, but the final product, often with provocative titles like "A Killer Speaks," played up the drama of murder and played down the humanity of any man foolish enough to provide his story. Lyle was tepidly willing to contribute to a book but earning his trust would be an ongoing battle.

And then Alim's letter arrived.

"When I first met you in class and I read my piece," he wrote, "I felt a passionate enthusiasm from you that made me believe you genuinely believed in me and wanted to help me get published. I can't tell you how much that meant to me, and it motivated me because you were a woman, you were white and educated and totally outside of my demographic, yet you were interested in what I had to say in my writing. Then, you got 'banned' from the prison, yet you still contacted me personally. I felt like this lady really wants to help me. Then, I got your last letter, and you talked about this idea that suddenly came to you about writing a book based on some of my experiences, and everything you had ever said before immediately sounded phony. I kicked myself for being foolish enough to believe that some agenda-free benefactor truly wanted to help insignificant old me. So, I threw all your letters away."

In a dramatic declaration, Alim prohibited me from contacting him. The letter knocked the breath out of me. In my naive belief that any help I offered would be welcomed, I'd been unprepared for accusations of ulterior motive and exploitation. I wrote a letter of effusive apology, promising that our friendship was more valuable than any book. He didn't write back.

Alim's rejection nearly scuttled the project. I felt ashamed of my assumption that the men would trust me, and I questioned whether I could move forward with so few contributors. While my other correspondents had supported the book idea, I equally feared betraying their trust by giving up after the first setback. Unsure what to do, I wrote to Lyle, Chanton, and Paul to ask for their help in recruiting other Death Row writers. If no one else expressed interest, I could cite lack of contributors as a face-saving exit strategy.

As they searched for writers, I explored the idea of including the voices of victims' families in the book. To tell the full story of the impact of these crimes, we had to acknowledge the gaping wound left in the lives of people whose loved ones had been killed. I reached out to a statewide victims' advocacy organization to ask their help in offering a space for the victims' families to tell their stories.

Here again, my naïveté became clear. I had assumed the victims' families would want to tell their stories, or might want to, if offered the opportunity. A staff member at the organization kindly explained that it would be inappropriate and potentially traumatic for the families if I contacted them, especially as someone sympathetic to the men convicted of those crimes.

"Don't seek them out," she advised. "Let them find you."

The book was challenging my preconceived notions before we'd even written a word; and I was about to be tested in new ways. A few weeks after I had asked my coauthors to search for more contributors, I received a letter from George, a friend of Chanton. His long letter revealed a sharp mind and skill with a pen, so I welcomed him onto the team.

George turned out to be more than just another contributor. He sailed into the project with remarkable energy and enthusiasm, filling my mailbox with essays, poems, and long, philosophical letters. With George as my prod, the book project picked up a slow, but steady, momentum. The men sent me essays about their lives and I pored over each, making suggestions to tighten for clarity or to expand for more emotional punch. My coauthors painstakingly rewrote each piece by hand and I typed them up, always at night after my day job was finished and my toddler fast asleep. All correspondence took place through handwritten letters as the men had no access to the internet, typewriters, or phones.

For a year, the work was progressing smoothly, but as evenings of tea and letters morphed into nights of rewrites and edits, I began to feel the warning signs of burnout. George picked up on my waning enthusiasm right away. His letters began challenging me not to give up.

"Tess, you are a symbol here," he wrote. "You broke the stereotype and showed us some people care enough to make sacrifices to help us…how you handle this situation, regardless of the actual results any book will/won't achieve, is going to have a real impact on the men here. Please keep this in mind."

I cut down my work hours and held burnout at bay as best I could. The book limped along.

In June 2016, Central Prison installed phones on Death Row. Previously, the men had been allowed only one ten-minute phone call per year. Every December, they agonized over how to spend those precious minutes, often forced to choose between a parent, a spouse, a child, or a beloved friend. Now, the men could call whomever they wished, restricted only by cost, a fifteen-minute limit per call, and the need to share a single phone with up to twenty-three other men on a pod.

Access to phones vitalized the dynamics between my coauthors and me. Communication that usually took weeks was cut down to days. Lyle called with updates on his college correspondence courses and aspirations to become a prison journalist. Chanton and I, trying to squeeze updates into fifteen minutes, constantly interrupted each other, apologized, laughing, and then interrupted each other again. George's more playful side came out over the phone, his Christian piety interlaced with irreverent humor. Paul never called, saying he didn't like to talk on the phone.

One night, a few months after the phones were installed, my cell phone rang. The pages of an essay were scattered on my lap as I leaned towards the coffee table to grab the phone.

"This is a prepaid call," said an automated voice. "You will not be charged for this call."

Before the voice announced the caller's name, I knew it was Chanton. Although I had deposited money into a prepaid account for the men to use, Chanton had insisted on paying for our calls himself.

I pressed "five" to accept the call. After a pause, Chanton came on the line.

"Hey, Tess," he chuckled. He often chuckled when he spoke, like he couldn't hide how happy he was to talk to someone else.

"Sorry to bother you," he continued. "I know you must be busy."

"You're not bothering me," I assured him.

"Right. How you been?"

"I'm good! Working on some new essays. How are you?"

"Keeping busy," he said. "But hey look, I got someone who wants to talk to you."

I cocked my head. "Who?" Chanton had already handed off the phone. There was a static sound, then a deep voice spoke.

"Hello?"

Pages slid off my lap and scattered onto the carpet as I stood up abruptly. "Alim?"

The line was silent for a moment.

"Yeah, it's me."

"What? Hey. I mean..." I stooped to gather the fallen papers as if collecting pages would also collect my thoughts.

"...I didn't expect to hear from you," I finished.

He cleared his throat. "Yeah, um...hey, look, I just want to apologize for being hasty with my judgment. I thought you was just trying to use me to make a buck, writing a book and all that."

"I'm sorry," I said. "I should have thought more before I wrote that letter." I paused. "What made you decide to reach out?"

He hesitated. "I guess I wanted to say something a little while ago. I just didn't get around to saying it. Then, when Chanton here said he was talking to you, I thought I'd come over and say hi."

For a moment, we were both quiet.

"Well, I'm glad you did," I said finally. "Does this mean you'll write to me again?"

"Yeah, I'll write. I'll do your book project too."

"You will?" Skepticism rang through my voice.

"Yeah, I figure it could be good to help get my writing out. Maybe you can help me publish my book of lyrics too."

I was glad he couldn't see me smile and shake my head.

"I'll help you publish the book of lyrics if you finish writing it," I said. "How's that?"

"Yeah, yeah. I know I got to finish." He let out a low laugh. Just then, the automated voice cut in to tell us our call time was almost up.

"Hey, look, let me give you back to Chanton," he said. "I'll write soon."

"I'll hold you to that," I said. "Thanks for calling."

"Peace," he said before the line went dead.

Alim's homecoming and the gift of phone calls with my coauthors rekindled my enthusiasm for the book. As our collaborative efforts increased, the personalities and quirks of each came into sharp focus.

Alim was the least predictable. On good days, he'd call brimming with new ideas that shot off his tongue like firecrackers. When depression hit, silence reigned for months. No letters, no essays, no calls. I could sense his mood from the energy in his greeting. Some days, his words had bounce, verve. Other days, he sounded smothered, as if a thick, wet blanket covered his face. No matter his mood, he was always kind. If I revealed in conversation that I was struggling with something, he would call again a couple days later just to check on me. As a writer, he procrastinated, and I frequently urged him to send me more essays.

George posed the opposite dilemma. By far the most prolific and enthusiastic contributor, he mailed me a blizzard of essays. I had to sift through fountains of words and reluctantly delete reams of artistry, just so his contributions wouldn't take up half the book. I often found myself pleading with Alim for more and with George for less.

Throughout most of the book project, George called every Sunday at ten o'clock sharp, and we'd chat about writing or share stories from our pasts. He was regimented, a man who woke up at 4 a.m. for two hours of exercise before launching into a self-prescribed schedule of creative work and ministry to other prisoners. Yet, for all his external discipline, he was open-minded and flexible, with a raunchy sense of humor that delighted me.

Chanton was the most accommodating writer, accepting feedback with openness and gratitude. He began every phone call with an apology for his intrusion into the more important people and activities to which I was surely attending. When conflicts arose between us, I never doubted his commitment to working through disagreements and preserving our friendship. With writing, he deferred to my editorial opinion to the point that I had to remind him that *he* had the final say over edits.

Lyle, in contrast, could turn every rewrite into a knock-down, drag-out fight with both of us battling over the direction of the essay. Smart, ambitious, and relentless, Lyle was constantly reaching beyond the prison cage: networking, planning, implementing, studying, challenging. With opinions like steel clamps and a strong independent streak, Lyle often chafed at the collaborative nature of the book project, preferring more autonomy and control of his work.

I struggled to build a relationship with Paul, especially since he didn't call. His letters were cheerful and short, and his essays, though poignant, were few. I liked him and wanted to be closer but wasn't sure how to bridge the polite distance between us.

The men were learning to navigate my dynamics as well. I'd often swing between generous moods, when I gave freely of my time and energy, to feeling overwhelmed and put upon, as if my coauthors were forcing me to do all this work. Some days, I felt energized by the project, and others, the desire to give up tempted like a siren call. In moments of doubt, a letter or phone call from one of the men would jar me back into focus, reminding me I could walk away from Death Row, but they couldn't.

In late 2017, the day arrived when the book felt complete. Though there was much more to each man's story than could be contained in a limited number of chapters, it was starting to feel more like a book rather than a loose collection of essays.

"It's done," I told my coauthors, barely believing my own words. "I'm going to write a book proposal and send it to publishers."

As I mailed letters of thanks and congratulations to George, Chanton, Alim, Lyle, and Paul, I took a deep breath and allowed my shoulders to relax. Two years of struggle to squeeze writing and editing into night hours was coming to a close. I anticipated the return of leisurely evenings with tea and letters.

Little did I know, we were only halfway through.

As we wrote the book, I think all the coauthors, on some level, were skeptical about publishing. Would we stick with the project? Would we complete enough essays? Could we find a publisher? Moreover, did we want to expose so much vulnerability to the world? And would our audience relate to their humanity or choose to focus only on their pasts?

These questions hung over us, suspended, as we slogged through each rewrite. For the most part, we ignored the doubts, choosing to take things one day—and one essay—at a time. Now that we were finished, or nearly so, these long-ignored questions came roaring to the forefront.

For some of my coauthors, the word "publish" galvanized a sudden, drastic shift toward perfectionism. They wanted to rewrite essays we had already finalized. They mailed me new essays we had never discussed. A misplaced word on a page would send some into a panic of negative self-talk and blame. Many voiced doubts for the first time about being involved in a collaborative project. They became suspicious of motives, both each others' and mine. They sized up the number of essays each man had written, their writing skills, the order of the chapters, who went first and who had the last word. They voiced concerns about copyright, compensation, public outcry, and retaliation from correctional staff, victims' families, or fellow residents of Death Row. My mailbox and voicemail glutted with angst.

For others, the word "publish" sparked a different association—fame. To many men confined before the advent of social media or even widespread internet access, selling a book seemed as easy as posting a tweet. Expectations about sales and promotion spiked alarmingly high and my scramble to puncture their dreams with the realism of first-time authorship seemed only to stoke suspicion.

These anxieties and expectations posed a challenge. Though my coauthors lived in the same prison, they were housed on different pods and had little contact with each other. We couldn't sit down in a room together to discuss our concerns. For each issue raised, I sent out five letters asking for feedback or explaining the difficulties of small press publishing. Often, I received five conflicting replies.

George later explained this process on a podcast: "Every one of us is so strong-willed and determined, and so every little issue was an issue worth dying for. [Telling our stories] was so important to each of us that we were unwilling to bend for a while."

Though I was often tempted to play the editor card and override their opinions, I didn't want this book project to be another example of a white professional making decisions for people with lived experience.

So back and forth, through letters and phone calls, we hashed out our differences as best we could. I clung tenaciously to the belief that the finish line was just weeks away and with a little more effort, we could cross it with the team intact.

The first casualty arrived in 2018. Paul Brown's exit letter was courteous. He was withdrawing his contributions, in order to focus on another book project; he wished me and the other coauthors the best of luck. Within the same week, I received letters from two other coauthors suggesting that they, too, were close to quitting—one over creative differences and the other over concerns about the book's effect on his legal case. The letters left me reeling.

For the next few weeks, I dreaded the mail. Whenever the prison phone number flashed across my screen, anxiety clawed at my chest. Conversations with the waffling coauthors were civil, but tense. I didn't urge them to stay because I'd rather have no book than a book with uncommitted coauthors. Mostly, I tried to listen. I answered their concerns. I held my breath and waited for their decisions.

How to end the book was a question that had always vexed me. Which coauthor would get the coveted "final word," and what would that parting message be? Though I'd received many brilliant essays over the years, none, I felt, outshone the others or represented a final message.

But that changed the day I received a special letter from Alim.

Since Alim had agreed to write to me a year earlier, most of our correspondence had been pleasant. Every once in a while something shifted in him: some raw wound opened up, and he sent searing letters of pain and poetry. This letter contained no hope. He was reaching into a pit of shame and wrenching out despair.

"I have cried and cried real tears from my soul out of remorse for the things I have done. The lives I took, the innocent families I have hurt," he wrote. "My tears, my grief, my sorrow, my dignity, my very spirit...this ongoing torment has taken it all."

Though I recognized the power and potential of this letter as an ending to our book, I hesitated to use it. Certainly, to end on a note of hopelessness would break the cardinal rule of all bestselling books, Hollywood movies, and American stories in general.

Yet what is hopeful about the death penalty? The system marches on as the carnage of unsanctioned murder is followed by the carnage of sanctioned murder. Yes, my coauthors were brilliant, insightful, and accomplished, but I didn't want to lull readers into imagining that Death Row is anything other than a place that chews people up and spits out the husks.

Apart from the hopelessness of the letter, there was also its vulnerability to consider. Clearly, it was a personal letter meant for my eyes alone. I didn't want Alim to suffer consequences if the wrong person read the letter, nor did I want him to stop showing vulnerability to me over fear I would try to publish his inner thoughts.

After stewing over the issue, I wrote to Alim asking permission to end the book with his letter. It took a while for him to respond. When he did, he said, "I have a lot of reluctance about including it...I'm not sitting in a comfortable enough place that I want people, particularly my peers, to see that sometimes the strong exterior isn't as strong on the interior...[but] being in a position of leadership, which is a byproduct of who I am, I felt like if somebody is going to do it, it's got to be me."

Alim's courage to show vulnerability took my respect for him to new heights. More than ever, I felt we had a book that showcased the complexity of Death Row, the daily tug-of-war between resilience and despair.

I typed up a book proposal, printed out a few sample chapters, sent the packet to publishers and to the four coauthors, and exhaled for what seemed like the first time in years.

*

The backlash over Alim's letter arrived swiftly and from an unexpected source—the other coauthors. One of them called me no fewer than eight times the day he received my proposal packet to urge me not to include the letter in the book.

"This doesn't represent us," he said. "We haven't all lost hope."

Another coauthor sent the letter back scarred with edits and deletions that quashed the unfiltered vulnerability of the original. Angry and disappointed, I defended the letter as an appropriate ending. A battle for the soul of the book ensued.

Using arguments and counterpoints, we thrust and parried, circling around the question of whether to end the book on hope. Alim, apparently embarrassed to be the object of such spectacle, stayed out of the fray and seemed willing to accept any outcome.

In one particularly tense exchange with Lyle, I told him if he didn't like this ending, he should write a better one. Not one to pass on a challenge, he delivered two new essays: "Learning to Die" and "Teaching to Live," one on the despair of executions and one on personal transformation in prison.

I demanded more changes and rewrites to those two essays than to the rest of the book combined, partly because they were vying for the last word and because I felt guilty for putting Alim in this predicament.

Although the editing exchange with Lyle was combative and exasperating at times, he put in so much work to improve the pieces that in the end, he won my respect. The final compromise was to include Alim's letter, unedited, but to move Lyle's new pieces to the end. When the dust settled, I felt pleased with the final manuscript. We had created a three-dimensional dive into the tangle of hopes and dreams, failure and redemption that is life on Death Row.

Although we weathered many storms throughout four years of writing and editing, the greatest threat to the book's publication came at the very end.

I spent much of 2019 shopping for publishers. Most ignored our proposal. The few that offered a personalized response told me somewhat patronizingly that I was doing a nice thing, but no one wanted to read a book about the death penalty. I had expected rejections; still, the stalled progress depressed me. The pendulum that had swung between excitement and frustration during the writing process now careened into indifference and immobility.

One summer day, the coveted offer of a publishing contract appeared in my inbox. I felt a rush of pins and needles from the roots of my hair to the tips of my toes. Euphoric, I dashed off a post on social media and received a flood of congratulatory messages. I was so jittery and excited I couldn't eat or work or think. I yearned to call my coauthors, but prison calls are one-way, so I waited for the phone to ring.

Alim called first.

"We're going to be on Oprah!" he crowed when I told him the news, and for once, I didn't try to drag him back down to reality.

The other coauthors were excited too, except Lyle, who wanted to know every detail of the publishing contract before he would permit himself an opinion.

My euphoria lasted a day, maybe two, and when my spirit returned to earth, it hit ground and kept plunging. The doubt and anxiety that had struck my coauthors during the final editing phase now sunk its claws into me. I began to question everything: my writing skills, my coauthors' writing skills, my ability or desire to promote the book. I worried no one would read it; I worried everyone would read it. I worried the book wasn't good enough. I worried I wasn't good enough. I deleted my celebratory social media posts and hoped people would forget.

The temptation to run away from the book pulled, stretching me thin. It felt like standing in front of an ominous steel door trying to decide whether to open it. I knew that whatever waited on the other side would change my life. I just wasn't sure if the change would be for better or for worse, or if I wanted change at all.

I considered, as I had many times throughout the writing of this book, that the mere fact I could choose to walk away from Death Row invoked a responsibility to stay. If I, who had years of contact and close relationships with several people on Death Row, declined to speak up, who else would?

In the end, the bond of friendship guided me to publish this book. I believe in my coauthors. I trust them. I am proud of them and who they have become despite the horrors of their pasts and present. Prison is not a place where personalities and priorities are time-stamped by a conviction date. Incarcerated people are constantly changing—some for better, some for worse. Each of my coauthors has used the gift of time for self-examination and atonement or, as Lyle once wrote, "to live my life as it should have been from the beginning."

This book is an attempt to share the gifts of their wisdom with others, as those gifts have been shared so generously with me.

MICHAEL J. BRAXTON,

A.K.A. RROME ALONE, A.K.A ALIM

Hymn of H.I.M. (He is Me)

Who could've seen it but the prophets?
The gun, the weed, the projects
A young seed blooms inside the darkness
With no light, his future unfolds
A broken rose
His soul's cold
He dies as he grows
With eyes closed
In blindness
Walking alone, searching for divine-ness
A heavy load
A narrow road
How can he find it?
Criminal-minded?
None of the teachers
Could reach him
The preachers scold him
But couldn't show him
The role of guidance
All alone in confinement
They point fingers, but he didn't mold the environment
He's just a crossbreed
The offspring of contradiction
The legacy of nigger lynching
The pedigree of mixing
Enemy blood
A four-century taboo that pretends to be love
But it was lust for forbidden fruit

And when sin is at the root
The offshoot's surely corrupted, plus his skin was tainted
The color of flesh that men degraded
He's an outcast, society's waste
The mixed race
Half-breed
Biracial, so many labels for this bad seed
Is he Black or mulatto?
Society still calls him a nigger, he drinks liquid from the bottle
To soothe the wounds that scarred him
Temporary escape from hell, his heart hardens
His everyday is a struggle
Who can relate to this young man who's troubled?
There was his father who never loved him
Fuck him, his mother would hug him
But hugs don't erase the drama
How could he face his problems
And explain
He was ashamed
Of his own persona
His flesh and blood and his own Mama?
He inhales a moment of hope
From the blunt smoke
But it's only temporary
Slowly reality
Begins to surface
To face defeat he feels is purposeless
He yearns for guidance, but this cold world is merciless
Feeling so worthless
His heart races and rages with wildness
They never see the lonely tears he wastes in silences
Placed in confinement

They label him violent
Blamed for defiling
Society's law of what they call goodness and piety
They chain his wrists up in iron rings
Claim that he's vomit to humanity, a monster, or some kinda thing
He only mimicked what he learned from them
I ask why as he waits to die as I cry singing this hymn of H.I.M

Cemetery in the Flesh

In 1982, when I was nine years old, I woke up to the ugly realities of race.

It was after midnight in the small home where I lived with my mother, grandmother, and two younger siblings. A loud commotion in the hallway woke me from a deep sleep. Groggy, I slipped out of bed and cracked open the door that led to the hallway.

My grandma stood in front of my mother's bedroom door holding a pistol. It was the first time I'd seen a gun. She'd been drinking, but I was too young to understand the effects of alcohol. All I saw was my sweet grandma, the one who would pinch my cheeks and tell me to give her some sugar, wielding a gun and cursing.

"I'm gonna shoot that goddamn nigger!" she screamed at my mother's closed bedroom door. I recoiled in shock. I'd never heard her utter such awful words. My mother's door opened.

"Give me the gun, Mama," my mother said in a calm tone.

Grandma waved the gun around. I was so afraid she was going to shoot Mama, I didn't know what to do.

Mama stared at Grandma and said if she was gonna shoot anybody, she would have to shoot her first. Grandma snarled.

"Goddamn nigger lover."

The scene blurred as hot tears spilled over my cheeks. I closed the door and sat on my bed. Grandma had called my mother a "nigger lover." While I understood this was a reference to the Black man in my mother's bedroom, whom she'd been dating for months, I couldn't understand why loving a Black person was wrong. My own father was Black and my light brown skin reflected his brief union with my mother, who was white. Did grandma think that Mama was wrong for loving me?

As I sat there and cried, I wondered why Black people were called "niggers." I wondered why we weren't supposed to be loved.

My mother, Linda Marie Braxton, grew up in Ayden, North Carolina, and she knew the pain of feeling unwanted. As a child, she lived with her parents on the Braxton family farm, which had been handed down for generations. Before she was nine, her father went blind. Her mother abandoned him and their children to run off to Florida with another man. Unable to manage the farm without his sight, my grandfather ceded the property to his sister, Selma, and at eight years old, my mother was sent to a foster home.

Eventually, Aunt Selma and her husband, Harvey Everett, who were unable to have children, adopted my mother and raised her as their only child. Through Selma's business sense and Harvey's hard work, the farm became prosperous. In their will, the Everetts named my mother sole heir to the Braxton farm and all the family wealth. They wanted her to go to college, become a teacher, and marry a man of good social standing and financial stature.

After graduating high school, my mother moved to Meredith College campus in Raleigh, North Carolina, to pursue a degree in English. Then she met my father.

Reginald Jerome Hunter was a married father of three. Sporting a gold tooth and dapper clothes, he was smooth, handsome, and street savvy. My mother fell hard for him and I was conceived soon after.

Before I was born, my father was sent to federal prison for trafficking heroin. I never got the chance to know my grandparents, aunts, uncles, or numerous cousins because his family never embraced me. I was the shameful bastard child of a white woman, conceived from adultery and scandal.

My mother turned to her adoptive parents for help but received only condemnation. Not only could they not believe she'd gotten pregnant out of wedlock; she was carrying the child of a Black man.

They urged her to have an abortion, but my mother refused. Already, she'd begun to feel connected to the life growing inside of her. They threatened to disown her if she kept the child. Surely, she understood that to raise a Black child was unthinkable. What would their friends say?

They gave her a clear ultimatum: give the child up for adoption or be disinherited.

My mother mulled over her future. Were her parents and fortune worth giving up for me? Was she willing to sacrifice everything for a half-Black child whose father was in prison?

In the end, she agreed to give me up for adoption. Her parents drove her to the Salvation Army home for unwed mothers in Durham, North Carolina, where she lived in secret until the day I was born.

I arrived June 1, 1973. I suppose I was reluctant for the journey ahead because I came three weeks late. My mother signed me into the custody of the Department of Social Services and returned to Ayden.

Once home, she couldn't shake thoughts of the son she had just named Michael Jerome Braxton. Could she abandon me like her own mother had abandoned her? She knew in her soul that she loved me. What difference did it make that I was half-Black or that my father was in prison?

As she inventoried her life, she realized that a stable home and financial security didn't substitute for love. She'd been given a six-month grace period by the social services department in case she changed her mind about adoption, so with new resolve, she packed her meager belongings and informed her parents that she was keeping her son.

Not long after my birth, my mother met another Black man, Willis Gore, who fathered my brother, Chris, and my sister, Keisha. Before Willis died unexpectedly in 1979, my mother reunited with her biological mother—

the one who would hurl the hateful invective "nigger lover" three years later—and together, my mother, grandmother, siblings, and I moved to the Kentwood housing projects in Raleigh, North Carolina.

My mother never gave up hope of reconciling with her adoptive parents. Year after year, we drove to Ayden to visit Uncle Harvey and Aunt Selma. At first, while Mama went inside to see them, Chris, Keisha, and I had to wait in the car. I knew it was because we were "half breeds." I'd heard Mama on the phone talking about how Harvey and Selma didn't want anything to do with us. I felt ashamed and rejected. I couldn't understand why our family would treat us so coldly simply because of the color of our skin.

After several of these no-contact annual visits, one year, Harvey and Selma ventured outside to look at us. They stared quietly through the car window. No smiles. No waves. No words. Mama forced us to wave, but our relatives stood expressionless with their hands in their pockets.

I hated going to Ayden, but Mama was persistent. Finally, after a few more visits, Uncle Harvey and Aunt Selma seemed to relent and they let us inside.

The first time we went inside the house, Mama fussed over us all day. She explained that Harvey and Selma were "old-fashioned." They didn't want a bunch of children running around their house, so we were to sit down, behave, and not speak unless spoken to.

I recognized these rules as the same that applied in public spaces occupied by white people. From an early age, I'd picked up on subtleties, such as impolite stares and whispers, whenever my siblings and I went out in public with our mother. Sometimes, Mama had to tell clerks, waiters, and hostesses that we were her children.

"Oh, I'm sorry," they'd say. "I didn't know you were together."

Other strangers would nudge each other, point, or nod in our direction. If my siblings and I talked too loud, ran around in a store, or goofed off like typical kids, Mama would hiss at us through clenched teeth. "Don't embarrass me out in public like you don't have no home training."

I understood the warnings to mean that we had to be on our best behavior, not only to reflect well on Mama's parenting, but to combat any stereotyping associated with race.

I despised going out in public with Mama. I felt like a spectacle, a circus attraction. And although Mama never spoke of it directly, I knew she felt it too.

Eventually, Harvey and Selma allowed us to hug their cold, stiff necks. But their hearts never changed. After their deaths, the Everetts willed their entire estate, including the Braxton family farm, to white people outside of the family. They even left a quarter of a million dollars to the next-door neighbors. Mama didn't inherit a dime.

Mama's efforts to help us "fit in" to white society in public often forced us to minimize our Blackness, but at home and in school, being accepted by my majority-Black neighbors and classmates often meant erasing my white half altogether.

One day in fifth grade, my mother came to my school for a parent-teacher conference. Later, a young Black girl asked me, "Who was that lady you were with today?"

When I told her that was my Mama, her eyes widened in disbelief.

"Your Mama is white?"

Hearing the shock in her voice made me feel like I'd been hiding something now finally exposed. The question seemed to imply, "How can you be one of us if your mother is one of them?"

Whiteness stood for oppression, the denial of rights, hatred, and slavery. I had never made that association with my mother. Now, I had to make room in my mind for the fact that even though she was just "Mama" to me, to the rest of the world, she was a "white person."

While I never denied being biracial if confronted, I didn't voluntarily divulge it either. Most people saw me as a light-skinned Black person and treated me like any other member of the race. I was "passing as Black," a weird reversal to the plight of light-skinned Blacks historically, who went to great lengths to pass as white to reap the social and economic privileges of whiteness.

Because I was generally accepted as Black, I could see and hear Black people in ways that white people never will. Once, I heard someone comment that white people smell like wet dogs when they get out of the shower. I'd never noticed my mother smelling like a wet dog. Hearing the blanket accusation felt insulting to Mama, yet I didn't have the courage to denounce it and risk exposing myself as half-white.

Other times, I'd hear Black men brag about how they used white women for sex and money. I'd wonder if that's how my dad felt about my mom. Was she merely a sexual conquest, a forbidden-fruit fantasy? Or was mom the evil, white seductress with an unquenchable desire for Black men, as the stereotype often portrayed?

During these race-charged conversations, I lived in fear that someone would single me out and expose that I was half-white. If friends who knew my mother were present, I'd wonder if they expected me to defend white people.

I didn't have the courage to speak for or against an entire race, so I stayed quiet. Even then, I feared that my silence might be construed as approval. Did my friends interpret my silence as agreement that white people really did smell like wet dogs after a shower? Maybe they thought I was a coward who couldn't stick up for his own mother. Is this how they thought I would react if I were among white people disparaging Blacks?

These thoughts and feelings gnawed at me constantly. I spent a great deal of time and energy concealing my half-whiteness for fear it might be used as a weapon against me.

Occasionally, however, a curious Black person would sniff me out.

"What are you?" they'd ask.

"I'm Black," I'd respond.

They'd scrutinize my hair texture and light skin before insisting I had "something else" in me. Maybe Indian? They were always reluctant to outright guess white.

"My mother's white," I'd respond.

My interrogator would light up like a dog that's just snuffed out a rabbit, declaring, "I *knew* you had something in you. You've got that good hair."

I felt like my membership in the Black race was revocable at any moment. Because of my light skin and "good hair," other Black males often emasculated me, slapping me with labels like "pretty boy," which meant "soft." In trying to defy these labels, I felt I had to constantly prove my Blackness, my toughness, my manhood. As I grew older, my methods of winning approval became more extreme.

Despite my attempts to fit in, I always felt alone, like nobody really understood me. I spent my entire childhood and early adult life hating my racial identity and never really knowing where I belonged.

This underlying storm guided me into the tempest that would culminate in my becoming a cemetery in the flesh, as I describe in one of my songs:

If a coward dies a million times, I guess I've died a million one
Every time my spirit died from fear, it's just like killing one
Scared of what other people would think, fearing that they won't relate
Made me hide the truth inside, wanting to be something I ain't
Tryin' to be something I can't, living lies, ashamed of my fate
So every time my spirit rise, I'd kill it 'cause it's me that I hate
But this is murder, nonetheless
Now, I'm a cemetery in the flesh

The Top One Percent

When I was a kid, my Mama told me that when I grew up, I could be anything I wanted. She showered me with praise even when I didn't feel like I deserved it. When I played on the school basketball team, my Mama would brag to her friends about how well I played—even if I only scored four points in a game and one of my teammates scored twenty-five. I took her words as encouragement, but when they didn't match up to actual performance, somewhere along the line, I stopped believing them.

This came back to taunt me in 1994 as a jury considered testimony regarding how they should sentence me.

In the courtroom, a social worker took the stand with a stack of my school records, test scores, and medical history in hand. He read the data and my attorney asked what he'd concluded from his findings. As he began to explain, the social worker's body language shifted and his tone changed from that of an analyst crunching numbers to the voice of a concerned father.

According to my test scores, in the fifth grade, I scored in the top one percentile of students my age in the nation. However, by seventh grade, I had fallen into the bottom sixty-seven percent.

I listened to the social worker in disbelief as he testified that academically, there was no explanation for this. The problem had lain outside the classroom. He was incensed that no one had taken notice. How, he asked, does a kid drop from the top one percent in so short a time and no one even notifies a guidance counselor to find out what is going on?

The Braxton family: Marie, Michael, Chris, Keisha, 1989.

I was stunned at this revelation. I had never known I'd scored exceptionally in the fifth grade. Yet the social worker was right. The period when my test scores dropped was one of the most turbulent times in my young life.

During this time, my homeboy, Pete, killed my good friend Mike. I had looked up to Mike. He was light-skinned and had curly hair just like me. Girls loved him, and he wore the title of "pretty boy" like a badge of honor. I hated whenever someone used that label on me, but Mike was cool and people respected him. He never seemed afraid of the guys who picked on me.

They say that during a fight, Pete stabbed Mike in the head and pierced his brain with a curling iron. They said Mike became a "vegetable." They said he was on life support until someone pulled the plug.

My young mind struggled to make sense of it all. What did they mean when they called him a "vegetable"? What was life support? How can you pull a plug on a person to make him die? Instead of schoolwork, these questions roamed my troubled mind. No one seemed to have satisfactory answers.

Pete never went to prison for what he did. I used to watch him from my bedroom window, afraid to go outside if he was there. I watched him and wondered if it was true what people said: if you killed someone, you would be haunted by his ghost. Did Mike's ghost haunt Pete? I'd gone to Mike's funeral and looked into his casket. I knew death was real. Mike wasn't coming back.

Two other people from my neighborhood weren't coming back either: Teresa and Karen. They were sisters who went missing about a year apart. Teresa went missing first. Some people suspected that she had run away, but a year later, her sister Karen went missing too and we all knew it was foul play.

A few months after, their remains were discovered. They had both been murdered. One of the sisters had been partially dismembered. The killer had lived among us all along. It was someone we knew.

The discovery of Teresa and Karen's killer sent shock waves through my head. Suddenly, I didn't know who to trust. Their brothers had been close friends of mine, but now I didn't know what to say to them. Though they still lived in my hood, they seemed to exist in a world of their own.

In the seventh grade, the most dangerous place in the world was school. My school was located right across the street from a housing project and every day at 3:00 p.m., students would hurry to get on the school bus before the guys from Chavis Heights projects spilled onto campus. Some days, they lined up at the school's edge to throw bottles and menace our bus.

One day, a girl yelled at them from a window and several of them stormed onto our bus. Kids screamed and cried. When some of the teachers came to our rescue, instead of fleeing, those guys started trying to tip over our bus.

No one at my school was immune to the violence. Even the principal was assaulted that year. A gang of guys ran onto the school grounds, beat her up, broke her arm, and threw her in the dumpster. How can you expect someone's test scores not to drop when school isn't a safe place?

I reflected on these events as I sat in the courtroom and listened to the social worker testify about my earlier potential. I wondered if it were possible that my mother had been right about what she had told me as a child. Absent the trauma, tragedy, and terror of the time, could I really have been whatever I wanted when I grew up?

The Butterfly Path

I grew up in west Raleigh in a housing project called Kentwood. Dead smack in the midst of middle- and upper-class affluency and mere blocks from North Carolina State University's campus, Kentwood was the tolerated blemish of the west side. We weren't hustlers or trendsetters in fashion like some of the other housing projects in Raleigh. Nor were our neighborhood girls the "project chicks" that every "hood was sweatin." In Kentwood, we were the bottom rung of the housing projects in terms of respect. Many in my generation would become the future crackheads, winos, and inmates of tomorrow.

Our culture was built on three main pillars: fightin', stealin', and gettin' drunk. Fightin' was a rite of passage and it determined your position in the hood hierarchy. The better you were at fightin', the higher your status.

Stealin' was our way of life. It was never considered in the context of right and wrong. It was just something we did. We didn't steal from one another most of the time, but everything outside Kentwood was for the taking: clothes, food, money, alcohol, accessories. Anything not bolted to the ground. In that case, we'd use bolt cutters.

Gettin' drunk was how we celebrated and mourned. We drank to gain courage, to have fun, and to fuel further excursions of thievery and daring. Usually, gettin' drunk ended in a fight that reshuffled the hood hierarchy.

Although Kentwood was my stomping ground until I was eighteen, I only lived there until I was almost thirteen. My mother decided to move after three people from my hood were murdered and someone burglarized our apartment while we were asleep. Besides, the rent had increased according to the rate of her income and it just made more sense to rent a house. After we moved, I was still in Kentwood after school every day until the eighth grade, and then, it was sleepovers every other weekend with one of my friends. Kentwood was my hood. It was in my veins. It was the only home I knew.

The house we moved into on Edmund Street was a block away from Glascock and Brookside Drive. We had a front yard and a backyard with a patio, a driveway, and a basement as well. My mom purchased a basketball goal and installed it in the backyard. We even had our very first dishwasher and garbage disposal. At first, it felt like we were rich and I couldn't wait for some of my friends to see our new house. I was so excited that I looked forward to starting a paper route or mowing the lawn.

However, I began to realize that our new house was far away from Kentwood. Once I changed schools, I rarely got to see my friends. The new neighborhood consisted mostly of adults and seniors, upper-middle-class whites, and people I had little in common with. My Mom said it was a "better environment" for us. A better place to raise kids.

I eventually made a few friends at school, but these kids were different from the guys I was accustomed to hanging around in Kentwood and I quickly realized I was at the bottom of the economic ladder. Even though I was now living in a house in a "better" part of town, all we had was the husk of what looked like comfortable living. Beneath the façade, we were still poor people from the projects. I never felt like I fit in.

My clothes still came from Kmart, Big Lots, Sears, and Roses, and my tennis shoes were imitation brands from Pic 'n Pay. This was no big deal in Kentwood, but on this side of town, the kids wore expensive jeans and deliberately tore holes in the knees. Their play shoes were Air Jordans, and they were getting dirt bikes at the age of thirteen or fourteen! They'd pop wheelies and race through trails in the woods, particularly one place we called "The Butterfly Path."

This was the path where I drank my first taste of whiskey: a bottle of Wild Turkey one kid had stolen from his parents. We would huddle there and puff cigarettes and joints of reefer, then emerge like monarchs with new attitudes and "I don't give a fuck" personas, searching for trouble like butterflies looking for nectar.

I was soon drinking and smoking every weekend and skipping school to get drunk during the week. It was during one of my drunken escapades that I called my high school and made a prank bomb threat.

The next day, my homeroom teacher told me to report to the principal's office. I strolled in with hardly a care in the world. It wasn't until I saw my school-skipping partner, Steve, and his mother waiting in the lobby that my heart rate increased. I cut a glance at him for a heads-up of what to expect, but Steve averted my glance.

The principal ushered me into his office and told me to have a seat. He had already spoken to my mother, he explained, and she was on the way.

I felt nervous. My mother hadn't been called to school on my account since sixth or seventh grade and that had resulted in my dad driving all the way down from Washington, D.C. to give me the worst spanking of my life, which turned out to be very reformative. Yet here, my mother was being ushered into the office by the secretary.

My mother's face was stone, etched with severity in the corners of her mouth and in her eyes. She took a seat next to me and clutched her purse tightly on her lap as the principal began to explain the nature of the meeting.

The school was aware that Steve and I had called in a bomb threat and the Raleigh Police Department had been called as a precautionary measure. This had cost a significant amount of time, resources, and taxpayer money. As a result, I was being expelled from all Wake County schools indefinitely. I would not be permitted to return for the remainder of the school year, and I would have to reapply the following year to seek admittance.

I couldn't believe it. The school year was barely two months in and I was already expelled for the entire year! I heard my mother inhale sharply, and I watched her from my periphery. I was sure she would lash out any second and slap me right out of my seat. I didn't want to be blindsided. Yet somehow, she remained composed in the presence of the principal, asking necessary questions in a business-like manner while occasionally glaring at me.

After the meeting was over, we walked to the car in tense silence. I could feel the fury emanating from her. I knew at any moment the sky would collapse on my head. When we got into the car, she didn't say a word on the short drive home, and neither did I.

She pulled into the driveway and I opened the door to get out.

"Don't think this is over," she said through clenched teeth. I looked at the ground and said nothing.

"I'll see you when I get off work. And you'd better not leave this house."

"Yes, ma'am," I responded with a formal respect I wasn't used to using. I closed the door and went into the house as my mother drove to work.

I just knew my world would be coming to an end. My mother was gonna kill me; there was no other possibility. This was by far the worst thing I had ever done in my life—much worse than the misbehavior that had incurred my father's wrath three or four years before.

Once, she'd been so mad at me that she grabbed up a hammer and slammed it against the washing machine, putting a dent in it. Another time, she picked up a knife and stabbed it into the cutting board with a scream of rage at one of my misdemeanors. What would she do now that my behavior had really driven her over the edge? I was afraid to find out.

I thought about running away, but that would only compound things for me when she found me. I played out all types of fatal scenarios of what she would do to me as I waited for her to come home.

Finally, she arrived. I knew she was still upset, but I could sense that her anger had settled down. However, what she said surprised me more than any scenario I had prepared for.

She looked at me with a stern face and said, "Don't think just because you got kicked out of school that you are gonna lay up in here on your ass! I'm so mad with you, I don't know what to do! But I guess you think you are grown now. Well, you are gonna get your ass up and go to work every day if you are gonna stay in this house. Do you understand me?"

"Yes, ma'am," I said, and just like that, the universe shifted. Not only was I still alive, I didn't even get yelled at! In fact, my only punishment was a reward from my perspective. I had to get a job.

At fifteen, I was an adult now, and after escaping what I'd been sure was imminent death, I wasn't afraid of my mother anymore nor her displeasure. Without that fear and her standard of approval to keep me in check, I could do anything I wanted with no concern for the consequences. I could smoke cigarettes at home, get drunk, and not even try to hide it. I could hang out all night, come home at five o'clock in the morning, sell drugs, and go to jail.

There were no consequences to deter me. I didn't give a fuck about anything and that seemed like liberation. I was free. Free like a butterfly to flap my wings, sip the nectar of intoxicating drinks, and flutter right into the path of crime.

God's Mercy

I used to be a despot
I shit you not
I was straight tyrannical
Before I got put in these manacles
I don't give praise to them ways
Nor do I say this to glorify
But there's people that's still horrified
Traumatized and scarred forever
To this day they'll never forgive me
Literally NEVER!
'Cause those I left my marks on
Will tell you straight from the heart
That they hate Rrome
And would love to see my date come
And truthfully how could I say that they're dead wrong
To a degree they got a right to see my head gone
And I don't say this to justify the things I've done
But I went through some shit when I was young
I was picked on and jumped on
Literally stomped on
And there was no one to help me so I would go home
Go to my bedroom and cry my tears
Beneath my pillow in silence so no one hears
And I would think about getting revenge
Fantasizing 'bout murderin' those that hurt me for days on end
I was the fuck-up at my school
The straight loser that wasn't cool
Although I excelled inside the classroom

The chubby-face half breed with the pudgy waist
I rarely smiled, my insides was an ugly place
Kids were teasing me
Treating me like being mixed was something evil to be
I was easily
Laughed and picked at
Punched on and kicked at
While feeling like a big fat
Piece of shit
And worst of all I was believin' it
I wanted so bad to even it
That this ain't no kiddin'
I snapped one day and this ain't no shittin'
I beat a muthafucka senseless
I tell you God is my witness
He was beggin' me and pleadin' forgiveness
But I ain't have not an ounce of mercy
Muthafucka, you goin' feel like I felt all those years they hurt me
It felt good releasin' all that hatred
Bottled up in my soul
Plus I was settin' examples
So they would know
I'm the wrong one to fuck with
So leave dude alone
Or else he'll try to beat you to death
Dude's gone!
Now, I'm grown
Much more mature
I came into my own
So now I'm much more secure
I get to reminiscing
And my feelings get disturbed

I think back on shit I did
People ain't really deserve
I'm like damn, you ain't have to do dude like that
It'd be fucked up if somebody did you like that
And that's true, that's why I recognize
And I feel true compassion from the hurt
That I caused when I was wreckin' lives
And it took time to realize
But now the torment and grief in my soul is eatin' me alive
I wanna make amends now
How can I right the wrongs?
Can I set the record straight
Lettin' the State inject my arms?
I place my fate in God's palms
This is to everyone I've ever harmed
You all deserve Justice
And truth is, I deserve to be where the dust is
But if by God's will I must live
I forgive
All the sins of those that ever hurt me
And for those I hurt
I ask forgiveness and for God's mercy
Amen

Mercy on My Soul

It took the jury only four hours to determine my fate.

I sat in silence at the defendant's hardwood table as twelve strangers filed into the courtroom to take their seats as my designated peers. I searched their faces for some clue of what they had decided, but their faces were stoic.

Sitting with his fingers entwined on his desk, his brow creased with austerity, the judge issued his command.

"Will the foreman please rise?"

Juror number four stood with a sense of duty. He was an older white man, perhaps in his early sixties. Tall, with casual polish, wearing a light-colored polo and tan slacks, he had the appearance of a man who might spend his spare time playing golf, a man I stereotypically envisioned brushing shoulders with the social elite. Certainly no peer of mine, yet an obvious choice for a foreman as his presence seemed to demand deference.

"Has the jury reached a decision?" the judge asked the foreman.

"Yes, Your Honor, we have," the foreman responded.

"Will the bailiff please convey the sealed decision to the clerk?"

The bailiff walked gracefully over to the foreman, received the decision, and handed it to the clerk. My eyes were transfixed upon this scene as the clerk passed it along to the judge.

His Honor was a plump man of about fifty years with rosy cheeks and a head absent of hair on the top. He carefully opened the sealed decision and looked at its recommendation. Glancing at me with the same look of severity he had worn throughout the trial, he pushed the bridge of his reading glasses up the slope of his nose and returned his gaze to the decision before him. Lifting his pen, he began to write as the entire courtroom, including its audience of seven spectators, waited in anticipation of the outcome.

Right behind me, in the second row sat my mother and my sister, the only people who cared enough about me to show up on this important day when strangers would determine my fate. My mother, with her dignified gray hair and blue eyes that smiled while concealing a lifetime of pain, held tight to my sister's hand.

Keisha and I had the same face. I could look into her eyes and see myself reflected in the best light. She was the only person in the world who saw me as a role model—someone she looked up to despite the accusations, despite the deeds; someone she took pride in calling her brother. In her eyes, I was forever her hero.

Behind the prosecutor sat the aggrieved family of the victim: a grandmother and mother who had both lost a man they'd called "son." The grandmother was graceful. Her light brown face still contained a youthful glow as she sat with dignity despite her grief. Her eyes, visible behind large glasses that covered almost a third of her face, had a quiet kindness to them. Her face showed mercy, yet compassion and empathy for her daughter's pain.

Her daughter, though an obvious version of the grandmother's younger self, had none of the kindness or mercy in her eyes. Instead, her eyes were like daggers I could not bear to meet lest they further torment the guilt-ridden heart of my conscience.

As I focused my attention on the judge, my heart seemed to rise up inside my chest. It reached the top of my throat and lodged there, holding me breathless as the judge finished what he'd been writing and handed what appeared to be the jury's recommendation back to the clerk.

Composing himself, the judge sat up from the perch of his throne and fanned out the sides of his robe, pulling it tightly around his shoulders like a cape.

"The jury, having found the defendant, Michael Jerome Braxton, guilty of murder in the first degree, sentence him to death..."

His words continued, but my heart sank from my throat down to the pit of my stomach as everything except my thoughts receded into the shadows around me. Words and sounds became nothing but background chatter in a movie I now seemed to be watching from outside myself.

I looked around at this theater of drama unfolding and felt my soul hovering above me as if it were fleeing to seek refuge from the tsunami of emotions inside.

Amidst the chatter, I heard the request for each member of the jury to stand and affirm their verdict. I watched in a clouded daze as the figures of men and women see-sawed up and down to acknowledge the decision. Suddenly, there was a pause.

A Black woman, perhaps in her thirties with a brown complexion and medium build, appeared overwhelmed by the burden of the occasion. She choked back heavy sobs and continued to sit even after her name was called. Every eye in the courtroom turned toward her.

I looked at her face and could see the difficulty etched in her features due to the battle waging inside her. My heart raised barely a micron from its pit. The juror sitting to her right, another Black woman of similar age, gave her a tender stroke on the back, perhaps empathizing with the difficulty of the task. Then, the woman looked at me, and a body-wracking lament erupted from her throat. Gripping the arm of the chair, she struggled to pull herself to her feet and utter a weak "yes" before falling back to her seat and sobbing.

I almost wanted to thank her and console her myself, seeing the pain she had to endure to stand behind a decision that she ultimately believed was right. It moved me that even though this woman had sentenced me to death, she recognized my humanity, and it caused her great pain to participate in my execution.

For a moment, I was lost in my thoughts, still numb to the reality of what was happening to me. Separated from the part of me that had feeling, everything became white noise again.

I could hear the drone of the judge's voice from a distance in my mind. Words and phrases were uttered about being handed over to the custody of the Warden of Central Prison to be held until my death was carried out. I heard a date of February 8, 1998, announced for execution. But in some weird way, none of it was happening to me. I was just another spectator observing the proceedings along with everyone else.

Until I heard my name.

"Michael Jerome Braxton!"

The sound roared as if shouted down from the expanse of heaven. My soul collided violently with my body, and once again, I was sitting at the defendant's table.

I looked up to see the eyes of the judge peering down at me over the rim of his glasses. He hoisted his gavel like a mighty weapon ready to smite the wicked. His face bore a look of the most frightening condemnation as he spoke words that sent tremors through my bones—words that indicated my judgment was no longer a concern of this world because now, I was to face the judgment of the divine.

With a thundering boom of his gavel, he intoned, "May God have mercy on your soul!"

My whole world came crashing through the roof of that courthouse and left me in a swoon. I was going to die.

I looked back at my family. My sister's face was a mask of torment. Never in my life had I seen a face so anguished and distraught as she wept until her cries became a wailing hiccup and her body convulsed in her seat.

My mother reached out to me, her hand pleading for a last touch of the son she had birthed into this world. As the guards surrounded me, her beautiful eyes became puddles of the saddest pain. She mouthed the words "I love you" as they took me away.

Welcome to Death Row

Intro [Talking in a sinister voice]
Welcome to Death Row. Please remove all your clothing and personal
    effects and place them into the white bag
as we dress you out in a one-piece red jumpsuit with Department of
    Corrections on the tag.
You will be fingerprinted, photographed, and assigned to a cell in this
    institution
where you will dwell for the remainder of your days until it's time for
    your execution.
Welcome to Death Row!

Verse One
Welcome to Death Row, this is your resident Deadman talking
Your host to guide you close inside this world that I am walking
Your tour guide to peep into the minds of those who live it
A sentence reserved for less than one percent of the murders committed
The odds which are similar to one being struck by lightning
Yet being stuck by poison is a prospect just as frightening
However, walk with me as I describe the insides
The state-of-the-art facilities designed solely to end lives
In fact, I'd have to say this place looks quite medicinal
Sanitized to hide its use for executing criminals
As you enter, two remote-controlled doors close right behind you
With an echoed metal clap perhaps just to remind you
That you can't leave so breathe and just leave that world behind you
As we walk through the valley of death, I'm here to guide you, this is
    Death Row!
… Welcome to Death Row [sinister laugh]

Verse Two

That first door, the one that's on your right, that would be the chaplain
The first office you come to and ironically the last when
Your date comes and perhaps you may need some spiritual guidance
To usher you into the next life, these accommodations are provided
The next door, the one that's to your left, that's a command post
For the sergeant and lieutenant and the first place every man goes
When he comes in to learn in which cell he'll be located
And also where the sergeant has you briefly orientated
Rules are rules! Now come with me as we walk through the hallway
See the cameras on the ceiling? They record and monitor all day
And to our left here is an alcove for therapeutic and medical health
To help you cope with the loss of your hope
For the next twenty years as you wait for your death
We have pills for that, don't worry you'll be fine
The exit door in the alcove is the door that will take you outside
To the rec yard for exercise for sport and jump and play
In an enclosed space with a stone wall for one full hour a day
And on the stone wall are towers, see the guards patrolling with guns
To ensure no one attempts to climb the wall or tries to run
That's a no-no, these guards are trained to shoot and aim to kill
So if anyone attempts to flee you best believe they will, cause this is Death Row
... Welcome to Death Row [sinister laugh]

Verse Three

Welcome to Death Row, now follow me as we exit the yard
Now make a right after the alcove so I can take you to what's called a pod
But first there is a control booth reinforced with shatterproof glass
Equipped with multiple monitors and two guards performing their task
Of operating the control panel which remotely opens the doors
And there is another directly above it to operate on identical floors
Each control booth sits on an island of four pods, together there's eight

And this is where the condemned are housed 'til executed by the State
Each pod has twenty-four cells with a toilet, a sink, and a bed
Well, actually a steel plank and a pallet for each of the dead
Don't worry you'll have your board games and puzzles to distract your mind
And even a snack from the canteen to help as you bide your time
Believe me we'll treat you humanely, you'll hardly suffer an ill
And before your execution you can choose your own last meal
And then when the moment comes you'll hardly feel a pain
During your 10-minute death injecting poison in your vein, 'cause this is Death Row
... Welcome to Death Row

Outro
Welcome to the death chamber. This is your executioner speaking. You may experience a bit of turbulence on your journey to the next life. But don't worry. We will paralyze you so that you cannot speak or express your pain. This is totally humane ... [sinister laugh]

Letter from Alim

October 7, 2017

Dear Tessie,

Hey, how are you? I got your letter and the chapter from your book. I enjoyed reading it and thought you did a good job. I especially liked reading your perspective of my family. It made me smile because they seemed really standoffish and short with words. In other words, they sounded like me (smile). You were correct not to view it as trying to be rude. We are just very self-composed and guarded in public. Perhaps that's the consequence of a lifetime of being gawked by everyone...

I don't know if you've realized this or not, maybe you wouldn't be able to, but every one of us that you correspond with or wrote about in your book represents a different stage in the lifespan of a Death Row inmate. It's hard to explain, really, but it's like I see a part of myself in each of these guys. With the exception of JT, I've been in prison longer than all of them. Some of them still have a lot of passion and drive, they want to make a difference, leave their mark, be seen and recognized as someone greater than the worst thing they ever did. In the life trajectory of being on Death Row, I've experienced all of this. It's like when you are young and you have an idea and you feel like you can change the world. You see the corruption in the system, you hear about some alternative theory, and you are fired up. But eventually, you get tired. You've heard all the arguments, you know all the theories. Nothing is changing, and you realize you are just another slave on the plantation.

At one time, you thought you were different, that you weren't like the rest. That they had lain down and given up. They stopped fighting. Some of them even volunteered for the needle. You swore on everything you believed in that you would never become one of them. Then, you wake up one day twenty-five years later and you realize you are barely the shell of the man you used to be. You get tired. You are beat down. You just want to go home.

I swear to you, I feel like Kunta Kinte! This is no lie!! I read the book *Roots* years ago, and it was like I was reading about myself. A young African, captured, and sold as a slave. When he arrived in America, he was shocked to see other Blacks walking around with no chains! Why weren't they fighting? Why weren't they revolting? He could not understand it. He was in full restraints, yet they were walking unescorted in the town and driving horse-bound carriages. I had that same type of fire in me once upon a time when I did ten years in solitary; everywhere I went, I was in chains. Every fiber in my body wanted to revolt, and I was constantly in a state of intense inner rebellion. I looked at all the inmates in the regular population willingly working to keep the plantation running as sellouts! Why were they helping the "authorities" keep us in bondage by cooperating and being obedient? As soon as they took the chains off Kunta, he ran. They captured him, rechained him, and after a while, removed the chains again. Every time, he tried to escape. He wanted freedom. Until finally, they chopped off his foot and left him hobbled.

They forced him to work in the fields. He would refuse, and they would whip him again and again. He felt like everyone else was a sellout for obeying. Then, one day, he noticed that some of the slaves weren't really working at all. They just acted like they were working when the overseer looked their way. When he wasn't looking, they'd rest or even sabotage the equipment, breaking it or destroying the crops. He realized they were keeping the whip off their back but still resisting in a different way. So, he began to employ these tactics, even down to the "Yessuh, massa." While inside, hating his condition, and secretly planning his escape. But you know what ends up happening? Degree by degree, it breaks you down to the point where one day you wake up and realize you've been biding your time for so long trying to keep the whip off your back that now you are one of them old broken-ass slaves walking around with no chains on, driving massa's carriage and making his tea. Every now and then, you see a young slave not too far removed from freedom, and he's full of all these ideas and ambitions just like you once were, and you don't even want to hear it. You've been there, done that. You're tired, and you realize with a sad recognition in your eyes that you are broken. They got you. They broke the spirit of Kunta Kinte, and the only thing left is that tired, weary body and the only escape you can envision now is death.

I feel like I needed to share that with you, and that is just a thumbnail. I pray that none of those other guys go through that feeling of just being beaten down and broken, but the truth is—the guys I know who have been in prison longer than me, you can see it in their eyes and know it happens to practically all of us. JT can relate to what I am saying, and it's unspoken—but he and I are kinda in the same space. It may be accelerated more based on your experiences. Like for me, I did so much time on lockup, and I have so much to shoulder by being looked up to and sought out for advice and counsel. It drains you. I'm at that point where sometimes I wonder *How much more do I have to go before it's all over?* I'm telling you all this because I need this demographic of inmates to be spoken for. In your book, I need people to hear that there are men in prison, and this is what happens to us. It is sad, Tessie. It is depressing when you have a system designed to break you down to the point where the only escape left is death. This is why I told you before that it would have been better to just kill me twenty or twenty-five years ago, but don't do me like this. [Don't] break my spirit to the point where death is now a relief. That's not humane. That's torture. I write this because it needs to be heard. I don't want to be the one to say it. I'm ashamed and embarrassed that it has happened to me. I guarantee you, JT feels the same way, and we've never even discussed it. I just know.

The reason why I went there at this particular moment is because you asked me about remorse, you asked me about the victims' families, and I wanted to say that there is a reason why I show you the side of me that I let you see. I'm complex. As a human being, we all are. I could easily mask my vulnerabilities. I could mask my exhaustion. I choose to let you hear and see the tired, beaten down Alim. I want you to hear the coarse language. I want you to peep into my mind a little and get a glimpse of what it feels like to be broken. Not for me. But for everybody who has been through this. Do you understand? I don't write you and talk about my faith in Allah although that is there. Everybody doesn't have faith. So that isn't the part of me I wanted to share with you. Trust me, there are people who only know me from the aspect of my religion—because that governs my daily life—and they would have no idea about the things I have shared in this letter.

I have cried and cried real tears from my soul out of remorse for the things I have done. The lives I took, the innocent families I have hurt. There was a time when all I could think about was how could I make amends for the things I have done. I talked to my lawyers about contacting the families. I wanted to apologize to them. I am truly, sincerely sorry for what I have done. I even felt that I would end my appeals if they wanted me to die to make amends for killing their loved one. All of that is still there. My tears, my grief, my sorrow, my dignity, my very spirit…this ongoing torment has taken it all.

Your friend,

ALIM

Execution Night

They put Ricky in the gas chamber—oh, God!
I watched the scene from my window, the COs was so hard
Protesters picketed, I couldn't sleep, I fidgeted
Mufuckas was celebrating—I witnessed it!
They ate cupcakes, shared hugs, exchanged handshakes
Congratulated each other, I mean, for God's sake!
I stood glued to the window
Subconscious saying, "Rrome, this is how it's going down when they get you!"
I wanna cry but I'm tearless
Heart tremblin' in my chest, but my mind sayin', "You gotta be fearless"
So I clinched my goddamn jaw
But I'm a give it to you raw—inside, I was beggin' for Ma!
Like Ma, I just wanna go home
I swear I'll be a good boy, Mommy, I don't wanna die all alone
That's when I heard the batons
And I was snatched back by the crack of the bones that the COs were
    beatin' up on
They claimed he was protesting, so they taught him a lesson
That tonight there would be no contesting
Or you will lose your life
And this is how it goes down at two a.m. inside on Execution Night!

Chorus
Somebody dyin' tonight
After lights out, somebody fryin' tonight
On death's watch, clock tick louder than life
Light a candle and pray for the dead—it's Execution Night!

Verse Two

When they executed Dawood, it was like a swoon came over me
His last words was spoken so nobly
Invoking the curse of Allah upon his killers
It was like I felt a quake in the prison's pillars
When they put him under anesthesia
Then they paralyzed his nervous system and injected the needle
The next shot made his heart stop
I couldn't breathe, suspended in thought, I felt my heart drop
To his death, he proclaimed he was innocent
I couldn't help but wonder how those who witnessed it
Could have peace and pretend that this was humane
While they were putting poison in a man's vein
Who swore upon his God that he was not guilty
That let me know for sure they was goin' kill me!
A glimpse of what my future's like
Strapped down at two a.m. on Execution Night!

[Chorus]

Verse Three

When they executed Syriani, it was like watching a scene that would taunt me
Over and over and over and haunt me
We was housed in the same pod
And it was odd watchin' for weeks as his date grew closer to God
Nobody hardly spoke to him
I mean, what do you say to a mufucka 'bout to get a needle poked into him?
I watched his face for a clue of what he was going through
In my mind sayin', "One day, Rrome, this goin' be you"
His demeanor was serene, but his features looked tortured
And his eyes looked so weary and clearly exhausted
I was sitting on the top tier when the squad came

Watchin' some inmates in a domino and card game
As the guards marched him right down to the death watch
Nobody spoke a word as his shoulders dropped
Slumped in defeat, but still seemly brave
He looked around the pod, and then weakly waved
For a second, the tension had the sounds muffled
But ten ticks later, cards were being shuffled
And things went right back to the way that they were
Like everything we witnessed ain't even occur
I guess that's how we cope when we feeling distress
We push it to the side and keep doing our best
Fearing what our future's like
When the death squad comes for your soul on Execution Night!

[Chorus]

Life after Death

Hope was my enemy. Hope was a fraud, just a trick the mind played on the heart to give it reason to exist. Every time I had walked with hope, it had caught me when I'd least expected it and stabbed me right in the heart, leaving me alone and groping in the darkness. So, into darkness I was determined to descend. Closing my eyes, I embraced despair.

The embrace began during my seventh year of solitary confinement in Central Prison's Unit One lockup. No matter how strong a person believes himself to be, everyone has a breaking point and I had reached mine. In those long days in solitary confinement, I had looked at myself in the mirror. The gentle flame that had once burned in the eyes of the little boy I used to be had slowly eroded.

Many nights, I lay on my bunk wanting nothing more than to bring this madness to an end. My soul was weary. The weight of the armor I wore to protect that frightened and sad little boy had ended up crushing him. The weight was now too heavy to bear.

Unlike some, I had no illusions of ever being released from prison. I had no claims of innocence to cling to. In fact, I had practically forfeited my life and my freedom for a warped sense of what I viewed as respect. In my self-taught logic, respect was something taken or earned—usually with a tightly clenched fist, the barrel of a gun, or the sharp edge of a knife.

A man was supposed to have principles that he stood for: a code of ethics and laws that he lived by to give him meaning and purpose. In my code, crafted from street life and prison wisdom, convicts laid down the law and every man was his own sheriff. To ensure security, anyone who violated my law could not be left unpunished—and the more severe the penalty, the greater the respect. Those principles caused me to value my own sense of respect more than I valued human life. I had killed for respect. Now, with my self-respect gone, I was ready to die.

I began preparations. If I was to die, I wanted my captors to die with me. I wanted my death to be something that would give a new meaning to my struggle and be memorialized for generations to come. If I went out in a blaze of glory, it could be painted as an act of defiance, resistance, and revolt. I would be the leader of the slave revolt against the masters, like my heroes Denmark Vesey, George Jackson, and Nat Turner.

I started preaching my deadly gospel to a handful of like-minded souls, including a guy named Willie Forrest.

Willie was housed in the cell right above mine and we often came out for indoor recreation together. He stayed on the top tier and I on the bottom. We spent our hour plotting.

Willie told me all about his case and how he ended up on lockup, eyebrow deep in the pit of despair right along with me. Willie was from Raleigh too and, although we both knew some of the same people, we had never crossed paths on the outside. He had been a small-time hustler who got caught up in the party life and became addicted to crack.

To hear Willie tell it, crack ruined him. He would sell everything he owned and then steal from his Mama just to get a bump. He didn't try to hide it. He wasn't proud of his addiction and what it drove him to do, but he never lied about it.

Willie was doing time for kidnapping his aunt after she had refused to give him money for crack. After years on solitary, he was a walking, breathing, seething rage.

I had been sentenced in 1994 to two life sentences plus 110 years for robbery, kidnapping, and murder. Three years later, I was sentenced to death for killing a fellow prisoner. The grave I had dug for myself was so deep, I could no longer see light at the surface.

In solitary, I had fashioned a sword out of a metal piece of table and fantasized about slaying the guards I felt were responsible for my suffering. Of course, I would most likely be killed in the process, but for me, that would be liberation from the constant agony that my every waking moment had become.

I didn't believe in the hereafter. Almost nine years earlier, I had become a follower of a brand of nationalistic, race-based religion taught by Elijah Muhammad that had reduced my faith in God to a belief that was as bare-bones as a tree without leaves. According to Elijah, God was just a man and so was the devil. There was only this life and after you died, everything was over.

Yet something inside of me yearned for more.

Elijah had insisted that Black people were the people of God and that the white man was the devil. According to him, all references to the resurrection in the Holy Qur'an were prophetic statements concerning the mental and spiritual resurrection of the Black nation, which was dead to the knowledge of self and God.

I had read the Holy Qur'an at least once a year during Ramadan for the past eight years, and I was aware of the many verses that spoke of resurrection and a life after death. Elijah Muhammad claimed the Holy Qur'an was the voice of God himself, but then, how to reconcile his disbelief in the afterlife with the book's clear descriptions of life after death?

> They say: "What! When we are reduced to bones and dust should we really be raised up (to be) a new creation?" Say: "(Nay) be you stones or iron or created matter in which your mind is hardest (to be raised up)—(Yet shall you be raised up)!" Then they will say: "Who will cause us to return?" Say: "He who created you first. Al Isra." (17:49-51)

I tossed and turned over the matter, unsure of exactly what I believed. Here I was with the possibility of death right around the corner and I stood confused on the subject of life after death!

It was with these thoughts that I was suddenly released from solitary confinement after seven and a half years. My mind was a whirlwind. I had never anticipated such a sudden turn of events. Now, I was free to execute my deadly suicide!

But something occurred that would cause me to re-evaluate my hopelessness and ultimately transform my life. A few days after my release, I was sitting at a dayroom table in the prison common area when a newsflash appeared on TV. A prisoner had been shot and killed in court after grabbing an officer's gun and shooting him in the chest.

My heart sank as Willie's mugshot appeared on the screen. He had gone out with a bang just as we had discussed, but instead of glory, I felt an even greater defeat. My conscience tugged at me. Had I led him to this end?

I looked around at the other men on Death Row. They seemed not to care about Willie. As the regular program resumed, they returned to watching soap operas or reading books and chatting amongst themselves. Willie's death had been as insignificant to the world as his life. His grand demise had merited no more than a news break.

I retreated to my cell to be alone. Pulling out my sword from under my mattress, I looked at it. Is this really what I wanted to do? I needed guidance. I needed direction and, above all, I needed to know if there was a purpose in life.

I took out my Holy Qur'an. There is a verse in Ali Imran (3:191) where the believers pray and say, "Our Lord! Not for naught have you created (all) this! Glory to Thee!"

Was it true that everything in the universe had a purpose? Even the trees and the plants? If there was purpose in something as inanimate as plants, then what about people? What about Willie? What about me?

I pondered. Life had to have a purpose and that meant there had to be a life after death. Otherwise, it wouldn't make sense if the righteous die after a lifetime of suffering and receive no reward while the wicked prosper and meet the same end.

After a while, I was no longer convinced that Elijah had been the messenger of God. If he was wrong about a matter as weighty as life after death, then he was also wrong about God, the devil, and his teachings about race.

Overcome by an urgency to pray, I went to my sink, performed the ritual ablution known as wudhu, and faced the direction of the Sacred Mosque in Mecca. I stood before my Lord and begged Him for guidance. I poured out the contents of my heart and cried until my beard was wet from tears.

Then, a calm came over me, and I knew I no longer wanted to tread the reckless and evil path. Long ago, I had chosen a path of crime and poor decisions. Each decision had brought me closer to where I stood on Death Row. If I continued on this path, I would end up with a fate similar to Willie's, but if I made different choices that were good and pure and righteous, I could alter the course of my life.

With a sense of peace growing in my heart, I saw a faint glimmer of hope—the first I had felt in many years. It was like the twinkle of a distant star, but I knew it was there.

I ended my prayer, wrapped up my sword, and marched down the top tier to the trash can to throw away my instrument of death. As soon as it left my fingers, it was as if a weight had been removed from my soul. This was the beginning of a brand new life, a life of total surrender to God. I had freed myself from death.

Hip Hop: Live on Death Row

You don't know me, you don't know the things I've done
The things I've seen, you can't understand me, son
You don't know why I trust none, you just call me violent
You don't know if I'm buck wild when I'm silent
You don't know my arrest record, you don't know how I've suffered
You don't know the ground I've covered
You don't know what I'm thinkin' when I'm filled with rage
You don't know what it's like in a cage, devastated

"Devastated," RROME ALONE

Hubie opened the rap battle with an eight-bar rip to draw first blood. I signaled for my beat boxer, Moon, to drop a beat and responded with sixteen bars of rhyme. All sounds of gum-popping, teeth-sucking, and teen chatter died down as the crowd of high school students clustered around Hubie and me, locked in combat heat. It was the last place I wanted to be.

Earlier, when Hubie had challenged me to a battle outside the school cafeteria, I'd tried to decline. The three or four raps I'd written were braggadocio I kicked around my friends. I'd never been in a battle before, but he'd thrown down the gauntlet, and I had to respond. So, that afternoon, surrounded by a charged crowd rocking gold caps and door-knocker earrings, Hubie and I volleyed back and forth with barbs and stabs until I ran out of raps. Hubie had just landed a head-banger with his last rhyme. I felt the eyes of the crowd zero in, squeezing me with their expectations.

What happened next was like an out-of-body experience. Moon kicked a beat, and I went into an impromptu rap, something I'd never done before, but the beat and the energy of the crowd seemed to conjure words from my mind that fit into all the right places. In that moment, I became a microphone controller. I could move the crowd. I was an official MC.

*

Ten years after my high school rap battle, I sat in solitary confinement sentenced to die. My aspirations to become an MC lay shattered, but in my loneliness and heartbreak, I kept writing. I wrote songs of pain and hate, love and war, death and rage. I wrote about politics and race, about conflict and peace. I wrote and wrote, amassing a treasure trove of lyrics that catalogued my evolving skills, my ever-shifting political views, the story of my life and struggles.

I rarely shared my songs. They weren't ditties to bop to or make people dance. They were reminders. Affirmations. Contemplations. Meditations. Declarations. Anyone I did permit to hear one was offered a privileged glimpse into my soul, something I vigilantly kept safe and preserved.

When I did let someone hear me rhyme, I always got the same response: "Have you ever thought about selling your rhymes? You'd probably make a killing as a ghost writer."

I usually brushed it off. I couldn't imagine anyone else performing my songs, especially without hearing them first. On paper, they were just words. You had to hear them to feel them, but I had no means of recording my voice.

On Death Row, our only access to music was radio, and our only contact with phones was a monitored ten-minute call once a year during the Christmas holiday. In prison, I wasn't merely out of sight. I was bound and gagged. Sitting behind a wall that thousands of people pass by every day, I wrote rhymes and rapped to an audience of four white walls for over twenty years.

*

Captivated, feeling like Kunta
State property is what I've now been reduced to
Sentenced by a judge to a fate of incarceration
Like a captive in a cage being auctioned to a plantation
Stripped of my possessions, I'm ordered to start undressin'
Struck with humiliation and naked, I face inspection
The overseer looks into my mouth just like I'm livestock
Inspects my scrotum as I slowly feel my pride drop
And my self-respect is shredded
Once I'm ordered to grab my butt cheeks, squat down, cough, and spread it
I ain't lookin' for no sympathy
I can't even look at myself after the raping of my dignity

"Devastated," RROME ALONE

On June 6, 2016, something happened that would give me an opportunity to pursue my long-suppressed dreams. The prison installed telephones in every pod on Death Row.

The phones opened a door to the world. It was the closest thing to freedom that I'd experienced in two decades of near invisibility. I could now communicate and establish connections with people on the free side of the wall. After twenty-three years of silence, there was a lot to say.

One of the first goals I pursued was recording my rhymes. In September, I was given the opportunity to record a monologue to accompany an outside art exhibit called *Serving Life*. An art and drama instructor, who was volunteering to teach at the prison, gave me the phone number of Michael Betts, a local audio documentarian. Michael recorded my voice over the phone.

The opportunity turned on a light bulb in my mind—perhaps I could record my rhymes over the phone! I called my mom and she agreed to help, but our recording sessions soon fizzled over the awkwardness of spitting my rhymes, many of which described scenes of violence and vulgar language, in front of my mom. Additionally, the poor sound quality of the phone recordings frustrated me. Disheartened, I stopped recording.

*

In summer 2017, I developed a friendship with a fellow prisoner, Stacey Tyler, whom I know as Sabur and who is innocent of the crime for which he is imprisoned.

As I listened to his story, I felt a strong connection that didn't revolve around posturing and trying to act tough. In fact, Sabur was quite the opposite of tough. Despite over two decades on Death Row, he was still a genuinely considerate, compassionate, and caring person. Some people in prison might judge him as soft or a bit timid and use those qualities to overlook him, but for me, Sabur stood out as real.

A killer knows another killer. There's a light that goes out in the soul. An innocence that dies. Sabur's underlying innocence hadn't been tainted by this cruel experience, which reminded me of something forgotten within myself. I was drenched in guilt. My filth ran so deep that I couldn't even remember what it was like to think or feel with an uncontaminated mind and heart. It was refreshing to be in the presence of such innocence. It reminded me of home.

After establishing this bond with Sabur, I slowly allowed him access to my world. It started with a rhyme. We were in the chow hall waiting for our trays when a couple of guys who had already gotten their meals jumped back in line in front of several others ahead of me. I shook my head in disgust and told Sabur I had once cracked a guy across the head with a steel-toed boot for doing that very thing.

Sabur seemed to doubt my claim since he had only known me as easy-going and friendly, but I assured him it was true. In fact, I had written about it in one of my rhymes and quoted him a line as proof: "At twenty years old, I won't simply boxin'/I put them steel-toe boots to a nigga noggin.'"

In fact, I spit the entire rap to him and assured him that every bar in the song was the truth. He was amazed, not only because I had done things he could never imagine doing, but because I was able to rap as well, something he'd never considered.

After that incident, he started coming to my cell for hours every day, wanting to know more about me. For the first time, I began to share my rhymes and the stories behind them. Sabur became my first true fan. In his eyes, I was like a character in a movie. I didn't sugar coat my past. I owned my mistakes. Admitted my crimes. Expressed genuine remorse and accepted responsibility for who I was and what I had done. Above all, he saw the day-to-day manifestation of my Islamic faith—not just great in word, but in deed. The past was a part of who I was and I wasn't afraid to talk about it.

About a year into my friendship with Sabur, I was sitting in my cell thumbing through several large manila envelopes stuffed with rhymes when a friend of mine, Mu'min, visited my cell.

"What do you keep them for?" he asked, indicating the pages.

I didn't understand the question. It seemed he was implying I should throw them away, as if they had no value.

I tried to explain. "These are my songs. This is my life right here."

"Well, what are you gonna do with them?"

"Nothing."

I began to feel agitated, but he continued.

"Are you gonna try to sell them or get them recorded?"

I told him I couldn't imagine anybody else performing my rhymes because they were about me.

"Well, what good are they if nobody hears them?"

His final question pierced like a dagger to the heart. What good were they? I wrestled with that thought for a couple of days, and realized that deep down, I wanted to believe I was good at rapping. In fact, I imagined that if I weren't in prison, I could've been one of the greats, the musical equivalent of Michael Jordan that, tragically, the world would never hear.

I felt some security in that notion. As long as prison restricted my ability to prove myself, I imagined I "could have" been great. I found comfort in fantasy. But if I actually recorded my rhymes and people thought I was wack, then I'd have to face the cold, hard truth that I was just a wannabe rapper on Death Row.

Inspired to act, I flipped through my phone book and called up Michael Betts, the man who had recorded my monologue. It'd been two years since we'd spoken and I wasn't sure if he'd remember me or accept my call. My palms sweated as the phone rang.

When he picked up, I asked if he'd be willing to help me record my rhymes. I explained I couldn't pay him for his time or effort, and I feared he had little incentive to help. To my deep satisfaction, he agreed. We set up a schedule beginning the following Monday at 8:30 a.m. It has grown to every Monday morning for the last two and a half years.

*

Kentwood! 'Round my way
Raleigh North! 'Round my way
Oakwood Villa! 'Round my way
Berkshire Downs! 'Round my way
Since Day One, I'm proud to say if I was locked up and got out today
It's Ruff Love till the day I die, Ruff Raleigh, boy, that's where I stay

"Round My Way," RROME ALONE

That first recording session, I spit a rhyme called *Round My Way*. It was a shoutout to all the hoods in my city, Ruff Raleigh. I wanted to pay homage to where I come from. I wanted old friends to know I hadn't forgotten them. After twenty-five years of silence, my first recorded words were: "I shout my hood out, I'm from Kentwood."

The feedback and response I received from friends and associates were unbelievable. They said *Round My Way* was fire, that they loved it, that it was an anthem. In the following weeks, I put out *All I Know, Prisoner of War,* and *Raleigh OGs.* People loved the lyrics, but they kept saying I needed a beat, so I began to seek out producers.

My brother, Chris, talked to a number of people online about putting a beat to my rhymes, but they all replied that it was impossible to sync my vocals with a measured beat. My tempo fluctuated too much in the acapellas. Without the ability to hear the beat from within prison, I couldn't time my rhymes to fit the music.

Eventually, a local producer by the name of DJ Dezerk agreed to work with me. He explained that we needed to figure out a way to get me to record in fixed time. First, we played a beat in his studio to see if I could rap with music in the background, but I couldn't hear the beat once I started rapping, so we tried to channel it through headphones. All I could hear was my own voice played back half a second later, which made it impossible to hear myself think. Next, he asked me to rap to a metronome. I tried, but the instrument gave off a bunch of clicks and beeps. I couldn't hear anything that sounded like a rhythm.

As I thought about how to record my lyrics in time, I turned on my radio and zeroed in on the beat. As I started rapping one of my songs, it occurred to me that I could use the radio to record my lyrics. After setting up a recording session with DJ Dezerk, I put my earphones in, turned to the local hip hop and R&B station, and waited for a song to play. I knew I didn't have the luxury of a second take, so when I heard a beat drop, I gave it everything I had. I was so focused that I had no idea what song I was recording to, but we got a clear take.

I was so excited! Even without hearing the final recording, I was sure it would be a success. DJ Dezerk synchronized the beat with my lyrics and we set a release date for May 18, 2019 under the MC name Rrome

Alone—Rrome, as a nod to my middle name, Jerome, and Alone to represent the isolation in prison.

I put together a promotional plan by listening to the local hip hop station and writing down the names of all the DJs. My niece helped me find social media accounts for the DJs and sent them a letter I had drafted with a link to the song, asking them to play the record at clubs and events. Once people heard the song, I believed they would fall in love with it and it would become a hit.

Chris and my sister, Keisha, posted links on social media as well. Keisha set up a Facebook account for me, and she and my wife, Jeannie, relayed messages and helped me network. I couldn't believe my good luck—I had a promotional plan and a support team to help me execute it. With the right push, we would make a big splash.

Then, one day, I heard my song for the first time. A staff member at the prison played it from an administrative computer. What I heard deeply discouraged me. My vocals were uneven, muffled, and hard to understand. The production sounded horrible, and there was distortion around my words. There was no way I could ask DJs to play this in the club.

I spoke to DJ Dezerk about my concerns and he said this was the best we could do because of the phone-recorded vocals. That took the wind out of my sails. If I couldn't record and release good quality music, how could I ever expect anyone to listen to it? No matter how dope the rhymes or the flow, if it sounded like garage music in a sea of digital perfection, then nobody would listen to it. I was ready to pull the plug on my recording career.

*

My man Henry did thirty years before the system ever found proof
Of his innocence and then set him free after robbing him of his youth
So I looked around and started thinkin' outward
How to use my voice and start speakin' louder
For those innocent and still in the trench like Stacey Tyler and Elrico Fowler!

Stacey Tyler, Elrico Fowler! Say their names and repeat 'em louder
And I pray to God that they get relief before God judge in that Final Hour!

"Unbreakable," RROME ALONE

The inspiration to pursue music again came from my first fan, Sabur. Throughout my struggles to record rhymes, I had shared every detail with him. He was a great listener, and sometimes, he believed in me more than I believed in myself.

One day, we were looking out of his cell window. Somewhere on the other side of Western Boulevard, the city of Raleigh was preparing for the Dreamville Festival featuring rapper J. Cole. Forty thousand people were enjoying a festival and not one of them had a clue that right across the street, Sabur, an innocent man, was staring out of a small window waiting to be executed.

"Right across the street from Dreamville, you are living a nightmare!" I told Sabur.

He looked at me and smiled with sad eyes. "Yeah."

Emotion lay heavy on my chest. "You know what? This year, they don't know you are here, but next year, the next time they have Dreamville, they gonna be shouting your name from the stage. I'm gonna make the world know Stacey Tyler!"

From then on, I saw my music in a different light. I now had a purpose. It wasn't enough that I could rap. I wanted to use that talent to do something good. I wanted to glorify Allah and use what he gave me to benefit others. Through rap, I could generate attention for innocent people on Death Row like Sabur, who inspired my next song, *Unbreakable.*

After that day, Allah opened opportunities through almost every door I knocked. In August 2019, I read an article in the *News & Observer* about a professor named Mark Katz, who oversaw The Beat Lab at the University of North Carolina in Chapel Hill. He'd assembled a few producers to teach young people how to create and produce music.

I took a long shot and wrote him a letter sharing my link on SoundCloud and the problems I had run into trying to record. I wanted to know if he could help me improve the sound quality of my vocals. Michael Betts got me his mailing address at UNC, and I sent the letter off.

It took six weeks to receive a response: a handwritten note on a Sierra Club notecard dated October 4, 2019.

Dear Mr. Braxton,

Thank you for your letter of August 19, and my apologies for my slow response. I listened to your acapellas with great interest, and I also consulted with some hip hop producers. The consensus was that there was not much they could do to improve the sound quality aside from some filtering and that the best thing to do (aside from re-recording them) is to add some good beats to them. I would also say that I personally like the sound quality— it gives the tracks a rawness and authenticity. I know some producers who would be happy to provide some beats for you. Please let me know if you would like me to connect you. Best wishes—Mark Katz.

I almost leapt with glee! This was the Music Director at UNC not only writing me a note, but willing to introduce me to producers! I responded right away and did not mask my excitement or enthusiasm.

A correspondence developed. I was amazed at the number of hip hop legends he personally knew: DJ Cash Money, Diamond D, Phife Dawg from A Tribe Called Quest, and Sadat X from Brand Nubians. He even introduced me to the Rock and Roll Hall of Fame producer and member of Public Enemy's infamous production team, The Bomb Squad's Kerwin Young, who wrote me a personal letter answering my questions about copyright and publishing.

Finally, Mark introduced me to Nick Neutronz, the producer who would become my musical partner and number one collaborator. Now with a producer to put beats to my rhymes, I called Michael Betts, and we devised an urgent schedule. Michael suggested I perform each song three times to make sure we got the best take.

The pace was hectic. By the time one of our recording sessions had ended, I felt physically and emotionally drained. I put everything I could into every song to ensure that my enunciation was clear, my volume high, and my flow locked in tight with the beat.

After a month, I had recorded thirty songs. I felt so relieved to get the songs that had been caged inside of me for over twenty years preserved on record. For the first time, I felt I could exhale. My legacy was safe.

Once Nick Neutronz had synced my tracks to the beats I selected, my family heard my music for the first time. My wife played *Land of the Profits* over the phone to me and my sister, Keisha.

"That's my joint right there," Keisha said. "I can bump that in my car!"

I felt so proud and grateful for what my team and I had produced. I could hardly believe I had made it this far from Death Row. One issue remained: the recording was still a phone vocal. It lacked the crispness of a professional recording.

Nick Neutronz wasn't sure if music listeners would be able to get past that. We listened to a few other artists who had recorded vocals from prison and agreed that quality-wise, our production sounded better than any other phone vocal. Michael Betts advised that we simply had to own it. When you hear Rrome Alone, not only is the content different, but the sound is unlike anything else in the industry.

I began to see my music from a different perspective. This wasn't merely entertainment. These recordings were like slave narratives that would have a place in preserving some of the stories and life of people in prison. I thought about slave songs. If one were ever discovered on record, it would sound scratchy because it wasn't polished and shined up in a professional studio. The type of music I make comes from the sparest of resources. It's supposed to sound gritty and, like Mark Katz said in his first letter to me, authentic.

*

Just as I was celebrating those first recordings, tragedy struck, and my music took on a purpose for which it was never intended—as a memorial. My baby sister, Keisha Braxton, my friend and supporter and one of my greatest helpers, died suddenly on February 5, 2020. She was forty-two.

Her boyfriend, the father of their four-year-old son—whom she named Christopher Jerome, after me—had found her unconscious when he came home from work that morning. Paramedics rushed her to the hospital where she was placed on life support. My brother, Chris, sat by her bedside every night to keep her company and he brought my mother to see her every day until the doctors confirmed that Keisha was braindead.

My family made the difficult decision to let her go. For our final goodbye, I called my Mom's cell phone. With me on speakerphone, Mom and Chris circled the hospital bed and held Keisha's hands as we played her favorite of my songs, *Land of the Profits.*

I remember Chris whispering, "Ride on out to this, Lucy," the nickname I'd given her long ago, and together we cried.

I know Keisha was proud of me and perhaps my biggest fan. She wanted to start a record label to protect the rights and royalties to my music. In fact, she started a music publishing company called Ahad Music Group and registered me as a performer and a songwriter with the American Society of Composers, Authors, and Publishers before she died.

All of this gave me even more motivation to succeed. I had to keep pushing. I had to accomplish my dreams and open doors for people like Sabur in the process. The music and the project had become so much bigger than just me.

My next breakthrough came from an unexpected source—the COVID19 pandemic. Once the virus hit, the prison restricted our movements, including closing the cafeteria, doing away with in-person visits and cutting back on outdoor recreation time, which we'd previously been allowed for an hour a day. Locked down on the pod, we passed the time by watching TV. It seemed that every other commercial featured a video conferencing software called Zoom. For years, I had been trying to figure out how to record my vocals separate from the beat. Watching the commercials, I wondered if we could set up a virtual studio using Zoom to record my vocals in isolation from the track.

I mentioned this idea to Michael Betts. I remember his total disbelief as he responded, "You just found the answer to the problem we've had all along. I can't believe that you figured it out and you've never even been on a computer. Dude, I'm amazed."

"So does that mean it's possible?" I asked.

"It's not only possible, it's something I can do right now. I just can't believe I never thought of it."

"Yeah, you never needed it like I needed it," I said, smiling.

Zoom changed the game. Suddenly, my production team and I were in the studio not only recording tracks, but listening to me on the playback. I felt like a real recording artist. My team had grown stronger and I could see that they believed in me. My vision was becoming their vision. My dreams, their dreams. All I needed now was a record deal.

*

In mid-2020, I connected with a successful Baltimore-based songwriter and performer named Wordsmith, who also owns his own label, NU Revolution Entertainment. We'd been introduced through his brother, who'd interviewed me for a podcast to promote the first edition of *Crimson Letters*.

During our first conversation, Wordsmith asked me to tell him my story, and I did my best to lay it all on the line, as I'd done with Sabur. Afterwards, he'd said he wanted to help get my music to a bigger platform not only because he believed in what I was doing, but also because he thought the music was good. Above all, he wanted to be my friend.

After that first phone call, my respect and admiration for him grew, along with our friendship. In December 2020, he offered me a nonexclusive recording contract, which meant that if someone offered a better deal, I could walk away, and nothing would bind me.

I talked it over with my Mom and she signed the contract. My first single, *Live on Death Row*, was released on August 13, 2021 as part of my upcoming debut album, *Mercy on My Soul*.

Words can't describe my gratitude to my production team, my wife, my family, my best friend, Sabur, and everyone else who has helped this prisoner on Death Row accomplish dreams he was never supposed to dream.

But I know it wasn't by my power or ability alone. All the praise, all the credit, and all the glory belong to Allah. *La ilaha ill Allah.*

They buried me beneath concrete eyebrow deep, you can't find me
And I sat there in that cold cell staring at the ceiling like "Why me?"
Now here I am after all these years, and I say Al-hamdu-lillah
Standing on the Sirat al-Mustaqueem, and that's all praise to Allah!
I never dreamed I'd make it this far, but now I'm raising the bar
Kickin' doors down on Death Row like waaaaah!

Chorus
They can't break me down, they can't break me down

"Unbreakable," RROME ALONE

The Phoenix

A decade later, still walking through the shadow of Death's valley
With a changed mentality
No longer buried under dirt
Beneath all the grime, I shine like a diamond in the earth
Birth from a death state
I emerge like a phoenix, no longer a victim of self-hate
Elevate from the low self-esteem
To glow like a beam of light where there's no hope it seems
I find peace through forgiveness
God is my witness, I prayed for redemption

"Deadman Walking," RROME ALONE

In 1995, I was thrown into solitary confinement at Blanch Youth Institution, North Carolina's highest security and most notorious prison for youth at the time. Blanch was an old prison, dark, with dungeon-style cells, the kind of place where prisoners were once assigned to work gangs busting rocks with sledgehammers.

My cell was so small, I could touch the walls on both sides by extending my arms. It was also filthy, overrun with roaches and rodents. On the rare occasions when I was allowed to leave the cell, I did so wearing full restraints—handcuffed by manacles on my wrists that were attached to a chain encircling my waist and shackles around my ankles.

Though I shudder to recall the physical conditions at Blanch, the psychological torment was far worse. Solitary confinement is, by design, an experience of intense loneliness and isolation. I remember the constant feeling of vulnerability, especially as I witnessed numerous instances of violence and brutality by the officers who oversaw our care. Sometimes, a prisoner might be upset and kick at his door or throw food or water at a guard. If officers felt that use of force was necessary, they responded with extreme beatings that often cracked bones. That cold, cramped house of horrors was my home for almost two years.

At Blanch, I began a journey that would forever alter my future. After a lifetime of self-hatred, the path to self-love and acceptance unfolded gradually through rediscovering a part of myself long since buried. It started with college.

One of the few amenities afforded to youth at Blanch was the opportunity to take college correspondence courses through the mail. In part to pass the time, I signed up for an Introduction to Psychology course offered through NC State University.

Reading through the course materials, I was struck by the concept of introspection and the argument of nature versus nurture. This was revolutionary stuff for me. I'd never thought about behavior as inherent or learned. I remember posing questions to myself: Why do I do the things that I do? Why do I think the way I think?

I became obsessed with trying to understand what made me *me*. I even wrote these initial reflections in a song, *Prisoner of War*:

Questions be on my mind
I stopped drinking wine and eating swine
Thinking divine no longer blind
But still confined to a cage, I'm in a rage
In the book of life, I'm stuck on this page
But can't you see I wasn't born killing, blood spilling, drug dealing?
So how I start this thug living?
It must be the way I think that causes me to do the things I do
Like smoke weed and drink brew
And cuss and steal and deal and rob and kill
Why do I think this way? Why is my mind state ill?

After being exposed to the Afrocentric worldview in prison, I began to see that the Eurocentric worldview I'd been taught by textbooks, school, parenting, society, media, and culture had shaped the way I viewed myself and the world around me, including my ideas about masculinity, aggression, women, and good and evil.

After the course finished, I continued searching for knowledge and understanding, devouring books to take my mind off the dirty cell and constant threat of violence at Blanch. Reading a book was often like sifting through mud until I found that one sparkle of knowledge. The jewel might be a single paragraph in a five-hundred-page book, but I'd put these jewels in my heart chest until I had a treasure-trove. After a time, the jewels mixed together and I forgot where I'd found each individual gem. They all became a part of the collection.

Several years later, once I was housed on Death Row at Central Prison and no longer in solitary confinement, a friend turned me onto a book called *Houses of Healing: A Prisoner's Guide to Inner Power and Freedom.*

I fell in love with the book because it affirmed what I'd discovered on my own about the path to emotional healing. At first, it was hard to admit that emotional immaturity and childlike behavior had been controlling the reins of my life for so long. It was a *Wizard of Oz* revelation to look behind the curtain of my own soul and find a scared and wounded little boy pulling the strings of this contrived persona mistakenly identified as me.

I knew instinctively that the little boy was the emotional and psychological part of me that had been hurt and wounded. He was the heartbroken nine-year-old crying in his room after hearing his grandma call his Mama a "nigger lover." He was the confused child who felt ashamed when a little Black girl announced in disbelief, "Your Mama is white?" He was the little boy who'd been rejected by his extended family and felt unwanted and shunned for having light chocolate skin.

In his pain and suffering, he had constructed a false identity to protect himself from a mean and uncaring world. He was pulling the strings that controlled the persona that ultimately led me to Death Row.

After this realization, I knew there was only one solution: part of me had to mature and heal. My injuries were old, but the wounds still felt raw and had infected almost every aspect of my being. In order to tend to those wounds, I had to be patient. I had to be kind. I had to be gentle. And, I needed the right medicine.

The medicine was the truth and it required large doses of honesty. Reflecting on the past, I saw that I had revised some of my memories to help me cope with pain or to give me a false sense of security. Instead of acknowledging fear or shame as drivers of my behavior, I had justified my actions with excuses that made me look strong and courageous. I'd repeated these revised accounts so many times that in some cases, the real truth was pushed beneath my consciousness and I had come to believe the invented versions.

The problem with this self-delusion is that it kept me trapped in the emotional state of that wounded child. Even as an adult, anytime I faced a similar experience, it triggered the same emotional response. To heal, I first had to acknowledge the truth and point out the wrongs.

Over and over again, late at night, in the solitude of my cell, I told the little boy inside me that I knew he'd been hurt. He hadn't done anything to deserve being hated, rejected, or ill-treated. I told him there was nothing wrong with him, nor was there anything wrong with interracial love. His existence wasn't something to be ashamed of—the people who made him feel that way had been wrong.

Once my inner child felt accepted and consoled, I moved on to forgiveness. I knew that to truly heal and grow, I had to set aside old grudges and resentments; otherwise, I'd be stuck in a cycle of hatred, anger, and blame.

It took many years to arrive at a place of forgiveness, but eventually, in my own heart, I forgave grandma for calling my Mama a "nigger lover." I forgave Uncle Harvey, Aunt Selma, and all the white people who had treated me wrong. I realized that just as I had told myself revised accounts of the truth, they had convinced themselves that being white made them something other than who they really were.

I forgave Black people too, many of whom had hurting and wounded inner children just like me who felt rejected and hated and mistreated. They'd created personas as well to protect their inner selves.

This forgiveness reverberated deep within me. I was not only acknowledging the wrongs done by the people who had harmed me and forgiving them; I also had to acknowledge the wrongs I had done and forgive myself.

This was no easy process. It took time, and it took faith. For the first time, I began to embrace everything that I was. I accepted all my faults, and began to love myself.

One book that had a profound effect on me was *Black, White, Other* by Lise Funderburg. It's an anthology with dozens of short memoirs from biracial people. Many were people with whom I could identify, but there were also people who had wonderful, loving parents and who grew up to be good and successful.

I realized that my childhood wasn't the defining experience of what it meant to be biracial, and the book reaffirmed the notion of being nurtured to think and act a certain way that I'd learned about in my psychology course at Blanch. Being biracial didn't mean you were destined to fail or that you were automatically an outcast or a reject, something loathed and despised. For the first time in my life, I felt a sense of belonging and community. I even felt proud to be biracial.

When I write about my journey toward acceptance and self-love, it sounds easy and straightforward. But often when you are on such a journey, you don't realize when you started or how you stumbled onto the path—even that you are on a path at all. When I was taking those slow, halting steps towards healing, I didn't recognize their significance—but I'll never forget the moment I understood how far I'd come.

In the twenty-four years I have lived on Death Row, my mother has come to see me every Friday. In the tiny visiting booth divided by Plexiglas, she and I reminisce, laugh, cry, and make new memories.

One day not long ago, my mother looked at me, her blue eyes wet with tears, and said, "Son, I'm proud of you."

I cast my eyes downward, afraid she was only trying to make me feel good and didn't realize the magnitude of her words. I hadn't yet been able to see the outward manifestation of what had developed inside me.

"Mama, how can you be proud of me? I've disappointed you on every level. I'm a convicted murderer. I'm on Death Row. I'll never get out of prison. How can you be proud?"

Holding her gaze steady, she said, "I'm not proud of the things you've done. You've done some terrible things and you've hurt a lot of people, including yourself. There was one time when you were filled with so much hate, I didn't even recognize you. But I've watched you over the years and I've seen you grow into a marvelous man."

Tears spilled as she continued. "You are a better person than most people on the outside because you've learned to acknowledge your mistakes and to own them and grow. It makes me proud to see you become the man I always knew you were: a deep thinker who is compassionate and cares about people—even in here, even on Death Row!"

She paused a moment before saying, "Son, it's not where you are in life that determines success, but how far you've come to get there. The things you've accomplished, the way you understand yourself and accept responsibility for your actions—most people never accomplish those things. Yet you've done it despite being in prison, despite being on Death Row. I'm proud of you."

Her words broke open a dam in my heart, and all I could do was sob.

§

Full Circle

TESSIE CASTILLO

In the final moments of a ninety-minute event to promote our first book, I was riding high. George and Lyle had called into the Zoom meeting for a moving Q&A session with a group of business leaders. Even through a computer screen, I felt the emotional electricity of knowing we'd connected with the audience.

As I asked if anyone had final questions, a woman who had been quiet throughout the event raised a hand.

"Do you feel that your work represents…" She paused. "…the full circle?"

She gazed directly at me from the screen, and I felt as if we were seated face to face. My skin prickled. Something about her hesitancy, her careful wording, suggested to me that the question was personal.

"Are you asking about the victims' families?" I inquired.

She nodded.

I took a deep breath and hoped my face wasn't flushed. My mind buzzed. Was she connected to one of the crimes associated with my coauthors?

Aware of the woman's gaze, I explained that staff at a victims' rights organization had advised me against reaching out to the families out of respect for their privacy and grief. I also explained that people convicted of violent crime are legally prohibited from contacting the victims' families—even to express remorse. The ban protects surviving family members from unwanted communication, but it also hinders opportunity for healing dialogue and atonement.

The woman didn't say much as I was speaking, but a few hours after the event, I received an email from her. Though she had no connection to my coauthors, she confirmed that she was a survivor of violent crime. Her father had been murdered several years earlier.

I wrote back and we developed a correspondence. Over the next few months, she recounted her story and even shared writings about her thoughts and experiences surrounding the murder. I was moved by her courage, the deep soul-searching and healing she had undertaken to piece herself back together—the forgiveness, even compassion, she displayed for the young man who had killed her father.

Since *Crimson Letters* was published, I've had many conversations with family members who have lost a loved one to violence, though none with any connections to my coauthors. In effect, the prohibitions on contacting victims' families forced me to choose between publishing a book without their contributions or not publishing one at all. Many times, I considered abandoning the book project for fear of its effects on these families, but I felt that to do so would weaken the bridge we're trying to build between all people impacted by crime—an effort that goes beyond "sides."

I've listened to the voices of people impacted by violent crime so if someone connected to my coauthors' convictions ever reaches out, I will be able to respond with presence and compassion.

In conversations with people who have lost a loved one to murder, they've described the heartbreak, the grief and rage, the wrenching, the crumbling and emptying, the despair, the disbelief. The endless wound.

"I was shocked and numb, almost in a stupor, like I couldn't breathe even," said a fifty-nine-year-old woman, describing her reaction to her aunt's murder. The two women had been close, like sisters. "I had no words. I couldn't cry. I couldn't do anything."

For many people, the loss creates a domino effect that knocks out the pillars of their lives—marriages, jobs, health, homes—all swept away by grief.

"We had life one day and it was joyful and vibrant, and the next day it was gone," said one mother. "It's like getting a terminal illness and being told to just go home and die."

Parents of a murdered child often describe to me a primal response to the news, howls and spasms beyond their control wrenched from their bodies. They speak of belonging to a "club" with exclusive, involuntary membership where strangers can glimpse each other and know, without speaking, that they share similar loss.

The long-term reactions to this loss are complex and varied. Some family members are furious; others dissolve into sadness and grief. Some oppose the death penalty; others would mete it out themselves. Some want to block out what happened; others step into the pain, grasping for answers and a sense of control. Some people forgive—many don't—but for all, the impact of murder lasts a lifetime.

My conversations with families of people on Death Row have been equally revealing. They too are innocent; they too suffer loss, though the fate of their loved one is tossed like dice onto the courtroom crap tables, gambled throughout decades of endless appeals.

"Can I love my child? Can I post my child's picture? Do I have to act like he is already dead?" lamented one mother I spoke with, whose twenty-three-year-old son is facing the death penalty.

Just as working with my coauthors has challenged my preconceived notions about the death penalty, speaking to people impacted by murder has forced me to confront my misconceptions about victims' families.

I'd always believed that crime victims had a voice. Their stories were splashed all over the media. Their words carried weight. Their testimony was central to the prosecution.

All fifty states have statutes protecting the rights of crime victims. These usually include the right to be notified of the legal proceedings regarding their case, the right to victims' support services, and the right to restitution. Yet, while listening to victims' families, I've seen a gulf between what exists on paper and what exists in practice. Even in states with strong victims' rights and compensation laws, victims' families may not be notified of legal proceedings. They may be unaware of available support services or unable to receive compensation for medical expenses, funeral expenses, mental health services, and lost wages. In fact, when I asked the families what support services they'd received in the aftermath of such reeling loss, the most common answer was "none."

Crime survivors are frequently revictimized by the legal system itself. In the adversarial courts, prosecutors and defense attorneys weave their opposing villain-victim narratives, sometimes distorting and omitting details to better fit their ends. Prosecutors might poke at the victim's tender places to elicit jury sympathy while defense attorneys might rip into the victim's judgment or memory or even suggest partial culpability, as often happens in sexual assault cases.

During the media scrutiny that follows a sensationalized murder, victims' families, who may be suffering shock or PTSD symptoms, are paraded in front of the cameras. Reporters zoom in on their tears or anger, bottling their grief for public consumption. Then, after the legal case is resolved or dismissed, the families are discarded, just yesterday's news. Few communities provide ongoing support services for victims' families. Even fewer help them heal.

The current legal system promises justice for the victim—in the exclusive form of punishment for the accused—but critical elements to recovery from crime or loss, including answers, atonement, and healing, are rarely offered, or even discussed.

For example, genuine remorse from a guilty person can facilitate healing for the victim and for the person who harmed them. However, people who commit crimes may face prison—a type of outward accountability—yet inward accountability is not expected or required. No one has to say, "I'm sorry." No one has to atone for the pain they've caused. No one has to change.

There is another approach to handling crime, one that prioritizes both outward and inward accountability as well as the critical need for healing.

Modeled after ancient and indigenous practices of gathering in community to discuss the harm of rule violations and then decide on an appropriate plan for repair, restorative justice shifts focus from merely punishing the person who caused harm to providing the person who was harmed with resources and support. Instead of asking, "What law was broken? Who did it? How do we punish?" restorative justice asks, "Who was hurt? What do they need to heal? How can the person who caused the harm show accountability and commitment to repair?"

In modern practice, restorative justice typically takes place in facilitated circles where the person harmed and the person who caused the harm, along with loved ones and community members, sit together to discuss what happened and how to restore the trust that has been broken. During these meetings, which are monitored by trained facilitators, the person harmed and their family members talk about what happened, how it affected them, and what they need to heal. The person who caused harm shares their perspective and commits to specific actions to help the victim with healing and closure. These actions might include an apology, community service, enrolling in school, financial restitution, or other terms as discussed and agreed upon by the group. Over weeks, months, or even years, the group works to ensure that these actions, called a repair agreement, are honored. Sometimes forgiveness, or even friendship, arises in these circles, and sometimes it does not. Still, the focus is where it should be: on healing and prevention of future crime.

"We have a lot of violence because we keep breaking people...and broken people hurt others," said one mother impacted by murder whom I spoke with. "Until we open our eyes to that, how are we going to fix things like racism—or value human life?"

By focusing exclusively on punishment and ignoring critical components such as atonement and healing for all parties, we risk enabling more people to hurt and to be hurt. We exacerbate conditions like poverty, unemployment, homelessness, mental health disorders, and trauma, all of which serve as lighter fluid for crime. To break the cycle of violence, we first need to stop adding to it.

There are challenges to the widespread adoption of restorative justice, including that all parties must agree to the process, but my coauthors and I have witnessed its extraordinary potential firsthand. A few years ago, Central Prison permitted some people who had lost a family member to murder—crimes unassociated with anyone on Death Row—to visit and tell their stories. One of these participants, Lynda, whose son Brian was killed at twenty-four years old, spoke to some of my coauthors.

Alim was in the room. Lynda remembers him pacing, brooding, and seemingly disengaged as she told her story, but the second time she visited the prison, he had composed a letter to her and wanted to read it aloud:

Dear Linda [sic],

I had no idea how I would be affected by hearing your story. I guess with everything we bring with us certain assumptions and expectations, so before I ever saw your face, I had a general expectation of what I assumed I would hear: a mother who has lost her son to an act of violence coming to address a group of convicted murderers. Coming to address me.

I expected some sort of rebuke. I expected to be spit on. I expected cursing and yelling and a mountain of pent-up rage to come thundering down on my head as you described detail by detail how some low-life scum just like me murdered your son.

I expected that this type of rebuke would leave me somewhat unsympathetic. Not uncaring, but incapable of feeling what you have experienced because my sympathies have been shaped by what it's like to be on the other side of the victim-murder relationship. Although I have always felt a deep sense of guilt for the wrongs I have done, when I felt the anger of those I have harmed, it caused me to shut down from feeling compassion and even hindered my remorse because I think there is a natural tendency in the face of perceived hate to hate back.

However, as you described your experience, something unexpected happened as I listened to you talk about your son Brian. I suddenly became Brian, and I listened as if you were my mother talking about me. I could see my mother's excitement and unbridled joy as she found me lying on her couch after being away from home for nine months.

I could see her tiptoeing down the stairs trying to be quiet and mouthing the words "he's here" so as not to wake me up. I could feel my cheek move as I tried not to smile while pretending to be asleep. I can see my mom's face as she realizes I'm not really asleep.

It was me taking those pictures with my mom that day and taking her to lunch and telling her I loved her at least five times that day. I can see my mom's joyful appreciation as I reminded her she was beautiful.

As Brian walked out of the house that day headed to visit his friend Alex, I could see myself rubbing my palms together in anticipation of having fun with my friends, never thinking that this would be the last time my mom would see me alive.

It's amazing how the mind records these details that we preserve and carry for the rest of our lives. My mother has memories as well, memories of my final days home. She too got one of those phone calls, and she cried and made noises that I am sure no human is supposed to make, but her son is still alive, and all I could think about was what if she was on the victim's end of the phone call, and I was the one who had been murdered.

I have a brother too. His name is actually Chris. How would he have reacted to my funeral? Would he go into a manic phase, and would my mother have the ability, strength, and motherly instincts left in her soul to console her other son? And all of this for what? Because of a few words or, in my case, a few lousy dollars or some misguided principles? It tears my heart to realize that I have caused a mother to hurt like you have hurt for your son, like the mothers of Emmanuel Oguayo, Donald Bryant, and Dwayne Caldwell. I thank you immensely for allowing me to hear your story.

ALIM

After hearing Alim's letter, Lynda told me she was surprised at how much the restorative justice process had helped her heal even though the men she faced were not connected to her son's death.

"I felt supported and affirmed by all the men in the circle that day," she said. "We all became surrogates for each other. It was powerful and truly unexpected."

My coauthors and I wrote *Inside: Voices from Death Row* because we want to live in a world where people share their stories, where those stories break down boundaries, where we see and honor each other's struggles, triumphs, and humanity. We want society to stop responding to the agony of murder by burying one person, warehousing the other, and leaving loved ones on both sides reeling from grief—without voice, without healing, without hope. We want everyone impacted by crime to face each other, not on two sides of a chalk line, but in a full circle, where we recognize that one break means rupture for us all.

LYLE C. MAY

Namaste

"Who's that?" I asked, pointing out the car window at a man whose stride betrayed an inebriated state. He did not move fast, but his rolling gait made it seem as if he were walking down a steep hill despite being on a level sidewalk.

My mother glanced through the window as we drove up Main Street in the late morning traffic. Spring had turned the thick grass of the park beside us a vibrant emerald.

"His name is Calvin," she said. "Be sure you stay away from him."

"Why?"

Ten-year-old eyes sharpening, I watched the man. His hair stuck out in greasy spikes of charcoal and ash while his matted beard was like a spill of salt across his jowls.

"Because I said," came my mother's typical reply.

Some weeks later, I asked Dad who Calvin was. His response was equally mysterious.

"Stay away from him, you hear? He's a junkie. A hobo."

It was the same instruction I got for most things my parents thought were bad for me. My curiosity poured contempt on such answers.

A few years later, I was on my paper delivery route and heard some stories about Calvin.

"He's crazy! Huffs glue every day."

"It's a wonder he's got a brain in his head."

"He's a drifter, moves from town to town then heads south for the winter. Never know where he's been or where he's going."

In the small town of Brunswick, Maine, people spread rumors about the time Calvin spent in AMHI, an asylum spoken of in the serious tone of a campfire story. One kid told me Calvin had killed a man for pocket change and spent a bunch of time at Thomaston, the state's only maximum-security prison in the 1970s. Others said police couldn't prove Calvin did it because the hobo had no fingerprints, having burned them off handling cans of food straight from the fire. Some said he slept under the trestle bridge, but when I went to investigate, there were only broken bottles, cigarette butts, and rocks.

I took to walking the tracks, hoping for a glimpse of Calvin. The tracks were a convenient shortcut from the high school through the downtown area and past Bowdoin College. Since many of the mills in Maine had closed, trains were infrequent travelers on the tracks—as rare as long summers in the Northeast. When a train did come, I would scramble aside and watch in fascination, wondering where it had been and where it was headed. In the wake of its mechanical noise, quiet rushed in. I'd think of how the horizon held another town where another kid like me walked on wood ties and threw rocks at tall weeds, perhaps also searching for an elusive hobo.

The harder it was to find Calvin, the more my desire grew to meet this mysterious figure who vanished at will and made others avoid the tracks. I enjoyed my treks among the crushed granite, discovering the edges of a forbidden world, one that swallowed my oldest sister and sent her to a place called "rehab." I picked up anything that caught my eye as my younger sisters and I had often done at the beach, searching tidal pools for the creepy-crawly things of the sea.

On the tracks, instead of hermit crabs, I found plastic lighters, half-smoked cigars, and empty wine bottles. Once, I dared open a full can of beer that had been lost amongst the weeds. I sipped and immediately sputtered, dropping the can and wishing for a drink of water. Once, I found a smashed nickel, the date distorted into an elongated 1978, the year of my birth. I put it into my pocket.

In this way, I finally met Calvin.

Jouncing down the tracks several hundred feet in front of me, he clutched a crooked cigarette to his face, hollowing his cheeks and exhaling pale exhaust. Seeing me, he held up a hand. I mimicked the action and stood waiting before he left the tracks and disappeared into the woods.

The next time we met, a plastic shopping bag ballooned from his face, then deflated as he huffed the contents. Legs fidgeting, he watched me watch him, finished with the bag, and stuffed it into his pocket. Calvin looked through me for a long moment.

"Can ya spahre some change, brother? Brother."

His breath came in fits and gasps, voice hoarse and throat full of phlegm.

Wary of the twitching blue-eyed man, I gave him the coins in my pocket and waited for the arcade to light up. He smiled a bit and shook my hand.

"Thank ya, brother. Brother."

I liked to imagine it was the Catholic charity of my upbringing shining through in that moment, but in reality I liked how he called me "brother," deep and gravelly like Hulk Hogan. I didn't follow Calvin as he staggered off, instead watched him mutter and run grubby fingers through wild hair. I wondered where he was going. The duct tape on his boots tapped the sidewalk as he went.

Calvin usually vanished in October and reappeared around May, sitting on a park bench and shouting at cars, or crossing the street with his rolling gait. One time, for a Boy Scout function, we delivered canned goods to the Tedford Shelter, the only homeless shelter in town. Expecting to see Calvin, I put aside some cans in a bag just for him— beans and franks, ravioli—but was disappointed to learn he rarely stayed there. Later, I discovered he survived long winters by getting arrested and thrown in jail for petty offenses or migrating south.

I did not realize that Calvin's lifestyle had a significant impact on how I chose to respond to the rigors of adolescence. Rather than try to make the right choices, I allowed events to dictate my actions. Generally, I leaned towards the least amount of responsibility and fewest ties to people. It was easier than trying, and what was failure if not another dirt road in life lined with broken bottles, cigarette butts, and discarded condoms?

When I dropped out of high school at the beginning of my sophomore year, consequences were the farthest thing from my mind—so too the lessons of the D.A.R.E. program, my oldest sister's struggle with addiction, and parental warnings against hanging out with the wrong people. Huffing seemed a natural choice when other drugs or even alcohol were unavailable. My world shrank to the pinpoint of each enjoyable moment without a single thought involving homelessness or mental illness. Walking the tracks as a sixteen-year-old dropout became the one familiar path in my life that made sense of everything. When I saw Calvin, he was no longer strange or pitiful. We sat under a bridge and hotboxed a joint before going our separate ways.

There were no profound conversations between us, very little talking at all. He didn't regale me with stories of a misspent youth as I poured mine out between the crushed rocks of the tracks. A word of thanks here and there and that familiar greeting: "Brother. Brother, can ya spahre some change?" If I couldn't, I gave him cigarettes or we smoked a joint, or we shared the poison destroying our thoughts—him, glue; me, aerosols. Alcohol was a rarity, but when I had a few extra dollars, I trusted him enough to get us both a forty-ounce of the god-awfulest malt liquor.

The last time I saw Calvin was the night my parents kicked me out of the house. I had been in and out of the Maine Youth Center and rehab; periodically at home, institutionalized, and homeless. I was eighteen and living at home on the conditions that I would work and not use drugs.

The former was easy enough; the latter, not so much. That night, Dad picked me up from the paper plant after I'd spent eight hours stacking inserts and adjusting the conveyor belt coming from the press. Though I'd washed up, there were still smears of ink on my neck and ear from errant itches.

He dropped me at the curb of the convenience store with everything I owned stuffed into a backpack. I had known this was coming and it felt just, but this did not lessen my sense of wonder as he gave me a quarter, told me to call one of my friends, and sped off in the family station wagon.

As I lit a cigarette, Calvin staggered around the corner and stumbled to a halt next to me.

"Can ya spahre some change, brother? Brother."

I gave him a cigarette. "I ain't got but some change. My dad kicked me out."

"That's a shame, that is. That is. Young fella like you ain't hurt hairs on a fly's ass."

Then, he surprised me by saying more. "You could go to the Tedford Shelter before it closes at midnight."

It was the best advice he could have given me at that moment. I thanked him, handed over a few cigarettes, and hurried to get a bed for the night.

By the time I began sharing experiences with Calvin—walking the tracks, huffing, homelessness, being institutionalized—it was too late to give any thought to negative influences or poor role models. He was neither and both. Something about him spoke to an indescribable otherness in me. I found it hard not to like a man who cared nothing for what other people thought even when they were right. He seemed to say that stubborn people learn hard lessons, but if you ignore it all and give them the finger, it hardly matters.

Except it does matter. Running away from home and spending time in the Maine Youth Center for various acts of delinquency were situations I could have walked away from. Rehab and brief stays in a mental hospital were challenges I could have overcome with a little dedication and self-reflection. What I could not have escaped was how my reckless choices grew acutely self-destructive.

It's hard to judge which mistake was the pivotal moment in a young life full of them. The easy answer should be whatever action caused my incarceration, and while I believe that is true most of the time, I also believe there were exits prior to the end of this particular road.

While my life at nineteen (the year I was arrested and convicted of murder) was little different from a life at sixteen, there was a subtle erosion—whether from drugs, alcohol, huffing, or a combination of circumstances—in my ability to respond and cope. The beginning of the end for me occurred when my girlfriend and I agreed she should have an abortion rather than carry our child to term. The decision affected me more deeply than I could have anticipated. I returned to self-mutilating, a behavior that had been absent for nearly three years. Where before the act of cutting and burning my arms had shocked me out of whatever emotionless vacuum I'd seemed to be in, this time nothing penetrated the fog.

I was hospitalized, drugged, and diagnosed, but it merely stirred my hatred of institutions. Those places made me feel like an animal; they were a driving force behind why I felt at home on the road: always moving, walking away from responsibility and the rest of the world. After experiencing a psychotic break, which led to an extended stay at Broughton Hospital, I knew I was not okay. Things were never going to be "just fine."

Maybe this is where I grew to dislike the meaningless, complex question "How are you?" What does that even mean? In the hospital, my world flipped from the undiluted freedom of an open road with my only concerns being food, cigarettes, and a drink, to a place with constricting jackets, four-point restraints, and "How are we doing today, Mr. May?" Screaming ninnies streaked the hallways as burly orderlies wrestled their naked bodies into the shower. Grown men crouched on the floor, caressing their scalps with palsied fingers.

There is no making sense of crazy. "Mental illness" was not a word back then any more than "iPhone" or "Arab Spring." I "stabilized" in the hospital because that was their goal. They pumped me full of drugs, stood me on my feet, spun me around three times, and pushed me back out into the world, a place that was too bright and shiny for my darkened eyes. Words had been thrown at me—"personality disorder," "psychotic break," "red flags," "schizoaffective"—but they meant nothing in the face of my one driving thought: I had to hit the road. Get moving. Out of this place where the mind raged with regret, self-pity, and sorrow. Hit the road and go find a place where it would be cool in the summer and tolerable in the winter, with a bottle to dull the sharper thoughts and a can to shatter the rest, everything I could need or want on my back and only the future to stop me. Would that I had given Calvin a thought then—he might have saved us all.

High Rise

The first time I ran from the police, it was for violating curfew, a condition of my juvenile probation. After the cop caught me, I was returned to the Maine Youth Center and put in solitary confinement. This punishment was administered to any delinquent who attempted to evade authority and was meant to instill fear and obedience—avoid the law and suffer the consequences.

At sixteen, the hole was a scary place where food was scarce, clothing a privilege, and kindness a rarity. There were no books or magazines. No TV or music. Silence smothered the cells and only a single light bulb pushed back the darkness. They called it ICU—Intensive Control Unit—and the staff were brutal. In ICU, even teenage bravado gave way to the despair of total isolation and deprivation.

Talking was forbidden, so when we communicated with each other, it was in whispers between the cracks under the doors. I remember lying on the cold concrete for hours, flicking ants and other insects out of the way as I listened to stories of street life from another kid. Pacing helped ease long days and nights in that cold hell, but so too did counting the cinder blocks and mapping the constellation of cracks in the floor. Sometimes, I sang half-remembered songs before trailing off into a hum. Even though forever was measured in seconds, minutes, hours, days, I knew it would end eventually.

The hardest part of doing time in ICU was hearing kids who acted up get beaten by adults who were supposed to be our legal guardians and caretakers. While most kids my age were thinking about prom or drivers ed, I was getting an altogether different education as a ward of the State. At the time, I knew there couldn't be anything worse than being in ICU on a Saturday night.

Two years later, I was charged with two capital murders in North Carolina and sent to the Morganton High Rise for safekeeping.

From a distance, the High Rise looked like an apartment complex jutting from a wooded valley in the Blue Ridge Mountains. Up close, the image changed with the appearance of razor wire coiled atop chain link fences, gun towers manned by rifle-toting guards, and prowling pursuit vehicles that stalked the perimeter fence. Within the sixteen-story building were hundreds of boys and young men aged twelve to twenty-one, incarcerated for crimes as varied as shoplifting, arson, and murder.

It was August of 1997 when I arrived at High Rise to await trial. Safekeeping is a common practice where county jails outsource high-risk, high-profile prisoners until they can be tried. Rather than send me to an adult prison as a nineteen-year-old, after six weeks the county shipped me to the Western Youth Institution in Morganton, North Carolina. Nobody called it that, though. It was simply the High Rise.

At the High Rise, safekeepers were segregated on the thirteenth floor in solitary cells without toilets or running water. Locked behind a wooden door with a small Plexiglas window for twenty-three hours a day, the confinement was harder than what I'd encountered in Maine. A single communal restroom with three toilets and a urinal served twenty-four people, but this did not guarantee access. Some staff loved tormenting any of us who needed to use a toilet, ignoring requests outright. Empty bottles, milk cartons, and Styrofoam cups were a must.

After I was strip-searched and dressed out in a mustard yellow jumpsuit, an immense guard over six feet tall handcuffed me. He led me to an open elevator with an older guard stooped from the weight of time. Through a haze of psych meds, I wondered what was next. The doors closed. In the hot metal space was a subtle smell of oil. The floor vibrated.

The elevator doors jumped open on a new floor. Kids in plastic chairs watched a music video on TV. When the gorilla pushed me into the room, a stocky guard snapped, "Go to your cells!" before spitting into a Mountain Dew bottle. He was more toad than man: wide, thick-lipped mouth, bulging throat, and no neck. A few of the kids in yellow jumpsuits spared me a glance before they scattered down the hallway into their cells, doors locked closed. Unease churned my stomach. I'd seen this before. Like people running to their cellars before a vicious storm, kids on State knew when to get out of the way.

A tall, lanky guard with a thin mustache and thinner combover narrowed his eyes, hooking thumbs in his belt loops. He had the swagger of a gunslinger, a man accustomed to getting his way and liking it too much. The toad nodded to the gunslinger, who snatched the property bag from my stiff hands and dumped its contents on the floor.

"Take the cuffs off," said the toad.

He kicked my things around with his boot. I knew the setup. Get angry or speak out, and they beat the crap out of you. Resist, and it gets worse. A familiar routine from the Maine Youth Center, one I didn't want any part of.

"What you in for, boy?"

It was such a deep question. I had no intention of answering it. My mind shied from the madness of being incapable of remembering a heinous double murder and unable to defend myself to such a response. Though heavy doses of imipramine and Zyprexa clouded my mind and blunted my feelings, the drugs couldn't stop a shudder from twitching my shoulders. Anyway, it was none of their damn business.

"Stealing cars and selling drugs," I said. "The usual."

"That right?" smirked the toad. "You a real smart mouth sum-bitch, ain't you? We know you're a killer. A fuckin' murderer. Your shit's been all over the news, boy. They gonna fry you up good and proper." He paused then and stared at my blank expression. "Got just the thing for you. Pick that shit up off the floor, and let's go."

The gorilla, gunslinger, and toad took me to the nearest open cell and pushed me in. The toad rushed me, grabbed two fistfuls of mustard yellow jumpsuit, slammed me against the wall hard enough to bounce my head from it, and backhanded me. He let go and whipped out his baton in a practiced move, jamming it across my throat and pressing hard as I flailed my arms at him.

The fat prison guard leaned in close enough that his bloodshot, blue-grey eyes were inches from mine.

"I hate punks like you," he said. I couldn't breathe. Panic squeezed my chest. "Did you like it? Was it fun?" His breath licked my face. "I'll show you fun."

The toad jammed his baton harder. I choked and gagged and weakly pushed against his arms. The gunslinger saw this and fired his baton into my ribs. Once. Twice. Thrice. Each impact buckled my knees. I needed air, but right then, oxygen was as far away as help or empathy. Still, I pushed against the toad, his club the only thing holding me against the wall. A fourth blow from the gunslinger's baton, and my bladder let loose with my consciousness.

The toad kicked me awake moments later, laughing as I sobbed in air. Tears, snot, and blood came with each broken gasp. The air was not sweet as some people claim it is after being without it for a while. It tasted of recycled fear, dominance, and degradation. I knew in that air that I was utterly alone.

Pulling the Mountain Dew bottle from his back pocket, the toad unscrewed the cap and pursed his lips, but when he saw me watching from the floor, he put the cap back on and spat brown saliva inches from my face.

"If we hear a peep out of you, we'll come back and string you up. Ain't nobody gonna question it or care about you dyin', boy."

In a falsetto he croaked, "I swear, detective, we offered to get the boy help, and he refused. I thought he might be suicidal, but when we let him out for showers, there he hanged." Blue-grey eyes bored into mine. "You understand me, boy? We straight?"

I nodded because it was all I could do beyond breathe and calm my hammering heart. They left then, slamming the door behind them.

I don't know how long I sat on the floor hugging my knees. My worldly possessions—four letters, a toothbrush and a tube of toothpaste, a pad of paper and a small pencil—lay strewn about. Boot prints marred the envelopes like canceled postage. The people who wrote those letters couldn't help me. Staring up at the bare lightbulb, I thought of breaking the glass and using a piece to cut my throat.

What if they came back? More time passed. I sat petrified, wishing myself far away from the High Rise. Wishing I had never traveled to North Carolina. Wishing I had a weapon to defend myself from the next person to come through that door.

Later, after a thorough search of the cell, I found that one of the long metal slats on the bunk was loose. It was thick, heavy, and cold. I pulled it up and knew it would be easy to break, then quickly pushed it back when the metal squealed. Listening for footsteps and hearing none, after a long moment, I climbed in bed, pulled the covers up to my chin despite the sticky August heat, and stared at the ceiling until the light went out.

There were two choices: the lightbulb or the metal slat. Me or them. I could hit the first one through the door. The others might get me, but I'd make certain the toad didn't. Despite my burgeoning hatred for their authority, I was drawn more toward cutting my throat. It would be so much easier to walk away from it all and save everyone a lot of trouble. I could escape this wretched place and move on to whatever came next. For the rest of the night and well into the days that followed, my thoughts flipped between the lightbulb and metal slat as the only two objects in my tiny seven-by-nine world that gave me power. Power over fear, isolation, helplessness, and despair. The only comfort I had.

It was enough. Finally, I slept.

All That Remained

When I was charged with capital murder, the jailors housed me on Four-High, a solitary confinement block in the county jail. Empty and sterile, Four-High was a box within a box. When all the cell and sally port doors were closed, I could almost pretend that nothing existed beyond the bottom of this pit. Silence was rare. The other confined men kept up a constant racket of banging, shouting, whining, singing, and screaming that filled days and nights. Time eked by in noisy increments measured only by a thrice-a-day meal cart.

Fourteen months into this confinement, my mind lost its brittle grip on reality. Thoughts of death eclipsed my future like a tsunami on the horizon, blighting all hope that tomorrow would be a better day. Tomorrow would not be better, nor the day after that. I stopped eating the bland, meager food pushed through the slot of my cell door. Rather than refuse it and draw attention, I flushed it down the toilet.

Self-hatred gnawed at me, a leaden weight that complemented my depression. I grieved for the victims and for the pain and shame my family endured. Coming from a small town, news of the double murder would have hit like an atomic bomb. Things like that just didn't happen in Brunswick, Maine. I thought of my parents, ostracized by friends and neighbors, and of my sisters having to answer questions about their brother, their adolescence tainted by mine. I grieved for my wasted life and struggled to understand how it had come to this point, but the cracks in the concrete provided a roadmap with only one destination.

One evening after the midnight count, I stripped a sheet from my bunk and tore it in half lengthwise. One end I tied to a crossbar over the window; the other end looped around my neck in a slipknot. Because the window was so high, I rolled up my mattress and stood on it. I looked out the window at blurry pinpricks of life, took a deep breath, and kicked the mattress to the floor. As the full weight of my body jerked to the end of the sheet, I swung once to the left and back to the right. My bare feet flailed against the wall as I choked—then the sheet ripped, dropping me to the metal bunk. I lay there for a few minutes catching my breath and massaging a burned throat, disappointed.

The next day during rec, I walked out of my cell and climbed the stairs with my soap and towel in hand as if heading to the shower. Once on the tier, I dropped the soap and towel, stood on the rail, and looked down. From the top rail, it was twenty-five feet to the concrete. I climbed the rail and crouched on top of it, then jumped.

Even in my emotionally wretched state, survival instincts kicked in, forcing my hands and feet out in front of me. I hit the floor in an awkward sprawl. The fall didn't knock me unconscious, but I felt as an insect might when it smacks into the windshield of a speeding car. The shock stunned me for a few seconds before pain lanced through my wrists, feet, and hips. I felt crushed and transfixed by the excruciating moment.

Jailors came rushing to the block. A smelling salt was shoved under my nose, but it was shame and defeat that burned my eyes with tears. Even at death, I had failed.

My high-flying act was punished by the jailors. It wasn't that I violated any rule against self-harm so much as caused a lot of paperwork and a trip to the hospital for X-rays and a cast. Upon my return, I was stripped naked and shackled to a bunk in an empty cell with frigid air. Several hours later, a folded paper gown slid beneath the door. It was to be my only covering for the next three weeks.

Days later, a shrink stopped by the cell block.

"Mr. May, I'm here to find out if you are a risk to staff, the residents at the jail, or yourself. Do you still want to harm yourself?"

"No." *Yes.*

"Are you having difficulty sleeping?"

"Yes."

"Hallucinations?"

"No."

"Mr. May, I am going to ask that you address my questions with 'no, sir,' 'yes, sir,' or, if you prefer, 'Dr. Graham.'"

I blinked.

"Do you understand what I'm saying, Mr. May?"

"Yessir." *Fuck you.*

"Do you still want to kill yourself?"

"No, sir."

I knew if I said anything different, he would keep me naked in that freezing cell for two more weeks. Giving him what he wanted meant that he might give me what I wanted—which, at that moment, was socks and underwear. He asked me a few more questions about my previous hospital stays and what medications I was taking, then prescribed an additional antidepressant and left.

After I was released back to my regular cell, jailors kept me on suicide watch. During my hour of rec, they would shackle me to a table near the phone or handcuff me in the shower while a guard stared as I washed. If I refused to shower, they threatened to use a fire hose, which wasn't an idle threat because I had seen them do it to a Mexican kid the year before. I ate because the alternative was a feeding tube. Day and night, they watched me.

As miserable as the situation was, the shock and pain of the fall cleared my mind of any delusions regarding death or escaping fate. I would stand and face the future. Whatever it held, I would live. All that remained, all that I needed, was to find meaning for my suffering, a purpose that would light my way out of the darkness.

Sleep

The sound echoed around the prison block, crashing against concrete walls with the force of each angry blow—somebody was mule-kicking the steel door of his cell with everything he had. Again and again and again.

It was 2 a.m.

The kicking stopped before the guards made it on the block and found out who was responsible. In the wake of the noise, squeaky boots and keys punctuated queries of "Who's kicking their door?" When no one answered, the guards left.

After a few minutes, a new sound ricocheted off the walls. Higher in pitch and frequency, it was easy to identify it as a bar of soap being slammed into the side of a commode like some demented alarm clock. BANG! BANG! BANG BANG BANG BANG BANG BANG BANG BANG BANG BANG BANG! It went on for a merciless minute. Then three. Guys started yelling. "Quit, man. Come on, stop!" Finally, the guards came. The banging stopped.

They walked around to each cell, looking in and promising a reward. "Come on, fellas, tell us who it is. We'll give you an extra breakfast tray. Tell us who it is, and we'll stick him in the drunk tank, naked."

Nobody spoke up though we salivated over the temptation of an extra breakfast tray. Two eggs rather than one. An extra shot of orange juice. A few more spoonfuls of grits. And sleep. Silence between annoyed keys and squeaky boots. After a while, they left.

"Hey, J-Will. What's up, man? Why you dragging us?"

It was as much a plea to stop as any I've heard. Everyone was awake now, and angry.

In prison, night's hourglass has extra holes in it. When sleep comes, gone are the plodding daylight hours, confining walls, and thoughts of letters. Sleep is relief for most of us. With this blessed comfort come dreams of love, companionship, peace, and life in all its complexity; desires so vivid and deep that reality is a disheartening comparison. Sleep cannot be degraded, beaten, or chained. In sleep lies our freedom.

When sleep eludes you, the beast within takes over and you act out, doing crazy, irrational things such as imposing your suffering on others. Why should they have peace? Why should they get to escape when you're in hell with the unrelenting demons of fear and regret?

About ten minutes went by before J-Will kicked his door again. The sound had gotten louder somehow. I realized the emergency exit was open and three guards had managed to sneak on the block without anyone taking notice. They carried a fire extinguisher filled with mace—industrial-strength, riot-sized, choke-you-to-death mace. They keyed open the food slot on J-Will's door, thrust the long nozzle through, spraying him like a troublesome cockroach.

J-Will screamed.

Two of the guards laughed and walked off as the other watched his victim writhe on the floor, choking, coughing, and crying. The two guards returned with a device known simply as The Chair. Black and boxy, The Chair is a restraint device used to punish problematic prisoners.

The guards sat it in the middle of the dayroom over a drain in the floor, dragged J-Will from his cell, and cut off his jumpsuit with a pair of scissors. He was a kid. Sixteen, maybe seventeen at most. No hair on his face or chest. So skinny, I could count each rib from twenty feet away. Cheeks sunken and pocked with acne, skin stretched taut around small bones. Just a kid a few years younger than me.

One of the guards handcuffed J-Will behind the back and jerked him upright by the wrists, eliciting a cry of pain. They forced him into the chair and strapped in his ankles, hips, and chest.

"Please," he begged.

The guards ignored him as a rubber mouthpiece was shoved between his teeth and what looked like a football helmet with a visor and earmuffs strapped to his head. Then, they left.

The Chair is designed to recline its occupant at such an angle that one's weight is entirely on the cuffed wrists. The legs are up high, so unless you're really tall, your feet don't touch the ground. It is agony in the way a pillory was intended to humiliate and the iron maiden to deliver a final, gruesome justice. The helmet immerses you in your suffering, shutting off sight and sound. J-Will would stay that way for four hours.

"Damn," said an old man. "They got that young boy hemmed up."

It was quiet except for J-Will's muffled moans. Laying on my bunk, wide awake in this nightmare, I wondered if sleep would ever come. The walls glowed with reflected fluorescent light, ridiculing notions of freedom in the night. I knew then that dreams are delusions, the only defense we have against anguish. As I began to drift, images of The Chair skittered through my skull, and when sleep arrived, it was dreamless.

In the Minds of Men

Since my incarceration nearly twenty years ago, I've thought about women a lot. As a heterosexual man, "a lot" is a number best described by scientific notation. I admit a touch of preoccupation with the subject, but no more than a blind man sees in his dreams or a crippled man envies a jogger. The opposite sex is a natural part of my thought process and being denied this element of life is one of the toughest parts about doing time.

When I got to Death Row in 1999, I was in a contentious relationship with a girl I loved and dated before coming to prison. Distance, attitude, mistrust, and circumstance made communicating impossible. We were too immature to understand that a significant part of our relationship involved sex, and with no way to give each other the physical comfort we craved, hope for a future together disappeared. My thoughts were poisoned with midnight executions, and hers were for moving on. My life had ended, not hers.

I didn't stop having a need for women because the State sentenced me to death, or my girlfriend took off. In those days, pornography was readily available, so I immersed my fantasies there. The women in these images were as unrealistic and unattainable as they were in the free world, and this, at least, was something with which I could identify. Trying to gain satisfaction from a picture or going through the mental gymnastics of what the ghosts of memory told me existed at one time was an empty feeling. Like a blighted field where nothing grows, feeling and wishing and dreaming doesn't put flesh on bones, and aching for the lushness of life means nothing. In the end, it is only a clearing: forsaken and barren.

Shortly after my girlfriend left, I got involved with an older woman I knew from the free world. It was flattering to be young and attractive to a mature woman despite everything about a death sentence screaming the exact opposite. Our relationship was based on a desire to love and be loved—but with no real understanding or ability to carry it out. Limitations to showing our affection eroded the connection we had, making desire a desperate thing corrupted by a golden ideal in the wasteland where I existed, and she dabbled.

Soon enough, she discovered there was nothing I could do to meet her needs. When the Dear John letter came in the mail, I threw it in the trash. I'd been expecting it. Our relationship was a sexualized dream that would never come true. She was the one who needed waking.

Time passed and this hard attitude remained. I grew to hate prisoners who begged the attention of female staff like dogs at the table—anything for a scrap or a scratch behind the ears. It was especially bad when, after an execution, you might see one off to the side discussing some inane bit of cultural trivia for a grin, wink, or whiff of perfume.

And when we confronted them for fraternizing with the same people who kept us from hugging our loved ones, who could one day strap us to a gurney and ensure the machinery of death worked, they replied, "Ah, man, she don't agree with the death penalty."

There was always a belief that with the right amount of game, the sexualized dream would become a reality. Maybe a few briefly accomplished such a feat, but for most, it was a bunch of tail wagging and hand licking.

Stockholm Syndrome was not a term I knew at the time, but when I grew to understand it, common sense never had a better champion. Of course, it was easy to identify with female captors, to feel sympathy and attraction for them when they were a missing link to another life, even if there was no real fulfillment. This in-between state of always wanting and never getting leaves many men bitter and hungry. From one side of the mouth spews misogynistic vitriol, but from the other pours desire for a woman—crocodile eyes tracking the movement of anyone with breasts. There is no shame or sense that the behavior is out of the ordinary because prison is full of deviants. It almost seems inevitable that something twisted rushes to fill the emptiness where intimacy should exist.

For some time, I failed to acknowledge that my hatred came from jealousy that certain others were favored—even if the attention was a fleeting glance from a female guard. Most of what I despised was the degrading circumstances of prison, the reminder we are considered "less than" and undeserving of having basic needs met. The incarceration experience punishes without exception or escape, and division from female companionship or consideration as equals is the most telling blow to our humanity.

The difference between what occurs in the minds of men locked away from love and compassion and how normal people think can only be described as mad despair to be touched and comforted. To be wanted. Normal people aren't stripped of the core necessities in life with the intent to inflict suffering. This is a circumstance specific to the idea that prison should be punitive. As a result, the prisoner must become inured to pain, loneliness, frustration, and heartache. Nourished by fantasy, hardened and hollowed out by the cancer that is every unfulfilled desire, the mind deteriorates, fixates, and objectifies.

Early in my sentence, I had one consistent penpal. She was my age and in college, choosing to write to me as an extension of her work with a local nonprofit. I took her regular letters to mean she really liked me, so I hit on her with a copy of a love poem taken from a book. I couldn't resist the idea that my desire for a close, caring relationship must mean I needed a girlfriend. After all, outside of family, I operated under an asinine belief that women served a singular purpose.

I soon discovered the depth of my ignorance and how socially inept being removed from society and human contact had made me. The young woman wrote back and kindly but firmly set me straight.

"I'm not writing to you because I'm looking for a boyfriend. I have one and we have been together for three years. I appreciate the poem although I'll understand if you don't want to write back."

I felt like an ass. The rejection was embarrassing. In my delusion, I thought a woman's interest in my life, a smile and a nod in my direction, meant I should pursue her like a trophy. Eventually, I summoned the courage to apologize and explained how she would be my first adult female friend. From then on, I resolved to ignore the part of my brain that had nothing to do with our relationship and see her only as a friend.

This relationship was a significant turning point in my maturation on Death Row, especially in how I viewed women. It seems like such an easy concept to grasp, but not objectifying women was difficult for me in practice because there really is a great emptiness in my life. Ignoring the need to fill that empty space, where desire can be fulfilled with a loving caress doesn't mean it stops being a need or is suddenly painless. It is, however, a process of growth in my recognition of women as people who deserve to be treated with the same consideration and respect.

Domesticated

About fifteen years ago, Death Row was housed in Unit Two, an older part of Central Prison. Toward the back of this section, an access road allowed ambulances to abscond with the bodies of executed prisoners, and the grass grew unchecked. This small, undisturbed area also attracted a variety of wildlife that made for some interesting entertainment. When nothing was on television, we often stood at the windows and watched spiders, pigeons, sparrows, hawks, mice, rats, a fox and possum, and a family of cats.

At first, the cats watched us. Our windows were holes through which we fed birds and vermin alike or passed contraband between the cell blocks with a weighted cloth line swung and grasped when it reached the right destination. Eventually, the cats figured it out and found willing hands to scratch their backs and provide food.

It was kind of cool to have pet cats on Death Row. They didn't judge or care about our crimes. They were oblivious to everything but their basic needs and once these were met, purring and lounging was the order of the day. The cats were affectionate in an unguarded way that made us feel human again. It's easy to see why we catered to them.

Gary and Mule, two old men who slept in adjacent cells on the ground floor and were close friends, named the first cats Sugar and Grandpa. They brought back some of their own meals from the chow hall to feed their furry friends—everything from tuna and chicken to scrambled eggs. The only food Sugar and Grandpa disdained was the mystery "meatloaf" patty, which they carried outside and buried.

Free to come and go through the ground floor windows, which had been cut to allow contraband to be passed, Sugar and Grandpa were royals treated with respect and awe wherever they roamed. When they weren't scaring off the mice and cats or chasing birds, the cats curled up on Mule's bunk and slept. They knew, either instinctively or by watching us, to scat when we yelled, "Man down!" to signify an approaching guard. Even cats understood that "The Man" was bad news and would take them away from us, nobility or not.

After a while, Sugar got pregnant, and we assumed Grandpa was responsible since the only other cat was Shadow, who wasn't inclined to come through the window. I finally gave in to the cats' affections when the kittens were born.

My resistance to playing with, holding, and feeding them was inconsistent at best. It reminded me I was far away from home. As a child, our family Siamese, Lilac, was my favorite animal. She ruled my room and beat up my stuffed animals when she wasn't hogging bed space— usually beneath the covers and behind the crook of my legs. When I left home as a teenager, she was part of the family I abandoned. Sugar and Grandpa resurrected this hurt, so I fought the lull of their acceptance.

Whatever veneer of toughness or indifference I maintained to deal with the executions crumbled with the arrival of Ginger, Pippy, Smokey, Strawberry, and Tommy. Their little kitten claws hooked deeper than the cloth of my red jumpsuit. Resisting their insistent curiosity and playfulness was impossible.

So I brought them milk and food, brushed the tiny fur balls, and helped give cat baths. With no access to a vet or medicine for worms, fleas, and whatnot, we used plenty of soap. The lye killed most of the mites, and the kittens stayed clean for as long as it took them to shake it off, sneeze, and run out the window.

Some of the guards knew we had cats on the cell block and threatened to call animal control or an exterminator, but they never did. They didn't need another reason for us to hate them and, at the time, several execution dates had been set. A couple of the more sociable female guards would ask after the cats, wanting to know if any were lurking about when they came to shake somebody down, but no one—prisoner or guard—went out of their way to hurt or run off our friends.

About six months after Sugar's second litter, some of the cats began to wander off or die. The first to go was Morax, a dusty black cat we thought was a descendant of Shadow. One morning, he lay in the grass, sluggish and growling. By lunch, he was dead.

Next, Sugar brought Mule a limp kitten, dropping it at his feet like some offering and meowing. While it was possible they got ahold of some rat poison, we had no way of knowing until another kitten died.

Some of the older cats were never seen again, so we hoped they took off to begin their families elsewhere. While we enjoyed their company and the affection, it was understood they did not belong at the prison with us, waiting for the eleventh hour.

The hardest day arrived when maintenance workers went around to each unit, installing thick panes of Plexiglas and metal grating over every cell window. Access to the wildlife ended—they even sprayed more potent pesticides and sealed the cracks where vermin entered the building.

For a while, we heard the cats cry at Mule's and Gary's windows, imploring sounds that twisted my chest. The last straw for me came when I overheard Gary talking to one of them through the barrier.

"I'm sorry, baby. Go on. I can't feed you anymore. You can't stay with us. You'll die here."

I immediately put my headphones on and blasted the radio.

A Window Between Worlds

Anticipation builds. As I sit on the metal stool, my elbows propped on the table jutting from the wall, my mind races with a question: Who is it? Who is coming?

It's hot in this cement box they call a visiting booth. The ventilation system is a smothering figment of the imagination. Sweat trickles down my spine; the blood red jumpsuit I've worn for seventeen years clings to my flesh like a second, uglier skin. Behind me, a guard shuts a door and turns the deadbolt. I am locked in this suffocating closet with its fetid odors.

It's worth it. I would sit here for half a day if it means a longer visit. Thirsty, hungry, back aching, hard seat biting—none of it matters once the visit begins.

The wall before me frames a window and a small, metal screen through which sound travels in a tinny sort of way. The window's filthy, scarred Plexiglas covers thick safety glass, and there are bars, but only on my side. This bridge between the inside and outside is the length of my arm and as wide as my foot is long. Hand and lip prints decorate the surface. This little window is the closest I will ever come to the free world, that place I forget about sometimes until, at last, the door opens on the other side, and the visitor enters.

I am transported. Death Row is temporarily forgotten and my troubles are pushed aside as we talk—conversation that informs, relieves, and excites. As I watch this person oh-so-closely, my chest aches with a longing that cannot be fulfilled except here, through this window between worlds. That need is only satisfied by my visitor's smiles and laughs and gestures. The weight of my sentence never leaves, but for a time, the burden eases, and I feel relief, pleasure. A genuine smile reaches my eyes; a laugh escapes with my grin.

Time is heartless, though—blind and deaf to my hunger for human contact. The visitor senses it: the grinding pressure that will close the connection between our worlds. When the visit ends, it is difficult to see the walls and the bars of that filthy little window that heals and strengthens as much as it pains me to remember where I am.

A Confirmation of Faith

If you believe and I believe
And we together pray
The Holy Spirit must come down
And set God's people free
TRADITIONAL ANGLICAN HYMN

Catholic Mass on North Carolina's Death Row was an oasis in the desolation of my confinement. None who attended were especially pious or reverent. Washing hands prior to service, not cursing in front of the priest, and participating at all the appropriate moments proved challenging enough.

Then, there was the singing. I generally like to sing and did my best to stay in tune, but most of the guys spoke or mumbled hymns through gritted teeth as if the act of making a joyful noise in prison was painful. Sometimes, it is.

When I arrived on Death Row in 1999 and began attending Mass, there were eight of us: Angel, Elias, Eric, Jeff, Mule, Pat, Terry, and me. We were a small group in a prison dominated by Protestant Christians and Muslims. For decades, the Protestant chaplains had refused to acknowledge Catholicism or to provide services to anyone claiming the Faith.

When Angel came to Death Row in 1996, upon discovering the anti-Catholic sentiment, he wrote a letter to Pope John Paul II expressing his desire to practice Catholicism, receive communion, and give confession to a priest. Though Angel never received a direct response from the Vatican, several months later the chaplain grudgingly announced that priests from the Church of St. Francis of Assisi in Raleigh would begin conducting Mass for us.

We met on Thursday afternoons for roughly an hour and sat at steel tables in the dayroom of the Church Block, so designated because all religious services were held there. We sang, read, and discussed scripture; received the Holy Eucharist and tried to develop our faith in God.

I wasn't new to Catholicism. My siblings and I had been altar servers at two Catholic parishes in Maine. Mom taught Sunday school classes for children. She had strong opinions about other parishioners and for a while resisted what she saw as the falsity of their faith. Eventually, it grew to be too much. She tried other churches in the area, but none seemed to fit. Ultimately, we stopped attending Mass because she did, and she gave us the chance to opt out. As kids, we chose the free Sunday.

Jeff comes from a background similar to mine—white, middle class—but his parents had been with St. Francis of Assisi since it was founded in Raleigh. Eric is completely different: a Costa Rican immigrant who served in Vietnam as a Marine then joined the Army. Both Jeff and Eric had received the sacrament of confirmation prior to their incarceration, which meant they had received the rite that sealed their entrance into the Catholic faith as adults. The rest of us—Angel, Elias, Mule, Pat, Terry, and me—hadn't been confirmed, but our consistent attendance at Mass prompted Father Dan to offer us the chance. We all accepted.

At first, I attended Mass on Death Row to escape the noise and cigarette smoke on my block, where people shouted to be heard over the TV, slammed dominoes on tables, squabbled, laughed, cursed, and made thinking impossible in the crowded space. Most people didn't want us to think. Not the guards who carried out executions. Not the doctors who participated and liberally prescribed opioids and toxic levels of psych meds. Not the nurses who gave out extra pills. Certainly not us.

Catholic Mass became a respite in the way an AA meeting in a church basement sobers some drunks. The priests mainly cared that we kept coming back. It didn't matter that Pat made faces while we sang or that Terry mixed scripture with pop culture or that Angel rarely said anything unless prodded by the priest. Father Dan and Father Mark were patient, politely correcting our misunderstandings and usually answering our obnoxious questions even though we knew better: no, Catholics don't worship Mary; they venerate her. Saints are not ghosts, and the Holy Spirit is neither a saint nor a ghost. Yes, even the people Mule called "heathens" could enter Heaven by the grace of God.

Father Dan gave us a study guide and a Rites of Christian Initiation for Adults book about choosing Catholicism as adults. Mule (who was only called "Henry" at Mass) and I lived on the same block and studied together when there was a lull in the noise and we were both sober, neither of which was often. Other than Mule, I didn't know any of the guys who attended Mass, but it mattered little once our discussion of scripture began.

I always sat on the priest's left. Angel and Elias, a short, swarthy man with a graying comb over, sat on my left. Then, Jeff, Pat, Terry, Mule, and Eric arranged in a horseshoe. Despite the books Father Dan gave us, I asked questions that would have embarrassed my mother. Pat's eyes would bug out or a shy grin would steal over his normally slack look. Angel said nothing, only interjecting if some historical fact was in dispute. Jeff jumped in on philosophical discussions, ready to argue a secular point, especially if it related to science. Terry, usually heavily medicated and nodding in his seat, woke only long enough to ask about secret societies in the Church. Eric was ready to argue with everyone. Sometimes, we directed questions at each other, shared bits about our background in the Church, got off topic, but the priests gently brought us back.

"Okay guys. Let's profess our faith."

Though I attended Mass as a refuge, I remained defiant and angry inside. Faith in God was a question in my mind that would not be easily answered. I think Elias saw this in me. He mostly listened to our discussions and only sometimes commented, but he was always attentive.

One day, after seeing me make the sign of the cross with my left hand, the older man pulled me aside after Mass.

"Lyle," he said, his Jordanian roots heavily accenting his English. "Why you make the sign of the cross with left hand? This is bad. You should make it with the right."

He demonstrated until I nodded.

"Good. You seem a nice boy."

Elias patted me on the shoulder, stern but pleasant.

I was one of the youngest people on Death Row at the time, having turned twenty-one a month before being sentenced to death. This meant I got called "boy" a lot, especially by the older guys from the South. Elias acknowledged my youth but he wasn't disrespectful, just kind.

Elias was generally quiet and unobtrusive. A machinist in the Jordanian Army before immigrating to America, he had a knack for finessing the few things we could have. For example, Elias would sharpen a disposable razor purchased from the canteen for fifteen cents. Whereas I might use one a few times and throw it away, he reused the same disposable razor for months.

He had a pair of black dress shoes he polished every day, only wearing them to Mass or visits. When the bottoms wore out, he re-soled the shoes with cutouts from a plastic rubber trash can. After the prison banned personal shoes and he had to send them to a friend, Elias was disgusted.

"Why do they do this? These people—they have no mercy. Praise God I have learned better."

Elias had been convicted and sentenced to death for killing his wife in the midst of a bitter argument over her cheating. He pled guilty, but the District Attorney charged him with first-degree murder, which until 2001 mandated a capital trial. The DA knew this when Elias pled guilty and so did Elias' attorney, but there was no offer of second-degree murder. Elias did not try to justify his actions, expressing only remorse and sorrow for his children, for whom he prayed at every Mass.

After twelve weeks of study, our 2000 confirmation class received the sacrament of confirmation. Bishop Gossman presided, wearing heavy robes and burgundy vestments, carrying an oak staff curled at the top like an unfurled fern, and greeting us like long lost sons, not grown men on Death Row. Father Dan and Father Mark served the bishop, one lighting incense in a brass censer while the other held a book containing the rite's liturgy, prayers, and vows.

We were allowed use of a small conference room for the occasion, barely big enough to contain eight Death Row prisoners, two priests, the bishop, chaplain, and a guard. It was nice to have a little privacy for a special moment in a place devoid of them. Elias looked harried and nervous. Pat cracked jokes about the bishop's garb and asked to borrow his staff. Jeff and Angel watched the priests and spoke in Spanish. Terry talked quietly with Eric while struggling to stay awake. Mule and I stood in a corner watching everything get set up and laughed at Terry when he fell asleep as Eric talked about the military.

Pursuing faith in God while elected leaders and the courts invoked the same God to kill us was difficult at first. It's like digging into rocky soil while looking for a place to plant a seed and finding more rock. Then, the shovel breaks and it refuses to rain. Part of the effort is desperation—a need that folds the body around it until ordinary thought becomes impossible.

Some people mock prisoners who experience come-to-Jesus moments and claim it's a pretense—anything to save one's neck and gain compassion from the secular world. Maybe there are a handful of people who mistakenly believe that works. They are usually the same people who learn about prison from TV shows and films. I returned to my Catholic upbringing, professing a faith I didn't completely feel, because I was suffering and needed answers from God.

Why? Why have you allowed me to suffer? Why did you abandon me?

As a child, when I was an altar server, the priests often sent me on errands that required crossing before the altar. A giant crucifix hung suspended from the ceiling and every time, no matter how much of a hurry I was in or whether the church was empty, I genuflected and made the sign of the cross with my right hand. If I forgot, my feet stopped of their own accord and brought me back to kneel. This ingrained obedience and reverence to a God who often seemed absent had waned over time, but enough remained to continue seeking Him out. I knew no quick answers would be forthcoming but at least I was not alone.

Others searched for the same reason, digging in the rocky ground of their lives even when it seemed impenetrable. Elias, Mule, Terry, Pat, Angel, and I, in receiving the sacrament of confirmation as adults, affirmed our dedication to that struggle.

Growing faith in God, even faith the size of a mustard seed, is as much persistence with little obvious effect as an evolution in identity supported by action. The lessons the priests taught us were simple: Love one another. Love God. Forgive one another. Read the Word of God. Repeat.

How we interpreted those lessons in our daily lives varied. I listened. Pat laughed. Terry and Eric reminisced. Angel dispensed kindness; Jeff, charity; Mule, devotion; and Elias, compassion. Together, we prayed, learned, and shared our strengths while connecting at Mass and beyond.

Sometimes, reality cuts so deeply and savagely you feel the cold numbness of loss before any blood appears.

It was like this on execution days. First, the executioner's meal appeared behind the large windows of a locked office. Two long tables were laden with food for a picnic: several two-liter bottles of soda, large bags of chips, dips, cold cuts, cookies, paper plates, solo cups, plastic utensils, and a colorfully frosted sheet cake.

Death Row prisoners filed by the display on the way to and from the chow hall. Staff claimed the snacks were for the guards serving the execution shift, but sheet cake is a strange snack unless you're an executioner celebrating a job well done. By the time an execution touched our confirmation class, I had already witnessed over a dozen such celebratory meals and knew enough to mentally prepare for what was to come.

Mule was put to death September 12, 2003.

The hardest discussions were the ones that never took place at Mass. During our first meeting after Mule's execution, Father Dan's homily was short and fell into a bottomless silence. None of us wanted to be there. Nothing was said for a few minutes. Being confirmed didn't alter our despair or make it less necessary to keep grief on a tight leash. More executions were scheduled for the year. In some ways, it was easier to embrace fatalism, the inevitability of death. It made talking about an execution a frivolous exercise for the living. We were already dead.

Finally, Elias spoke.

"Father, you know, it's hard to live in this place. They have no mercy. They kill us—young, old, Black, white, sick, healthy—then call it justice. Prison is justice, but still they kill us. Where is the Church, Father?"

It may have been the hardest question any of us had asked. Father Dan attempted to explain the disconnect between Vatican teaching and America's love affair with capital punishment. That devout Catholics could be totally against abortion, contraception, and embryonic stem cell treatment yet support the death penalty was baffling. Diocesan bishops were too quiet on the matter, appearing more like bureaucrats than disciples of Jesus Christ.

In the early 2000s, the loudest and most consistent voice cutting through Catholic hypocrisy and calling for the right-to-life from conception to natural death was not the Pope, cardinals, or bishops, but a nun from Louisiana. Sister Helen Prejean's advocacy for the men and women on Death Row forced anyone who kneels before the cross to answer a question: can you really be a Christian, a follower of the Son of God, and support the death of your neighbor?

The governor would have to answer this question when Elias received his execution date in 2005.

At his last Mass with us, before being taken to death watch, Elias received the sacrament of the Last Rite. When it came time to say prayers and intentions, my friend prayed for his children and asked for mercy, as he always had. Then, he spoke to us.

"Thank you, brothers, for being with me. For accepting me. Peace be with all of you and your families."

After the service, we each gave Elias a hug and said our goodbyes.

I was naively hopeful that Governor Easley, who professed to be Catholic, would commute Elias' sentence. There was room to believe he might since Elias' adult children, who were also the victim's family, advocated for clemency.

They met with the governor and begged him to spare their father, saying they didn't want to lose another parent to the same murder. They spoke with local media, again pleading for the governor to show mercy. They pled with the DA who had prosecuted Elias, rightly arguing that as victims of the crime, they should have a say in the punishment.

Absent from their public pleas was any support from a victims' rights group. Also absent from the quest for clemency was Bishop Gossman.

Elias Syriani was put to death on November 18, 2005.

Pat had a fairly insouciant attitude about executions, including his own.

"There's no need to get worked up over it," he'd say. "It's gonna happen whether I want it to or not."

Before he left for death watch after his final Mass with us, Pat cracked jokes about going to see the big leprechaun in the sky.

"I'm part Irish, and they're executing me on St. Patrick's Day—that has to count for something."

Patrick Moody was put to death on March 17, 2006.

Celebrating the Last Supper often feels like a distant flourish of faith passed down over two thousand years. Connecting to its true meaning is a tenuous act made even more difficult by faulty institutions and flawed

Lyle May confirmation photo. Standing left to right: Lyle May, Angel Guevara, Elias Syriani, Bishop Gossman, Eric Marillo, Henry Hunt (Mule), chaplain, Patrick Moody. Sitting/kneeling left to right: Fr. Mark, Fr. Dan, Jeff Meyer, Fr. Jim.

human beings. Early in my faith journey, I thought the answers to my questions lay beyond my reach, but then, I grew up on Death Row.

In less than seven years, I lived while thirty-three human beings, some of whom were friends and brothers, were exterminated. It changed how I understood life and death, a terrible knowledge that drew me closer to God. Slowly, I have come to realize we were never abandoned. The answer had been there all along in the Eucharistic Prayer:

On the day before he was to suffer,
He took bread and, giving thanks, broke it,
And he gave it to his disciples, saying:

"Take this, all of you, and eat of it, for this is
My body, which will be given up for you."

In a similar way, when supper was ended,
He took the chalice, and once more giving thanks,
He gave it to his disciples, saying:

"Take this, all of you, and drink from it,
For this is the chalice of my blood,
The blood of the new covenant,
Which will be poured out for you and for many
For the forgiveness of sins.
Do this in memory of me."

When I was an altar server as a kid, I had to watch the priest during this prayer. As he raised the bread and then the wine, my task was to ring a set of brass bells.

"Ring them as hard as you can," one priest told me. "Make sure everyone hears them."

Many years later, on Death Row, sitting at a table and watching the priest perform this rite, I still knew the exact moment at which the bells rang. Their clangor crashed into the silence then and now, awakening those who had fallen asleep as the sounds reverberated throughout the Church. Clear in their reminder. Absolute in their purity. Certain in their promise.

In memory of the Catholic Community of St. Francis of Assisi 2000 Confirmation Class, Central Prison, North Carolina:

> *Henry "Mule" Hunt: sentenced to death 1985; executed September 12, 2003*
> *Elias Syriani: sentenced to death 1991; executed November 18, 2005*
> *Patrick "Pat" Moody: sentenced to death 1995; executed March 17, 2006*
> *Terry Ball: sentenced to death 1996; died of natural causes October 18, 2017*
> *Angel Guevara: sentenced to death 1996*
> *Lyle May: sentenced to death 1999*

Learning to Die

In June of 2002, nearly two hundred prisoners moved to Central Prison's newly constructed Death Row building. Compared to the old Death Row blocks on Unit Two, the new pods on Unit Three are sterile, capacious, and vermin-free. Bright fluorescent lights banished all shadow; white walls and steel tables touched a light gray dayroom floor. Red lacquered paint coated doors, rails, and stairs.

Before the move, I knew only a few dozen guys on Death Row, mostly from the two blocks I had lived on before our exodus. In the old building, the only chance we had to intermingle between blocks occurred at Bible study, and not many willingly suffered through an hour of biblical excoriation just to hang out. But Unit Three's pods sat adjacent to one another, so we could wave through giant Plexiglas windows, shout through cracks in the doors, or stand in the hallway and talk when the pod door opened for chow and outside recreation.

Assigned to Pod Eight, I only knew about half of the guys there. Settling in proved easy enough because getting to know people in prison is only hard if you've never been there. Once in prison, you can get a feel for whom you might be able to talk with and who should be avoided. It remains something of a process, though—a tricky dance reminiscent of high school, but more dangerous.

When I met Eddie for the first time, he sat hunched over a dayroom table playing a card game my mother had taught me as a child. From what I observed, Eddie was quiet and mild-mannered. No signs of sudden psychosis or cruelty. No frothing at the mouth or telling twitches. He appeared to be a normal, middle-aged, pasty-faced white guy with a perpetual three-day beard. He didn't talk too much or too loudly. (Loudmouths, braggarts, and know-it-alls are the bane of every cell block in America.) Mainly, Eddie looked forlorn.

"You play cribbage?" he asked me and gathered the cards. In jail and prison, playing cards and other tabletop games has less to do with leisure and more to do with an opportunity to learn people's characters.

I hesitated before sitting. I didn't know this guy and, despite needing to learn more about my new neighbors, caution was always necessary. Was he a predator? A bully? Or worse, someone who would draw people like that? In my first few months on the Row, I'd had to prove to others I would not be punked or bullied.

Eddie quickly dealt the cards as I set pegs in the cribbage board. Rules of the game returned along with memories of rainy summers spent playing cards in a tent that my siblings and I had set up in our backyard. While Eddie and I played, he asked where I had lived before becoming incarcerated.

"Maine," I said. "And I regret ever leaving."

His eyes widened a bit. "Maine? No shit. I should've stayed in Newport News or Virginia Beach."

"I've been to Virginia Beach. I took a Greyhound there in November of '96 thinking it would be crowded. The place was deserted."

"Yeah. You should've gone in August or earlier. The nightlife is amazing."

After the first game, Eddie and I continued to meet to play and talk. Over the next few months, he told me about a pawn shop where he had worked. I soon discovered the pawnshop stood central in Eddie's life. Whenever other guys on the Row—Dan, Tim, J.J.—or I sat with Eddie at chow, he would find a way to interject, "That reminds me of this one time at the pawn shop..." and immediately launch into a story that lay on a shelf in his mind, marked at a discount: buy one, get three free.

I always felt disadvantaged swapping stories from the outside. The amount of time I'd spent away from the sheltered world of my parents' house in Brunswick, Maine, spanned only three years. Between the ages of sixteen and nineteen, my freedom had been perforated by stints in a group home, drug rehab, hospital stays, and juvenile detention at the Maine Youth Center. I know more about life inside institutions than life on the outside. So, I listened to certain older prisoners like Harvey, Mule, Earl, and Roper to rid myself of naiveté. They stood in for uncles and mentors in a place with few role models. Eddie was more of a peer, so his stories about selling everything he owned as cocaine and alcohol consumed his life were relatable.

"Man, I stayed high and drunk every day," he told me. "Three- and four-day binges where I couldn't even remember my name or where I put my car. When I started shooting cocaine, it was over. I'd wake up in a different zip code, in a strange house, struggling to remember anything."

I nodded, overcome with a sense of kinship and discomfort because of the similarities to my own drug-hazed journey to Death Row. Beyond a shared addiction, Eddie and I held no expectations for each other aside from quiet conversations about books, movies, or songs on the radio. Our conversations, like those with others I called "friend," were devoid of the posturing and lies typical of prison. And of course, we discussed the executions.

In December 2002, Ernest Basdon and Desmond Carter were put to death. Questions about Basdon's innocence helped him get a few stays of execution, but they were not enough to save him. During execution time, Unit Three's atmosphere was tense, brittle, and oppressively quiet, as if too much noise would break loose the scream of terror trapped in all of us. We suspected the State would make up for the low number of executions the following year; we were right. That year, 2003, became the deadliest year for Death Row prisoners since North Carolina had reinstated the death penalty in 1977.

Typically, the warden schedules executions ninety days in advance of the date, but the condemned prisoner is notified forty-five days into that period—after the court, attorneys, and State are informed.

The condemned is summoned to the warden's office, informed that an execution date has been set, and asked if he or she needs anyone to be contacted. About once a week until the final twenty-four hours on death watch, the warden summons the prisoner back, willing or not, to ask after his or her state of mind. Because prisoners with an execution date have nothing left to lose, they are considered a significant security risk and closely monitored.

By the end of July 2003, William Quentin Jones had been scheduled to die on August 22, Henry Hunt on September 12, and Joe Bates on September 26. As their dates approached, Eddie grew increasingly distracted and nervous. When I asked him about it, he said, "I'm out of appeals, and I think I'm next."

I didn't pay much attention at the time. I was concerned about Henry Hunt, or "Mule" as most of us knew him. A full-blooded Tuscarora Indian from Robeson County, Mule was a good friend and someone who taught me a lot. He and I had received Catholic confirmation together in 2000 when then-Bishop Gossman came to Central Prison for the ceremony. Mule had introduced me to the stray cats in the old building and showed me how to make potato wine. He was serious and funny, giving, and slightly wild. My favorite uncle in and out of prison, Mule liked teaching me things because I listened, especially when it came to home remedies and finessing limited resources in prison.

One day after playing with the cats, I noticed I'd caught ringworm on my shoulder. Worried, I asked Mule about filling out a sick call but he stopped me.

"Boy," he said, "don't you know that ringworm comes from animals? What you gonna tell them people? I got worms in the shower? Come here."

He then took a rag, dipped it in bleach, and rubbed the infected spot until it burned.

"If that don't fix it, fill out the sick call and tell 'em you've been playin' with a mouse. Leave my cats out of it."

Surprisingly, his remedy worked, leaving a light, ring-shaped scar on my shoulder.

Though Mule lived on another block when they gave him an execution date, I saw him at Mass every Thursday and was present when Father Dan gave him viaticum—the last sacrament of a Catholic. If Mule was worried, I never saw it. He seemed resigned to his fate, as if peace came with faith and the understanding that a new journey was about to begin.

A week before the state killed William Quentin Jones, Eddie received an execution date for October 3.

"What are your lawyers saying?" I asked, but Eddie just sighed.

"You know. Same bullshit they tell everyone. Clemency is my last best chance."

I had little faith that the governor would grant clemency and halt Eddie's execution. Former Death Row resident Harvey Green, who had demonstrated rehabilitation through Christian ministry in and out of prison, and Ronald Frye, who had provided reams of documents detailing childhood abuse, had both been denied clemency and put to death. My faith in clemency died with them, but I still clung to the hope that Eddie would get that golden ticket.

Even though I had known it was coming, Mule's execution was a gut punch that left me numb and breathless. I tried to read but just stared at the page, waiting for the trapped feeling to pass.

It never did. Since I also lived on the pod with Joe Bates, the next to die, seeing him withdraw as his time grew short was unnerving. Normally, Joe played poker, talked about sports, or religiously watched *The Young and the Restless*. All of that stopped after Mule's execution. Joe sat on his bunk flipping through magazines, stood at a narrow window looking at the sky, or leaned against the wall, arms folded, frowning at the TV. He spoke little in the final days and then only in terse statements.

When the death squad came for him, Joe gave out some hugs and handshakes. On his way out the door, he said, "All right. Y'all be easy."

The day before they took Eddie to death watch for the final seventy-two hours of his life, we sat in his cell smoking cigarettes. Smoke streamed through a rectangle of sunlight, thick and poisonous with the things we avoided in conversation. On death watch, he would be visited by attorneys, family, and friends, many of whom suddenly wanted to visit after years of silence.

Eddie's time on Death Row had been harder than most since he rarely received visits or money for the canteen. What little he had he received from those of us kind enough to give it. People on the outside might not give much thought to what prisoners do to get by, assuming meals provided at the chow hall are enough, but State food doesn't always relieve hunger. Eddie went hungry for years.

As we sat in his cell in silence, I watched a curl of smoke roll up the wall and hit the ceiling. Was it like this for all the condemned? This awkward, terrifying time we awaited the state to murder us and there was nothing that could be done to stop it, or the slow inevitability of that death.

Finally, Eddie spoke. "Can I tell you something, man?"

He stared at the floor, hands on knees, his face slack and unshaven.

"I'm scared. I don't want to die." He looked up. "Why does it have to be this way?"

How could I answer that? Over the last nine months, seven people had been released from Death Row with reduced sentences. Eddie was convicted and sentenced under the felony-murder rule, which triggers a death sentence if a murder occurs in the course of another felony, such as a robbery. Hundreds of murder cases like his end up leading to life sentences because the additional felony is dropped in exchange for a guilty plea. Eddie refused to plead guilty and received death for exercising his right to a jury trial.

My faith in God was not strong enough to share with Eddie. Besides, we all prayed for deliverance from this nightmare only to awaken the next day, our lives leaking through cracks. Doubt and an overwhelming sense of helplessness made it hard to speak.

"I don't know, Eddie. It just is."

I didn't know what else to say.

When they came for Eddie, a sergeant pushed an empty handcart onto the block. The warden, unit manager, and shift captain walked behind him. The brass represented a display of North Carolina's will that Eddie be put to death for the murder of Herman Larry Smith. Eddie put a white plastic property bag on the cart: old pictures and letters to be collected by whomever came to pick up his body.

One by one, guys went over and gave Eddie a hug or a handshake. A few offered brief words of encouragement.

"Keep your head up, Eddie."

"All right, my friend. I'm gonna miss you."

When my turn approached, I struggled to think of something profound or symbolic of our friendship, but words failed.

"Take it easy. You're good people to me" was all I could say. I hugged Eddie and turned away, not wanting to see him cry—not wanting him to see *me* cry.

The brass escorted him from the block and out of sight down the hallway.

I heard later that after the lethal injection cocktail was pumped into Eddie's veins, it took him nearly an hour to die. His attorney and other witnesses reported seeing him gasp and jerk against the gurney straps, despite being supposedly sedated and paralyzed by the drugs.

The prosecutor who attended the execution, who could just as easily have given Eddie a life sentence, declared, "Justice has been served."

The day after an execution is like a hangover: your head throbs and your stomach churns, laughter grates on every nerve and the lights seem too bright. After Eddie's execution, the State scheduled three more: Joseph Timothy Keel, November 7; John Daniels, November 14; Robbie J. Lyons, December 5. In the same period, four prisoners had their sentences overturned and were resentenced to life without parole.

I find myself unable to reconcile the randomness of who is allowed life and who is given death. Instead, I think about Mule, Harvey, Eddie, and all the rest who were executed. I try to overcome bitterness, anger, and despair—and fail. Their faces rise and engulf my thoughts in the quiet moments, leaving me to wonder who will be next.

Teaching to Live

In my early days on Death Row, I struggled to process my capital murder trial. After twenty months of pretrial solitary confinement, the anger and anguish I witnessed in the courtroom from the victims' family, my family, and others, overshadowed my own thoughts and feelings. After the trial, as the transport van rocketed towards Central Prison, I sat numb and unable to think. I felt much like a rock might after being hurled to the deepest pit on earth, completely at the mercy of gravity. Then, I landed at the bottom.

During my first few years on Death Row, I kept busy by reading fantasy novels and occasionally exercising. A fellow prisoner, Earl Richmond, trained me in calisthenics and life. Earl, or "E" as we knew him, had been an army drill instructor before coming to Death Row, so E trained me like any recruit: pushing me hard, testing my limits, and teaching me how to live no matter what the circumstance.

"It's easy to be a man in front of people," he once told me. "But who are you when no one is watching? Who are you at night when the cell door is shut, and nobody can see or hear you but God? That's what counts."

E looked at me to make sure I'd heard, then dropped to the ground to execute a set of precise pushups.

Though I did not always understand his lectures on faith and ethics, I listened, hoping to glean answers, trying to keep up. Had anyone told me I would find a mentor like E on Death Row, I would not have believed it. I was fortunate to have him and some of our peers to help me mature.

My initial years on the Row were also spent learning not to hate myself. I wrestled with addiction and depression; my mind twisted with the finality of my sentence and thoughts of self-harm. Despite an ever-changing regimen of medications that left me lethargic, I still cut my arms and legs with a razor. Self-mutilation is something I had dealt with since childhood, never really understanding why I did it, but turning to it in dark moments like the worst kind of drug. On Death Row, the behavior continued as a way to pierce the mind-numbing horror of executions.

E helped me turn to exercise as a safe alternative to drugs and self-abuse. Physical exercise helped a lot. This simple activity could be done on my own and allowed me to push myself to exhaustion. As my body developed, it improved my self-esteem enough that I quit taking psych meds and cutting myself. E showed me how hard work builds character, confidence, and mental strength. I began questioning why I continued to hurt myself when it undermined any attempts at physical improvement and solved nothing. My mental illness, both the overt self-harm and covert self-flagellation, was a battle with self-perception. Because my life consisted of failure, self-destruction, and impulsivity, it seemed obvious that reasoned judgment and success would be antidotes.

But finding reasoned judgment in prison is not easy.

Catholic Mass on Thursdays in the multipurpose room was a place I felt challenged because in those early days, I had little faith. The execution of my friend Mule in 2003 weighed heavily on those of us who regularly attended. His empty seat served as a constant reminder we might all share the same fate. We usually took turns reading the Scriptures before listening to Father Dan read the Gospel; then, we discussed the readings together. I always asked questions: What did Jesus write in the sand? Wasn't Lazarus the first resurrection? Did Christ know he was God? I understood the readings well enough, but my questions were combative. After being condemned to death and living through twenty executions, I had a beef with God—and more questions than answers.

Father Dan took most of the questions in good humor, answering with practiced ease and steadfast faith. The coolest priest I had ever met, Father Dan had no problem calling us out if he felt we were being dishonest or mentally lazy. When he didn't know the answer to a question, he admitted as much.

After an early September Mass in 2004, with two executions scheduled for October, we were discussing the Ascension of Christ when I asked Father Dan, "Who sits on the left?"

Father Dan frowned. "What do you mean?"

"If Jesus sits on the right, does Satan sit on the left of God's throne?"

At the time, it seemed like a good question.

"You know," I continued. "Kind of like the angel and devil do in the cartoons. They fight over the mind of the person whose shoulder they sit on."

Everyone stared at me.

"So, you think God worked with the devil? That he is not omnipotent and omniscient or, at least, that he created evil?" Father Dan raised both brows. "I'm sure that's not what you meant."

Embarrassed, I apologized. "No. Sorry. Never mind."

In confession a week later, Father Dan said, "You're a bright kid, Lyle. I don't know how you got here, but it would be a shame to see you waste your potential. You need to get something on your mind. What would you say to taking a college course or two?"

I paused. College? Me?

"I only have a GED," I said. "Besides, I dropped out of high school my sophomore year."

"A GED is enough. Does it seem like something that would interest you? It would occupy some time and answer a lot of those questions you have." Father Dan smiled.

I looked away. School had never been my thing. Bullies, drugs, poor self-esteem, and a lack of interest had made it seem impossible. I had needed help then, while I drowned in adolescence, but there had been no lifeguards available.

"I can't afford anything like that, and neither can my parents," I replied.

"You let me take care of that. Can you get a copy of your GED?"

"Yeah." The Maine Youth Center kept records for all their juvenile offenders.

"What do you say?"

I thought about it. This would be an opportunity to learn. It had to be better than wasting the rest of my life watching reruns on TV and waiting to die. Death Row did not have rehabilitative programs or much of anything else. The only organized activity beyond religious services was the annual basketball tournament that E had begun in 2002.

"Sure." I shrugged. "I'll try one."

About seven weeks after accepting Father Dan's offer, course materials arrived from the University of North Carolina at Chapel Hill. Higher education was something I had never seen in my future. Not for high school dropouts. Not for Death Row prisoners. Fortunately, my first course, social interaction, contained chapters about stereotypes, relationships, groups, and the interconnectivity of communities. Though the expectation of failure hovered in the back of my mind, I grew determined to defy every label, stereotype, and negative expectation leveled at me. I would succeed.

When E heard about the course, he encouraged me to ignore the idea of failure, but if it happened, to work harder.

"Giving up is easy," he said. "Do your best from beginning to end. Stay consistent and persistent."

In the time it took me to complete my first course, four people were executed; twelve others had their death sentences converted to life or less. During this time, Alan Gell, who had been on North Carolina's Death Row for eight years, was retried, acquitted, and released. In the wake of Gell's exoneration, nearly three times as many death sentences were overturned as were carried out. Many of us believed the end of capital punishment neared, and I drew strength from the tiny hope that the future was not fixed.

But shortly after I passed my first final exam, E received an execution date for May 6, 2005. The news hit Death Row hard. E was the pillar of our community, a man that everyone—staff and prisoners alike—looked to for kindness, approval, and guidance. Though E freely admitted his guilt and remorse for his crimes, he used it as a catalyst for change instead of a scourge, living the remainder of his life as we all should have from the beginning.

In the weeks prior to his execution, E quit his job as hallway janitor to spend more time with the guys on the pod. He cared how his execution would affect us. Friend, brother, confidant, and mentor, Earl Richmond exuded peace even as the state prepared to take his life. Throughout the time I knew him, E gave money to those who had none, resolved conflict before it grew violent, asked after family, and remembered details for future conversations. Earl made all of us better people.

At his final Bible study, seventy-two hours before his execution, E stepped up to the podium. Our expectant faces watched his calm and smiling one. Anguish and anger gnawed at my stomach but I ignored it, waiting to hear E speak. Staff clustered at the edge of a crowd of roughly forty Death Row prisoners. They too wanted to hear what Earl would say.

"I really appreciate everyone coming. Y'all do me proud."

Earl paused, scanning the group.

"You know me. You know I have always accepted responsibility for my crimes. I was wrong to kill those people, and I am here to pay for it. The Lord Jesus Christ knows my heart. By His grace and mercy, I received salvation from a life of sin because I asked for forgiveness. Since receiving that gift, I've done my best to live as a Christian should. I'm not perfect by any means. I've stumbled along the way, but I know my God forgives me. Now, it's time for me to go home to Him."

A few people muttered and grumbled under their breaths. There had been talk about what could be done to disrupt E's execution. When he found out, E had made sure to put a stop to it, but the sentiment was still in the room.

"Now, y'all listen up." Though he had not raised his voice, E's order cut through the room like a whip crack on a parade ground, reminding everyone of his military background. "These folks are coming down here to carry out the sentence handed down to me by a jury and authorized by the law. You don't have to like it, but I'm going with them. None of you can stop it, and anything you try to do will not be for my sake."

He caught gazes until a few people looked away.

"I know y'all love me," he said. "I know this hurts. It hurts me too, but love and respect me enough to keep calm. Help one another through this like we have done for other executions—because we're family, and that's what family does."

E continued for a while, selecting passages from the Bible that backed up everything we already knew about the man standing before us. Eventually, he named each person in the room and talked about what he would miss.

"Pit's 'truths.' Wayne's boxing. Lyle's workouts."

A few people walked out when it became obvious he would not condone violence. The room drew closer to Earl as he spoke, hanging on to his words for as long as we could, wanting to remain near this light shining in the heart of our darkness.

After Earl Richmond, seven more people were put to death in the fifteen months before North Carolina halted executions. Even as these deaths crowded my thoughts, E changed how I responded to them. Regardless of where, this was my life to live. No excuses. Death would always be in my future; why should the possibility of execution make me surrender, especially when hope for a different outcome always exists?

In 2007, I transferred my studies to Ohio University's Independent Studies program to pursue a degree in the social sciences. The Church continued to support me and, in 2013, I graduated with an Associate in Arts degree. The process, both plodding and exhausting at times, took longer than usual because I could only enroll in two or three courses each year.

Over the years, a number of people supported and encouraged my pursuit of a degree while others did not. Some wanted to know, a bit sarcastically, if I thought it would spare me from execution. Others believed I was wasting my time. The prison administration provided proctors for my exams, but they were often grudging, believing that no prisoner on Death Row should be allowed the privilege of an education. At times, their attitude caused me to doubt myself—why did a man sentenced to die by lethal injection need an education? But rather than totally discourage me, the negative sentiment made me feel increasingly responsible to make the most of my education, especially for my parents. I had done so little in life to make them proud; at least I could give them this.

If education was my panacea, writing became a way to communicate that experience. Though I wrote a lot for college, two friends on the outside helped me maintain a blog. Initially, it felt like throwing thoughts down a well, but I continued anyway. After a year, I branched out and published articles on some criminal justice websites and the *J Journal*, a quarterly journal produced by the John Jay College of Criminal Justice. These publications were reassuring, but they never felt like enough. Success in school bred the expectation that if I could attain a degree on Death Row, more was possible.

Over the years, education and writing became my life, raising and changing my standards for how a typical day in prison should unfold and completely altering my worldview. The person I had been upon becoming incarcerated—that mixed-up drug user prone to self-mutilation—disappeared. Gone were any self-destructive thoughts or apathy; in their place existed an iron will to defy every odd.

By the fall of 2017, I was accepted into Ohio University's Bachelor of Specialized Studies degree program with a concentration in Criminal Justice Administration. My acceptance into the BSS program was not automatic and served as a reminder that each step of my journey on Death Row was a test and an opportunity.

As my writing took on greater depth and intensity, I contributed essays to *Scalawag Magazine,* a Southern social justice publication that reports on civil rights issues. Through *Scalawag,* my writing reached a local audience, which is how I ultimately connected with Frank Baumgartner, a Richard J. Richardson distinguished professor at UNC.

Despite being enrolled in a degree program, I had never had the chance to speak with any professors. When I needed to ask questions, everything was relayed through academic advisors. The advent of phones on Death Row in 2016 may have advanced the ability to plan my degree program, but it also provided a significant new tool for networking, an ability that is ordinary to people on the outside but lifesaving for prisoners.

Professor Baumgartner learned of my writing and shared it with his undergrad class entitled Race, Innocence, and the End of the Death Penalty. After a conversation about the class one day, he asked, "Hey, Lyle, what do you think about talking to my students over the phone about some of your writing?"

The question echoed one I remembered Father Dan asking years before.

"Absolutely," I said. "I would love the opportunity."

But there was no way I would talk to a group of students off-the-cuff. Too much could be missed, and I didn't want to sound like an idiot or ruin the chance to challenge the narrative told about people on Death Row.

Before the call, Professor Baumgartner had his students read two of my *Scalawag* essays, "Beyond the Wall" and "Life Without Parole is a Silent Execution," as well as the North Carolina Supreme Court's decision on my direct appeal. His students created a list of questions for me to answer when I called in.

I had written a few speeches before, but nothing as important as what I believed these students needed to hear. I was nervous, writing several drafts of the speech, reading it to friends, and reading it aloud in my cell.

In the end, I put together an argument for education and prison reform. I hoped the students would take it to heart.

The day of the call, I worried that something would go wrong—some emergency would cause us to be locked in our cells. The phone would be broken. A hundred catastrophic scenarios played out in my mind until the time of the call arrived. My body shook with nervous energy as I dialed the number.

When Professor Baumgartner answered, I took a few deep breaths and tried to block out the dayroom noises from the prisoners behind me. My sweaty palm clenched the phone.

"Hi there, Lyle," said the professor. "We are ready when you are."

Over the phone, I heard a cough, then some papers rustling like dry leaves in the background. It did not sound like nearly three hundred undergrads were waiting for me to speak, but I had never done this before, so who knew?

"Hello," I said into the phone. My voice was amplified by a microphone held to the professor's phone. My heart thrummed, I grew short of breath. Pushing aside my fear, I read from the paper, ignoring any advice about memorizing the speech.

"Thank you for giving me this opportunity to speak with you. First, I'll answer the most important question you asked: What is the single greatest reform needed in the prison system?"

I had less than fifteen minutes to convey what had taken me years of painful, heartbreaking lessons to learn. Mentors and friends had given the best of themselves so that I could carry on and enhance their message.

"Higher education must no longer be viewed as a privilege," I said. "By maintaining this status quo and limiting college education to those who are free and can afford it, a permanent underclass will continue to fill America's prisons. Educating prisoners helps to end the poverty of thought that begets crime and violence. We represent the most needy and marginalized sub-citizens in the U.S. To break this cycle, there must be a greater investment in the idea that people go to prison to learn more than 'a lesson'—they are sent to become better human beings and productive citizens."

The anxiety disappeared as I continued, replaced by confidence that I spoke the truth. When I had finished, enough time remained for two questions from students and a brief dialogue about my capital trial. Professor Baumgartner spoke on the inequity of a trial where the younger defendant was sentenced to death while the older, equally culpable co-defendant was given fourteen years and released because he had testified against me. I listened, wishing I had another fifteen minutes to discuss this thorny topic.

After the call ended, I returned to my cell, mind awhirl with the awesome responsibility of teaching students about education in prison and the need for criminal justice reform. I immediately knew that I wanted to do it again. Within weeks, a friend of mine put me in touch with Professor Joshua Page at the University of Minnesota, and we made plans for a call-in to one of his criminal justice classes. I finally felt that I was putting my education to good use.

Throughout it all, I thought of Earl. He had defied stereotypes and expectations in a place where human potential is sent to die. E showed us that life is defined daily through our effort and aspirations. I keep this lesson in my heart, striving without excuse, reaching higher with every goal, and hoping to shed some light along the way.

§

Unpacking the Death Penalty

TESSIE CASTILLO

When I walked into the classroom on Death Row to greet the shy group of men in crimson jumpsuits, I had no idea how much that first meeting would change my life. I didn't know that I would develop real friendships with several of the men—friendships strong enough to weather time, misunderstandings, arguments, and distance. I didn't know we would one day write a book together. I was not at all prepared for what writing that book would expose—a death penalty system so costly, complex, and arbitrary I could scarcely believe the statistics even as I read them.

Through my years of correspondence with George, Chanton, Alim and Lyle, I learned about the specific circumstances that brought each of them to Death Row. Certainly, they had many things in common: poverty, family dysfunction, poor role models, and a whirlwind period of youthful recklessness that had landed each of them on Death Row before the age of twenty-six. While I sympathize with the trauma they endured, I also recognize that lionizing them or excusing their actions because they had difficult childhoods equally distorts the truth.

In compiling this book, I envisioned a collection of stories that explore the complexity of how personal choice and extraneous circumstances combine to lead people to Death Row. I wanted to illuminate these men's virtues and failings, their capacity for self-reflection, and their search for hope and purpose while living under the shadow of a death sentence. I wanted to challenge the inaccurate and simplistic portrayal of people on Death Row as monsters.

The death penalty persists partly because we value human life—in particular, the lives of innocent victims. Then, ironically, we deny humanity to those whose lives we wish to take. We reduce complex people into caricatures and paint portraits of devils to justify killing them, yet a closer look at the troubled lives of people incarcerated on Death Row reveals them to be as human as any of us. The monster is not inside the prison, but all around it in the people and systems that perpetuate violence, trauma, and brutality from generation to generation.

In addition to illuminating personal and societal forces that pave the way towards prison, I also wanted to detail the legal processes that brought the men to Death Row. Why do some people receive the death penalty for homicide while others do not? Why were all four men still appealing their death sentences years, even decades, after the original convictions? Why had one man in my journaling class at Central Prison been sentenced to death when he hadn't killed anyone at all?

These questions, and more, launched an exploration into the processes of capital punishment. In particular, Frank Baumgartner's book *Deadly Justice: A Statistical Portrait of the Death Penalty* provided me with an exhaustive collection of facts about capital punishment across the United States and throughout the decades.

Before writing this book, I believed, as many people do, that the death penalty in the United States is reserved for the worst of the worst crimes, that it is more cost effective than locking someone in prison for life, and that it is applied as selectively and fairly as possible so mistakes are rare. But in researching capital punishment in the United States, I found that none of this is true. The death penalty is not reserved for the most heinous murders, it is more expensive than a sentence of life in prison, and sentencing errors are not only common, but rampant.

How can death penalty rulings be so different from what most of the public imagines? To answer this, we need to understand how the capital punishment system was designed to work versus how it actually works. Key features of the death penalty are puzzling, even disturbing, but it is important that we know them. If we are going to take a life for a life, we should at least understand the mechanics of the exchange.

The death penalty process begins when the District Attorney, or chief prosecutor, in the county where the crime occurred, decides to seek capital punishment rather than a regular prison sentence for murder.[1] Each state that allows the death penalty has certain categories of crimes that are considered eligible for capital punishment—for example, murder committed for monetary gain, murder involving more than one victim, murder by someone in prison or attempting to escape from prison, murder of a law enforcement officer, murder that is especially heinous or cruel, and, most commonly, murder committed during the course of another felony, such as a robbery.[2]

Capital cases are complex and require specialized attorneys, separate trials for conviction and sentencing, and unique rules for jury selection.[3] Most capital defendants cannot afford a lawyer, so the courts assign a defense attorney to the case.[4] At first glance, the setup for capital punishment looks fair: there are specific crimes that make one eligible for the death penalty, and there are a prosecutor and defense attorney who argue both sides of the case to an impartial judge and jury.

Here the process breaks down. Both the prosecution team and the defense team in a capital case are paid using public funds, which they utilize for staff, investigators, experts, and other necessary expenses to build an adequate case. Politicians and elected judges hold the purse strings for these funds. Naturally, most elected officials are keener to spend taxpayer dollars to convict suspects than to defend them (letting

1   Baumgartner, Frank R. *Deadly Justice: A Statistical Portrait of the Death Penalty*. New York: Oxford University Press, 2018. (pp. 28–29)

2   Baumgartner, pp. 94-100.

3   Baumgartner, pp. 27–47.

4   Baumgartner, pp. 29–31.

an alleged murderer go free could be a ghastly public relations mistake), so in nearly all states, more resources are provided for prosecution than for defense. It is not uncommon for courts to appoint a defense attorney who does not specialize in capital cases, to vastly underpay them for the amount of work required, and deny them adequate funds to hire experts and investigators to build a solid case for the defendant.[5]

Because prosecutors typically have more resources to investigate a case than do court-appointed defense attorneys, they are likely to run across evidence that could point to a defendant's guilt or innocence. Recognizing the danger in allowing prosecutors to access—and potentially destroy—exculpatory evidence that the defense hasn't seen, the U.S. Supreme Court has tried to correct this imbalance. In 1963, the *Brady v. Maryland* ruling required prosecutors to turn over evidence favorable to the defense before trial.[6] Yet, prosecutors are often reluctant to follow a rule that works against their self-interest and many have continued to suppress exculpatory evidence even after the *Brady* ruling. A study of exoneration cases, or findings of innocence, from 1989 to 2015 revealed that seventy-eight percent of exonerations involved prosecutor misconduct[7]—the most common of which is to suppress evidence that could point to the defendant's innocence.[8]

Prosecutorial misconduct is notoriously difficult to discipline, thanks to another Supreme Court case, *Imbler v. Pachtman* in 1976, which upheld that prosecutors have "absolute immunity" from liability for certain actions undertaken in the course of their official duties. The Court explained:

> Although such immunity leaves the genuinely wronged criminal defendant without civil redress against a prosecutor whose malicious or dishonest

---

5   *Ibid.*
6   Baumgartner, pp. 188–189.
7   Baumgartner, pp. 174–178.
8   Baumgartner, pp. 188–189.

action deprives him of liberty, the alternative of qualifying a prosecutor's immunity would disserve the broader public interest in that it would prevent the vigorous and fearless performance of the prosecutor's duty that is essential to the proper functioning of the criminal justice system.[9]

The Supreme Court reasoned prosecutors must be able to perform their duties without fear of being sued, but the downside of absolute immunity is that in certain circumstances, prosecutors can also perform their duties without fear of accountability. Although state bar associations can discipline corrupt prosecutors with reprimands, fines, or, in extreme cases, disbarment,[10] these accountability measures are rarely imposed.[11] For example, a 2016 report by the Innocence Project studied cases of prosecutorial misconduct in five states from 2004 to 2008. The researchers documented 660 cases of misconduct, most occurring in murder cases. Of these 660 cases, many of which led to wrongful imprisonment, including wrongful death sentences, only one prosecutor was disciplined.[12]

With both resources and legal immunity on their side, prosecutors wield great power over the decision to pursue capital punishment for murder crimes. Whether for personal, political, or financial, reasons, they seek the death penalty more rarely than one might expect. Since 1976, over 700,000 homicides have occurred in the U.S., yet just over 8000 of these (1.1%) have resulted in death sentences.[13] Reading a statistic like this, one might assume that prosecutors reserve the death penalty for the cruelest and most heinous murders. However, studies show that the death penalty is *not* typically

9   *Imbler v. Pachtman*, 424 U.S. 409 (1976). supreme.justia.com/cases/federal/us/424/409.

10 Gordon, Neil. "Misconduct and Punishment." Center for Public Integrity, 24 Jan. 2018, publicintegrity.org/2003/06/26/5532/misconduct-and-punishment.

11 Baumgartner, pp. 44–46.

12 "Prosecutorial Oversight: A National Dialogue in the Wake of *Connick v. Thompson*." Innocence Project, 2016, innocenceproject.org/wp-content/uploads/2016/04/IP-Prosecutorial-Oversight-Report_09.pdf.

13 Baumgartner, pp. 33–35.

reserved for the worst of the worst. While judges, juries, and prosecutors do consider heinousness in the decision to apply the death penalty, there are so many other political and personal factors at play that in practice, the application of the death sentence more resembles a lottery. The outcomes have little to no correlation with the heinous nature of the crime.[14]

When I taught the journaling class at Central Prison, one of my students had received a death sentence for participating in a robbery during which an accomplice had killed someone. However, my student, who was the getaway driver, had received the death penalty while the actual shooter had not. By law, any major participant in a felony murder, such as a robbery that leads to homicide, is eligible for the death penalty. The theory is that all parties involved should be assigned equal culpability, but in practice, the felony murder rule can lead to some pretty bizarre outcomes: the United States has executed 10 non-triggermen while sparing the lives of the real killers.[15]

Heinousness or participation in the crime might not predict the outcome of a capital trial, but one surprising factor can: the District Attorney who prosecutes the case.[16] If you look at a map of capital cases in the U.S., they are clearly clustered in specific geographic areas. In fact, the majority of executions occur in only two percent of U.S. counties.[17] The clusters have no relation to higher or lower murder rates in those counties,[18] but they are likely correlated with the local District Attorney's personal zeal in favor of the death penalty.[19]

North Carolina offers a prime example of what one pro–death penalty prosecutor can do. From 1974 to 1988, Joe Freeman Britt served

14 Baumgartner, pp. 87–115.

15 Baumgartner, pp. 109–111.

16 Baumgartner, pp. 130–131; 82–83.

17 Dieter, Richard C. "The Two Percent Death Penalty: How a Minority of Counties Produce Most Death Cases At Enormous Costs to All." Death Penalty Information Center, 2013, deathpenaltyinfo.org/documents/TwoPercentReport.pdf.

18 Baumgartner, pp. 122–130.

19 Baumgartner, pp. 130–131.

as District Attorney for rural Scotland and Robeson counties. A strong proponent of the death penalty, Britt sentenced forty-seven people to death during his tenure, earning him a slot in the 1978 Guinness Book of World Records as the deadliest prosecutor in the world. However, due to errors and misconduct during the investigations and trials, only two of the forty-seven people whom Britt sentenced have been put to death.[20]

I witnessed firsthand the product of Britt's zeal—and his capacity for error—during my time volunteering in Central Prison. In 2014, the year I taught the journaling class, brothers Henry McCollum and Leon Brown were found innocent and released from prison after serving more than thirty years each. In 1983, the brothers had been convicted of the rape and murder of an eleven-year-old girl in Robeson County. A tip from a schoolgirl had led police to question the teenagers and, under duress, they had signed documents confessing to the crime. Later, they stated investigators had coerced them to sign the confessions, but this did not stop Britt from pursuing capital punishment. The teenagers were both sentenced to death, and Leon Brown, then sixteen years old, became the youngest person to have ever received the death penalty.[21]

In 2014, the North Carolina Innocence Inquiry Commission discovered through DNA evidence that the true killer was Roscoe Artis, the victim's neighbor, and a judge ordered Brown and McCollum's immediate release. The governor later pardoned them. In response, Mr. Britt called the governor "a damn fool" and continued to insist that the brothers were guilty.[22]

20 Schudel, Matt. "Joe Freeman Britt, Prosecutor Who Sent Dozens to Death Row, Dies at 80." *The Washington Post*, WP Company, 16 Apr. 2016, washingtonpost. com/national/joe-freeman-britt-prosecutor-who-sent-dozens-to-death-row-dies-at-80/2016/04/15/b246f27e-025b-11e6-b823-707c79ce3504_story. html?noredirect=on&utm_term=.9298cdc6eade.

21 Katz, Jonathan, and Eric Eckholm. "DNA Evidence Clears Two Men in 1983 Murder." *The New York Times*, The New York Times Company, 2 Sept. 2014, nytimes.com/2014/09/03/us/2-convicted-in-1983-north-carolina-murder-freed-after-dna-tests.html.

22 *Ibid.*

Henry McCollum and Leon Brown lost thirty years of their lives to wrongful imprisonment. How were they able to avoid execution for so long? This brings us to another interesting and unique aspect of the death penalty. Because execution is so severe a punishment, most states provide Death Row prisoners with appellate attorneys to help appeal their sentences after conviction.[23] During the appeals process, appellate courts look for errors made during the original trial. Additionally, in a separate process known as post-conviction or habeas review, courts examine potential issues such as incompetent defense attorneys, prosecutorial misconduct, jury bias, or suppressed evidence that could have pointed to the defendant's innocence.

These appeals move from state to federal courts and, sometimes, even to the Supreme Court.[24] The process is glacially slow. In fact, the average delay between the original trial and the execution date (set after prisoners lose their last appeal) is eighteen years.[25] Innocent people on Death Row wait even longer because prosecutors will fight hard against evidence proving they have put an innocent person behind bars. Between 2010 and 2015, exonerated prisoners had spent an average of twenty-four years on Death Row before courts discovered they were innocent.[26]

Filing decades of appeals doesn't come cheap. In fact, a death sentence costs $574,000 to $3.83 million more *per case* than a sentence of life in prison.[27] The long appeals process, combined with the high cost of a capital trial (which is lengthier and requires more specialization than noncapital trials) and the price of maintaining maximum security prisons for Death Row residents, means that, in general, it is more cost effective to incarcerate prisoners for life than to execute them.

Some might argue that there is a simple solution to the high cost of the death penalty: simply cut or eliminate the appeals process. After all,

23 Baumgartner, pp. 37–41.

24 *Ibid.*

25 Baumgartner, pp. 164–166.

26 Baumgartner, pp. 179–181.

27 Baumgartner, pp. 289–305.

people on Death Row have been convicted of murder. How often do they win appeals, anyway? Surprisingly, appeals are often successful.

Around the time we started writing this book, one of my coauthors from Death Row cited a research paper claiming that seven out of every ten people sentenced to execution in North Carolina eventually win their appeals and are removed from Death Row. When I first read this statistic, I didn't believe it. Such a high error rate seemed inconceivable. Imagine a hospital botching life-or-death surgeries nearly three quarters of the time!

However, when I combed through U.S. Department of Justice reports on capital punishment, the data confirmed it was true. In North Carolina, seventy-one percent of people sentenced to death have had their original sentences overturned, meaning either the defendant was found innocent or, more commonly, the sentence was changed to a lesser one, such as life in prison.[28] Sentence reversals are not unique to North Carolina. Across the United States, sixty-five percent of death sentences wind up reversed and only twenty-five percent of people sentenced to death have been executed. (The remaining ten percent died of suicide or natural causes while in prison.)[29]

One could point to the high rate of sentencing reversals as proof that the system is working. After all, the courts are catching mistakes and correcting them, but consider that as appeals drag on for decades, the state wastes millions of dollars only to admit that the majority of its original verdicts were wrong. Cutting or eliminating the right to appeals could mean that two-thirds of capital cases would not only result in wrongful imprisonment on Death Row, but in wrongful execution.

I understand why many people support the death penalty. The idea of condemning someone to the same fate he inflicted on others has a certain appeal. Yet, how we imagine the death penalty—as a justly meted punishment reserved for the worst of the worst—is not the reality. Politics, bureaucratic inefficiencies, and power imbalances have corrupted the system to the point where it does not function the way it was intended.

28 Baumgartner, pp. 148–149.
29 Baumgartner, pp. 140–141.

It is tempting to argue that the answer is to reform the system—to make it more predictable, more efficient, and less prone to error. We have already tried. In 1972, the U.S. Supreme Court declared the death penalty unconstitutional due to damning evidence of arbitrary application and bias in sentencing. Just four years later, the Court reinstated the death penalty with new measures to improve the predictability of who receives a death sentence and to ensure that it is applied to only the most heinous crimes.[30]

In the decades that have passed since these reforms were enacted, little has changed. Capital punishment is just as capricious. The only notable difference is that the wheels of justice grind more slowly than ever. Since the death penalty was reinstated, the average delay between sentencing and execution has nearly tripled.[31]

In *Jones v. Chappell*, a 2014 federal district court case which invalidated the death penalty in California, Judge Carney described the death sentence as one "no rational jury or legislature could ever impose: *life in prison, with the remote possibility of [execution].*"[32]

He continued, "As for the random few whose execution does become a reality, they will have languished for so long on Death Row that their execution will serve no retributive or deterrent purpose and will be arbitrary."[33]

When a justice system is invested with the power to take a human life, we should impose higher standards to ensure that its principles and processes are sound. We should challenge a system that places more weight on a prosecutor's personal zeal for the death penalty than on the nature of the crime. We should contest a system that prosecutes defendants but frequently grants its functionaries absolute immunity from prosecution

---

30 Baumgartner, pp. 1–27.

31 Baumgartner, pp. 164–166.

32 *Jones v. Chappell*, CV 09-02158-CJC (2014). s3.amazonaws.com/s3.documentcloud. org/documents/1222115/order-declaring-californias-death-penalty-system.pdf.

33 *Ibid.*

themselves. We should suspect a system that refuses to invest in adequate defense teams and then finances decades of costly appeals at taxpayer expense only to reverse its original verdict two-thirds of the time.

We should also question the presumption that underpins the justice system's deadly function—namely, that all people on Death Row are monsters, incapable of redemption, undeserving of second chances, and unworthy of life.

The process of writing this book with my four coauthors and getting to know their distinct personalities, strengths, and flaws was frustrating at times, but also illuminating. Even amidst the challenge of managing different opinions and egos, I have never ceased to marvel at how my coauthors are working to change the culture of life inside prison and to redefine assumptions about men convicted of murder. Lyle is pursuing a Masters degree and advocating for higher education as a form of rehabilitation in prison; George is an award-winning writer and poet; Alim has released the first ever hip hop album from Death Row; Chanton brings laughter and love to his family even from behind prison walls. The interests and relationships these men have developed in prison allow them to maintain a sense of normalcy and humanness despite the inhumane conditions around them. They are a part of laying down a legacy that is different from the one assigned by the crimson jumpsuit.

Lyle wrote once, "I will always be judged by the worst things in my life, but if people never know any of the good, then the greater fault lies within me."

In writing this book, I have come to know these men as complex and flawed, but also redeemable. The question is: can we redeem the capital punishment system to the point where it can be relied upon to justly impose a sentence of death?

I do not believe we can. Politics, power, and the drift towards inefficiency will find ways to corrupt even the most careful design.

I believe the path forward lies in accepting this fact. This does not mean giving up the push for reform, but it does mean accepting that reality will never quite live up to our ideals; therefore, no person or system can be entrusted with the immense responsibility to end a human life.

All of us—inside or outside prison—are more than our worst crime, but also less than our highest ideal. The challenge is to navigate this space with grace, self-reflection, and respect for life in all its complexity.

Afterword: A Brief History
of the Death Penalty in North Carolina

North Carolina's Death Row fills two tiers of Unit III at Central Prison in Raleigh, with 192 cells divided among eight pods, organized around a glassed-in guard booth. The cells open onto a common area furnished with metal tables, a shower at one end and a television at the other. A recreation yard is available twice a week.[1]

The execution chamber itself, with its gurney and tools of lethal injection, occupies a separate space. A room with a glass window provides a view for witnesses. Several days before a scheduled execution, those condemned to die are moved to one of four adjoining cells to await their death.

No one has been put to death here in 16 years.

Just four months after the most recent execution, George Wilkerson, whose essays begin this book, arrived on Death Row. The other authors have lived there long enough to remember. They write of talking with friends about the terror of their approaching executions, of the awkward goodbyes and the silence that follows, and of the despair for those left behind.

In the abstract, capital punishment serves justice by taking one life to repay the loss of another. In theory, it is reserved for the most monstrous of criminals and the most heinous of crimes.

But that's not how it plays out.

1   NC Department of Public Safety, "Death Penalty," https://www.ncdps.gov/our-organization/adult-correction/prisons/death-penalty.

At last count, 5,801 men and women imprisoned in North Carolina were serving time for murder.[2] They'd been convicted of, or pled guilty to, taking another life during a botched robbery, a drug deal gone badly, or a drunken fury. Some beat their wives to death or even their child. Of those, just 135 are facing a death sentence.

As a reader, I was moved to tears by the clarity and grace of the essays in this book. I think often now about the flock of birds that gave Wilkerson so much hope. I am moved by Lyle May's love of learning, by Michael Braxton's despair, and by Terry Robinson's letter to his son. After reading their stories, it's hard for me to see these men as the worst of the worst for whom supporters say the death penalty is meant to be reserved. Despite their convictions and the conditions of their imprisonment, the book's authors live with courage, curiosity, and faith. They love their friends. They cherish phone calls and visits. They regret their pasts. I cannot believe that these men are, indeed, the monsters the death penalty was meant to punish.

Still, the crimes they were convicted of are terrible, with victims and families who deserve justice for their anguish. Braxton was sent to Death Row in 1997 for stabbing another man imprisoned with him. They were both serving time in Caledonia, a prison farm known for violence, Braxton for two additional murders and the other man for a drug conviction. May was convicted in the 1997 deaths of an Asheville woman and her 4-year-old son. Robinson was convicted of murder during the robbery of a Pizza Inn in Wilson. Wilkerson was convicted in the deaths of two Asheboro men over a drug dispute. But, with the exception of the prison killing, these crimes are not unusual. The deaths of other children, of other victims of robbery, of others involved in drug disputes have been punished with a life sentence or less. So, what separates the 135 on Death Row in North Carolina from the other 5,666 men and women serving time for murder?

---

2   NC Department of Public Safety, Office of Research and Planning, A.S.Q. Custom Offender Reports, https://webapps.doc.state.nc.us/apps/asqExt/ASQ. Retrieved July 28, 2002 for first and second-degree murder.

Scholars who study this question look to history, judicial precedent, and reams of statistics related to crime and punishment and have concluded that the answer lies not in reason, which the law claims to follow, but in a legal system born of racism and shaped by chance.

As Tessie Castillo so clearly explains in her closing essay, the power given to prosecutors introduces chance from the get-go. North Carolina law defines 11 aggravating factors[3] to use in deciding whether the murder deserves to be punished by death. These include such specific circumstances as the killing of a law-enforcement officer, or a homicide committed while the accused is in prison for another crime. Other aggravating factors are clearly defined but not unusual, such as a killing during a rape, robbery, or another crime. Some are open to interpretation, such as whether the crime put others at risk of death or was "especially heinous, atrocious or cruel." These factors leave prosecutors with enormous discretion, easily influenced by political forces nowhere mentioned in the law. A study by the North Carolina Coalition for Alternatives to the Death Penalty found that only a handful of counties in the state were responsible for the majority of cases on Death Row. Most urban counties punish no more than 3 percent of those convicted of murder with a death sentence. Nineteen counties haven't sent anyone to death row in modern times.

Once the decision to seek the death penalty is made, district attorneys also have the leeway to change their minds with the offer of a plea deal. This can happen at any point during the months, even years, of trial preparation, or at any point during the trial. That's because the prosecutor is balancing the principle that allows for the death penalty against the reality of a trial. Perhaps the evidence is not as strong as it once seemed, or a witness falters while testifying. The terms of any plea deal are also at the discretion of the prosecutor. An offer could include first-degree murder

---

3   NC General Statutes. Capital Punishment Law, chapter XV, subsection 100, 15A-2000, section e. https://www.ncleg.net/EnactedLegislation/Statutes/HTML/ByArticle/ Chapter_15a/Article_100.html

and a sentence of life without parole, or a lesser charge of second-degree or manslaughter, which carry lower sentences. One analysis by the Office of Indigent Defense Services of capital cases between 2007 and 2015 found that 70 percent of capital cases were never heard by a jury but instead were resolved by a plea bargain.[4] Critics argue that prosecutors use the threat of the death penalty to extract a guilty plea, even in weak cases. With death as a possible punishment, the offer of a plea deal is hard to refuse.

Arbitrary factors also shape the way a capital trial unfolds. In other felony trials, a jury determines guilt while a judge sets the punishment. But in a capital murder case, the burden of sentencing falls to jurors. Courts select potential jurors randomly, from voter registration rolls and a list of people with driver's licenses. During jury selection, any potential juror who expresses opposition to the death penalty, or even ambivalence, may be disqualified, on the theory that jurors must be willing to apply the law. That means that the pool of potential jurors is greatly reduced in capital cases, leaving those who hold more conservative beliefs to hear the evidence. Each side is also allowed to excuse jurors without cause. Race is not supposed to factor into that equation, but numerous studies show that it does. If the jury finds the defendant guilty, the trial moves to the final sentencing phase, when jurors hear from the prosecutor about the aggravating factors that make the crime worthy of the death penalty, and from the defense about any mitigating factors that make the defendant deserving of mercy. That decision, with all the weight it carries, depends on 12 men and women who, apart from living in the same county, share one trait—a willingness to apply the death penalty.

More than any of these arbitrary factors, however, is the pernicious fact of racial bias—conscious or unconscious—that at every level undermines any expectation of fairness from a system entrusted with such grave decisions. Racial bias taints police investigations. It can shape the decision by a prosecutor to seek death. It plays out in jury selection,

4 North Carolina Office of Indigent Defense Services. "FY 15 Capital Trial Case Study, Potentially Capital Case Costs at the Trial Level," November, 2015.

even in decisions appellate justices make when deciding appeals. The result of such bias is clear. The likelihood of landing on Death Row is highest for those convicted of killing a white woman and lowest when the victim is a Black man.[5] Across the country, Black people are far more likely to be murdered than white people, but the punishment for killing someone white is more likely to be death.[6] A study of more than 15,000 homicides in North Carolina, between 1980 and 2007, found that killings of white people were more likely to be punished by a death sentence than killings of Black people. A narrower study of just seven years of executions leading up to their halt in 2006, found that most of the victims of those executed were white, and only 22 percent of victims Black.[7] Put another way, the system values the loss of white life more than the loss of Black life. The statistics also show that it is more likely for a Black defendant to be sentenced to death than a white one. Of the 133 men and two women on North Carolina's Death Row, 54 percent are Black[8] compared to the 22 percent[9] of the state's total population comprised of Black people. Bias also excludes Black citizens from deciding who deserves this ultimate punishment, which means that a Black defendant is rarely judged by a jury of peers. In a study of cases between 1990 and 2010, 20 percent of death penalty cases in North Carolina were decided by all white juries and 21 percent by juries with only one person of color.[10]

5   Kotch, Seth, and Mosteller, Robert P. "The Racial Justice Act and the Long Road Struggle with Race and the Death Penalty in North Carolina," *North Carolina Law Review* 88, no. 6 (2010).

6   Baumgartner, Frank R. *Deadly Justice: A Statistical Portrait of the Death Penalty*. New York: Oxford University Press, 2018.

7   Robinson, Matthew. "The Death Penalty in North Carolina, 2021: A Summary of the Data and Scientific Studies."

8   NC Department of Public Safety, "Death Row Roster." https://www.ncdps.gov/our-organization/adult-correction/prisons/death-penalty/death-row-roster

9   U.S. Census Bureau, "QuickFacts: North Carolina." https://www.census.gov/quickfacts/NC

10 Weeks, Gregory, order, *State of North Carolina v. Marcus Reymond Robinson*, April 20, 2012

These skewed statistics are no accident. Historians of capital punishment argue that North Carolina's modern death penalty system is rooted in slavery and Jim Crow, both institutions that relied on the threat of execution as a tool for asserting white supremacy. Law professor Robert Mosteller and historian Seth Kotch established this clearly in their 2010 law review article, "The Racial Justice Act and the Long Struggle with Race and the Death Penalty in North Carolina." During slavery, slaveholders were free to beat, maim, and torture those they enslaved but it was left to the state to order executions. Between 1726 and 1865, 71 percent of the 242 people executed in North Carolina were Black. After the Civil War, the racial disparities continued. Throughout reconstruction until 1910, 74 percent of the 160 executed were Black, even though Black people never exceeded 38 percent of the population. In 1910, the state assumed responsibility from county officials for executions, centralizing them in Raleigh. During the next 50 years, even as the Black population declined to 25 percent, 78 percent of those executed were Black while 75 percent of the victims were white.

During most of this period, murder, rape, first-degree burglary and arson were capital crimes, but as a punishment for rape, the death penalty was used almost exclusively for Black men convicted of raping white women. Between 1910 and 1961, of the 78 men executed for rape, 66 were Black. The race of the victim was not always recorded, but when it was, at least 58 of the victims for which Black men were executed were white women. In North Carolina, no white man was ever executed in the rape of a Black woman. The authors also make the case that this pattern of legal executions worked with lynching to terrorize Black people. Death penalty trials were rushed to avoid a lynching by a mob. And the racism inherent in the legal system of capital punishment justified the hysteria that led to lynching, which while illegal was rarely punished.

During the 1960s and early 1970s, executions across the country were halted as public support for capital punishment fell and several cases challenging it wound their way through the courts. One of these cases involved a mentally disabled Black man on Georgia's Death Row named William Henry Furman who broke into the home of a white family in Savannah. When the father woke up and came downstairs, Furman fled through the back door, tripped and fell, discharging the gun he carried and killing the man.[11] He appealed the sentence and in 1972, the Supreme Court ruled 5–4 that the death penalty was imposed with such randomness that it violated the 8th Amendment prohibition against cruel and unusual punishment. Some justices, at least those in the majority, were also concerned about the disproportionate number of Black men on Death Rows across the country but found that the statistics alone did not prove racial bias. In his majority opinion, Justice Potter Stewart wrote:

> These death sentences are cruel and unusual in the same way that being struck by lightning is cruel and unusual. For, of all the people convicted of rapes and murders in 1967 and 1968, many just as reprehensible as these, the petitioners are among a capriciously selected random handful upon whom the sentence of death has in fact been imposed. My concurring Brothers have demonstrated that, if any basis can be discerned for the selection of these few to be sentenced to death, it is the constitutionally impermissible basis of race [see *McLaughlin v. Florida*, [McLaughlin v. Florida 379 U.S. 184] (1964)]. But racial discrimination has not been proved, and I put it to one side. I simply conclude that the Eighth and Fourteenth Amendments cannot tolerate the infliction of a sentence of death under legal systems that permit this unique penalty to be so wantonly and so freakishly imposed.

The ruling reversed all 630[12] death sentences in the country and temporarily halted any new ones while states rewrote their laws to

---

11 The National Constitution Center, "On this day, Supreme Court temporarily finds death penalty unconstitutional," June 29, 2022. https://constitutioncenter.org/interactive-constitution/blog/on-this-day-supreme-court-temporarily-finds-death-penalty-unconstitutional

12 *"Furman v Georgia."* https://en.wikipedia.org/wiki/Furman_v._Georgia#:~:text=Georgia%2C%20408%20U.S.%20238%20(1972,majority%20writing%20a%20separate%20opinion.

comply with the ban on a random imposition of the death penalty. To that end, legislators in North Carolina at first required the death penalty for all first-degree murders, and when that was ruled unconstitutional, they set up a system that required prosecutors to seek the death penalty in murders that met at least one of 11 aggravating factors. Executions resumed in North Carolina in 1984 and since then 42 men and one woman[13] have been put to death. North Carolina reformed its capital punishment system again in 2001, giving prosecutors more discretion both to seek a prison sentence instead of the death penalty and to negotiate pleas. Legislators also banned the death penalty for defendants with intellectual disabilities. Despite these reforms, the central question remains of whether North Carolina's death penalty is fairly applied. In *Deadly Justice, A Statistical Portrait of the Death Penalty*,[14] University of North Carolina politics professor Frank R. Baumgartner and his coauthors say no. They make the case that in the 27 states including North Carolina that allow the death penalty, the discretion given to prosecutors, accidents of geography, and the deep-seeded racism that infects our justice system mean that arbitrary factors separate those on Death Row from the thousands of others imprisoned for murder.

I have seen the random nature of this system up close through my reporting over nearly 20 years on the case of Darryl Hunt, a Black man wrongly convicted in the murder of a white newspaper editor in Winston-Salem.[15] The victim, Deborah Sykes, was attacked on her way to work early one morning in August 1984, raped and stabbed 13 times in a crime that clearly fit the legal standard for punishment by death. After years of studying this case, it's clear to me that racial bias infected it at every

---

13 NC Department of Public Safety, "List of Persons Executed." https://www.ncdps. gov/our-organization/adult-correction/prisons/death-penalty/list-persons-executed/executions-1984-present.

14 Baumgartner, *Deadly Justice: A Statistical Portrait of the Death Penalty.*

15 Zerwick, Phoebe. *Beyond Innocence: The Life Sentence of Darryl Hunt.* New York: Atlantic Monthly Press, 2022.

level, fueling the hysteria over the crime, leading to the rush to judgment once Hunt was arrested, and keeping him imprisoned for 19 years despite overwhelming evidence of his innocence. In interviews long after the verdict, I learned from the foreman that the jury was never fully persuaded of Hunt's guilt. When they could not agree that the evidence against Hunt met the legal standard of "guilty beyond a reasonable doubt," they compromised by convicting him then saving him from Death Row with a sentence of life in prison. Had they followed the law, the lingering doubt would have led to an acquittal, but in this case, as in so many, the decision seems to have been driven more by emotion than by reason. It took 19 years for Hunt to be exonerated by DNA evidence that identified the real killer. After his release in 2003, Hunt went on to become an advocate for social justice, using his story to show the unfairness inherent in the system. Ultimately, the full trauma of the injustice he endured caught up with him and in 2016 he died by suicide. While Hunt never served time on Death Row, I see his tragic death as part of a capricious legal system that claimed his life and those of so many others.

In North Carolina, executions have been put on hold since 2006 while the courts resolve a series of lawsuits that challenge the state's method of lethal injection. Lawyers for those on Death Row argued that the three-drug cocktail the state used did not work as intended, with those condemned often suffering a painful death. Soon after, the N.C. State Medical Board threatened to revoke the license of any doctor who monitored an execution, as required by state law, because doing so violated the most basic tenet of medical ethics to do no harm. Litigation over lethal injection is still pending.

In 2009, the General Assembly took a hard look at the racial bias in capital cases and passed the Racial Justice Act, which allowed those on Death Row to appeal their sentence if they could show discrimination in their case. The law explicitly allowed defendants to back their claims with statistics about the race of victims, defendants and, as importantly, of jurors. In other words, they no longer needed to prove racist intent. A pattern of bias was enough. Darryl Hunt lobbied tirelessly for the law, with his case a clear example of racial bias both in the decision by the prosecutor to seek death and during jury selection. So far, four death sentences have been overturned and replaced with sentences of life without parole. In 2013, after Republican legislators won majorities in both houses, the Legislature repealed the Racial Justice Act, but two years ago, the N.C. Supreme Court ruled that the cases filed before that repeal could go forward. Most of the 135 on Death Row, including the four authors in this book, have racial bias claims pending.

North Carolina courts continue to sentence people to Death Row, but the numbers are falling, with 16 death sentences since the last execution in 2006.[16] Public support for the death penalty is also falling. A 2019 poll by Public Policy Polling[17] found that three quarters of North Carolinians reject death as a punishment for murder, preferring instead life in prison or some combination of prison, work, and restitution. Those polled said they worried about racial bias and the risk of executing an innocent person. That risk is no longer theoretical. Across the country, 189 men have been exonerated from Death Row.[18] Most have been proven innocent by DNA testing. In North Carolina, which ranks fourth after Florida, Illinois and Texas, 12 men on Death Row have been exonerated. As with so much about capital punishment, Black people are at greatest risk of landing on Death Row for someone else's crime than anyone else. All but one exonerated from North Carolina's Death Row was a person of color.[19]

16 NC Department of Public Safety, "Death Row Roster." https://www.ncdps.gov/our-organization/adult-correction/prisons/death-penalty/death-row-roster
17 Robinson, "Death Penalty in North Carolina, 2021."
18 Death Penalty Information Center, "Policy Issues: Innocence." https://deathpenaltyinfo.org/policy-issues/innocence.
19 North Carolina Center for Alternatives to the Death Penalty, "Innocent People are Sentenced to Death." https://nccadp.org/reasons-to-end-the-death-penalty/innocence/

Guilty of nothing except perhaps bad luck, these men lost more than 157[20] years of their lives, years they will never regain. It's hard to know with certainty if any of the 135 on Death Row today are wrongly convicted, but there's a good chance some are. Recent studies suggest that as many as 4 percent[21] of those on Death Rows are innocent, which means that in North Carolina we run the real risk of executing more than one innocent man or woman. It also means the real perpetrator of a crime that a prosecutor and a jury determined was worthy of the most severe punishment our system provides has gone unpunished.

The last person executed in North Carolina was a man from Clemmons named Samuel Flippen, who was sentenced in the murder of his 2-year-old stepdaughter. Flippen maintained his innocence all along. Lawyers have now turned up evidence of wrongful conviction and the girl's father also questions whether the right person was punished for his daughter's death, but the chance of correcting these errors has long passed. Flippen died by lethal injection in August 2006,[22] just weeks before his 37th birthday. May his execution be the last.

PHOEBE ZERWICK
Author of *Beyond Innocence: The Life Sentence of Darryl Hunt*

20 *Ibid.*

21 Gross, Samuel R., et. al. "Rate of False Conviction of Criminal Defendants Sentenced to Death," *The Proceedings of the National Academy of Sciences*, vol. 11, no. 20 (May 20, 2014), https://www.pnas.org/doi/full/10.1073/pnas.1306417111

22 Hewlett, Michael. "Nearly 15 years ago, Samuel Flippen was executed for his stepdaughter's death. Now girl's father wants answers about his daughter's death," *Winston-Salem Journal*, June 9, 2021. https://journalnow.com/news/local/crime-and-courts/nearly-15-years-ago-samuel-flippen-was-executed-for-stepdaughters-death-now-girls-father-wants/article_42589a92-c954-11eb-8cbc-673e2629c15c.html

Listen to the Authors

George T. Wilkerson reads "Limp Gray Fur"
https://soundcloud.com/user-642844422/wilkerson

Terry Robinson, a.k.a. Chanton, reads "Boondocks Country"
https://soundcloud.com/user-642844422/robinson

Michael J. Braxton, a.k.a. Rrome Alone, a.k.a. Alim, reads
    "Letter from Alim"
https://soundcloud.com/user-642844422/braxton

Lyle C. May reads "Learning to Die"
https://soundcloud.com/user-642844422/lylecmay

Discussion Questions

George T. Wilkerson

1   Some people might point to George's abusive childhood as the reason he ended up on Death Row. Others may say that despite his past, he is still responsible for his actions as an adult. What do you think?

2   In "Missed Amends," George and Mike fight back against their dad, after which he says, "Finally...my boys have become men." What does this say about cultural expectations of masculinity? How do you think these words affected George's ideas about being a man?

3   In "The Huggy Boys," George reflects on the possibility of his own execution: "Would my family come witness my final moments? Would I want them to?" If you were executed, would you want your family present? Why or why not?

4   Do you think it's appropriate that the victim's families and the families of people on Death Row are permitted to witness executions? Do you think members of the general public should be allowed to witness executions? Why or why not?

5   George writes, "[In prison] we avoid touching one other emotionally the same way we avoid seeing each other naked, and for almost the same reasons." What do you think he means by this? Why do you think that in prison, a place where many are starved for human contact, many residents might avoid connecting with people around them?

6 In "The Huggy Boys," George realizes that although he'd considered himself a person of few emotions, his intellect was actually enslaved by emotions. What does this say about human behavior? Do you notice people around you being this way? Do you notice yourself being this way sometimes?

7 In "Limp Gray Fur," George reflects, "I want to feel that I'm no longer the scared little boy who entered prison quick to fight battles with fists, but am now the man of God I claim to be—a man who is quicker to forgive than to fight, though no less scared sometimes. Maybe I'm scared to find out I haven't changed that much." Why do you think he's afraid to discover he might not have changed? Do you think there's something else he may actually be scared of?

8 In "Vacant Lots and Aviaries," prison administrators deny requests for educational opportunities because people on Death Row "are not here to be rehabilitated." Do you think rehabilitation should be a goal of the prison system? Why or why not? How about for those on Death Row?

9 In "Vacant Lots and Aviaries," George says, "Our identity is an empty lot onto which we can build anything we wish, but if we don't fill it ourselves, somebody will fill it for us." What does he mean when he writes, "we realized that by default, many somebodies had already filled it while we stood by in ignorance"? To what extent do you feel that others create your identity? What steps have you taken to create your own identity?

10 In "Vacant Lots and Aviaries," George mentions reading the memoir of an incarcerated science teacher who noted that wildlife "stayed true to itself" whether inside prison confines or out. Do you think you would be able to transcend prison life by staying connected to your true self? If yes, how would you do so? If no, why not?

Terry Robinson, a.k.a. Chanton

1 In "A Letter to My Son," Chanton writes, "It's the belief that prisons are dangerous that makes the people in prison act poorly to protect

themselves." How do our ideas about our environments affect how we act in them? When do you feel you have to protect yourself?

2   In "Salvation," Chanton describes his first days on Death Row. Is his depiction of Death Row what you expected? In what ways is it different?

3   "Chatty" describes Chanton's first encounter with his granddaughter. What do you think it would be like for people you know to continue their lives—getting married, having children, etc.—without you being closely involved? If you have experienced this before, how can you relate to Chanton? How might it be different for him?

4   In "Mending Fences," Chanton states that until 2016, men on North Carolina's Death Row were permitted only one ten-minute phone call per year. If you had only ten minutes per year to speak to a loved one, who would you call? What would you say?

5   In "Boondocks Country: A Eulogy from Death Row," Chanton writes, "I believe that all people are inherently good and that even our worst mistakes can invoke positive change." Do you share Chanton's beliefs? Do you believe there's such a thing as a truly unredeemable person? Who do you feel has a chance to redeem themselves, and what might that look like?

6   In "Life over Law," Chanton states, "Adam wasn't killed because he had a gun. He died because of a systematic imbalance that holds some people's lives with the highest regard while dismissing the humanity of others." Do you agree or disagree? Why?

7   Do you think it's appropriate for police to use force against people exuding "typical suspect behavior"? Why or why not? How does "typical suspect behavior" differ with regards to race, age, ability, gender, sexual orientation, and neighborhood?

8   If you were locked away from the world for sixteen years and then let out for one afternoon, what do you think you would notice first? What would you notice most?

9   In "Humanity Undenied," Chanton describes an interaction with a hospital nurse: "there was a politeness and professionalism in her disregard for me that did not seem spiteful. As quickly as the thought entered my mind, I realized that my lesson in being dehumanized had already taken effect." What does he mean by this? How can politeness and professionalism dehumanize others?

10 In "Humanity Undenied," Chanton writes that Death Row isn't a place that lacks humanity, "it is where humanity is rediscovered and restored. On Death Row, the meaningfulness of life tremendously exceeds the inevitability of death." What do you think he means by this? If confronted with a death sentence, how do you think you would find meaning in life?

Michael J. Braxton, a.k.a. Rrome Alone, a.k.a. Alim

1   In what ways does Alim's story illustrate the school-to-prison pipeline?

2   Alim spent much of his childhood minimizing his Blackness when he was with white people and minimizing his whiteness when he was with Black people. In what places and at what times does American culture encourage this kind of code-switching? When do you find yourself code-switching?

3   In "The Top One Percent," Alim describes a moment during his trial where he learned for the first time that he had scored in the top one percent of students in fifth grade. His grades later plummeted due to violence and instability in his school and neighborhood. How much do you think the environment in which children learn affects their performance? Should this information be considered at criminal trials?

4   At trial, Alim was given an execution date of February 8, 1998. (The date was extended due to court appeals). How would it feel to know your date of death? If you had only a few months left to live while incarcerated, how would you spend them?

5   In Alim's letter to Tessie, he likens himself to Kunta Kinte, a slave who spent years defying his captors only to accept servitude in the end. Why do so many people—both those within the system and those upholding it—come to accept captivity and injustice? Is it the same for white people as it is for people of color?

6   In his letter to Tessie, Alim writes, "I could easily mask my vulnerabilities. I could mask my exhaustion. But I choose to let you hear and see the tired, beaten down Alim." Why do you think he wants this part of himself to be seen? How does that kind of vulnerability change a friendship or relationship? Have you experienced this before?

7   In "Life after Death," Alim describes his former code of ethics as one where "convicts laid down the law, and every man was his own sheriff. To ensure security, anyone who violated my law could not be left unpunished—and the more severe the penalty, the greater the respect." How might this code of ethics contribute to cycles of violence in communities, especially for those who've done their time and been released? Consider the code of ethics in one of the spaces where you interact with others—the workplace, school, home, the grocery store, etc. Who administers punishment or consequences for breaking the code? How does this compare and contrast with Alim's former code of ethics?

8   In "Hip Hop: Live from Death Row," Alim describes his journey to record music from inside prison. Why are creative outlets so important in a place like Death Row? How might it be difficult to have a creative outlet while in prison? How was it difficult for Alim?

9   In "The Phoenix," Alim writes, "Reflecting on the past, I saw that I had revised some of my memories to help me cope with pain or to give me a false sense of security. Instead of acknowledging fear or shame as drivers of my behavior, I had justified my actions with excuses that made me look strong and courageous. I'd repeated these revised accounts so many times that in some cases, the real truth was

pushed beneath my consciousness, and I had come to believe the invented versions." Can you relate to any of this in your own journey towards maturity and healing? Have you changed any of your own memories to fit a certain view of yourself?

10 Alim writes that he learned to forgive white people who had harmed him because "just as I had told myself revised accounts of the truth, [white people] had convinced themselves that being white made them something other than who they really were." How does this attitude contribute to ongoing racism in the United States? What can be done about it? What is Alim implying about who white people "really" are?

Lyle C. May

1 In "Namaste," Lyle writes that during his time in a mental hospital, "they pumped me full of drugs, stood me on my feet, spun me around three times, and pushed me back out into the world, a place that was too bright and shiny for my darkened eyes." How do you think the mental health system, or other systems or programs, could help patients with their transition back into society? In Lyle's case, how do you think the mental hospital should have treated him? What other systems fail the people they are built to help?

2 Lyle admits in "Namaste" that his girlfriend's abortion had a much more significant effect on him than he had originally thought, and that it led to his self-mutilation. Why do you think it took Lyle so long to realize this? In what ways do we tend to overlook the causes of our own mental health problems?

3 In "All That Remained," Lyle describes a suicide attempt in jail. After the failed attempt, he was taken to the mental health unit, stripped naked, and forced to earn back his clothing piece by piece by assuring a mental health professional that he was no longer suicidal. Why do you think this type of treatment is considered acceptable for people in prison? How does reading about it make you feel?

4   Do you believe that keeping incarcerated people in solitary confinement is necessary or ethical? Why or why not?

5   What do you think it would be like to sit on a jury at a capital trial? How would you feel if you and eleven others had to decide whether a stranger should live or die?

6   In "Learning to Die," Lyle says that in November and December of 2003, four men were executed while four more were removed Death Row and resentenced to life in prison. In the United States, 65% of death sentences are overturned, usually after the defendant has spent decades in prison. What does this say about our death penalty system? Do you think the system should change? Why or why not? If so, how?

7   Do you think people on Death Row should have access to higher education and rehabilitative programs? Why or why not?

8   In "A Confirmation of Faith," Lyle describes the search for faith on Death Row as "a need that folds the body around it until ordinary thought becomes impossible." What does this mean to you? Why do you think faith is so important to many people on Death Row?

9   What was your reaction to Lyle's description of the "celebratory meal" laid out for correctional officers before each execution?

10 Elias Syriani was put to death in 2005 even though his children, who were also the victim's family, begged the governor for clemency. Do you think victims' families should have a say about whether someone is executed or not? Why do you think they so often don't?

Tessie Castillo

1   What surprised you most about the stories you read in this book? Did any of them resonate with you? Which ones and how?

2   In "Gifts," Tessie states that she didn't want the book project "to be another example of a white professional making decisions for people with lived experience." What do you think she meant by this? Where do you see these types of power dynamics play out in your life?

3   In "Gifts," Tessie writes that "the mere fact I could choose to walk away from Death Row invoked a responsibility to stay." Would you have felt the same way? To what extent do people outside the carceral system have a responsibility to the people inside? What does that responsibility look like?

4   In "Full Circle," Tessie explains that in North Carolina, people convicted of violent crime are legally prohibited from contacting victims' families even to express remorse. She herself was advised not to reach out to victims' families to ask for their input on the book. What are some of the benefits and drawbacks of policies like this? If you were or have been a victim of violent crime, would you want to speak to the person who hurt you? Why or why not?

5   In her argument for restorative justice, Tessie writes, "By focusing exclusively on punishment and ignoring critical components such as atonement and healing for all parties, we risk enabling more people to hurt and to be hurt. We exacerbate conditions like poverty, unemployment, homelessness, mental health disorders, and trauma, all of which serve as lighter fluid for crime." Do you agree with this statement? Why or why not? What are some ways we can break the cycle of violence?

6   Do you think the criminal legal system should strive for inward accountability, such as remorse and atonement, as well as outward accountability, such as prison and punishment, for crimes? Why do you think the focus of the current criminal legal system is, by and large, only on outward accountability?

7   Tessie describes her vision of a just world: "We want society to stop responding to the agony of murder by burying one person, warehousing the other, and leaving loved ones on both sides reeling from grief... We want everyone impacted by crime to face each other, not on two sides of a chalk line, but in a full circle, where we recognize that one break means rupture for us all." How is "one break... rupture

for us all"? How do we recognize others' humanity? Is this a goal you think we should have? What is your vision of a just world?

8 In "Unpacking the Death Penalty," Tessie explains that the death penalty is not, in fact, always reserved for the worst of the worst crimes. Was this a surprise to you? Do you think the criminal legal system should change because of this? Why or why not? If so, how?

9 Do you research candidates' positions on the death penalty before elections, including judges and district attorneys? Why or why not? Where can this information be found?

10 How has this book changed your understanding of people in prison and on Death Row? How have your ideas about the criminal legal system changed, if at all? What are some of the main things you learned?

Acknowledgments

Michael J. Braxton, a.k.a. Rrome Alone, a.k.a. Alim
I begin by giving all praise to Allah and prayers and salutations to His Prophet Muhammad.

Also, I thank my mother for her unconditional love and support in my darkest and brightest moments. I thank my brother, Chris, and my deceased sister, Keisha, for loving and believing in me. I also thank my wife, Jeannie Bunch, for her love and commitment to me.

To my team: Michael Betts, Mark Katz, Nick Neutronz, and Anthony "Wordsmith" Parker. Thanks for believing in me. And to all my people on the inside and all the believers—I see you.

Also, thanks to all the editors who pored over my words and helped to hone them into what they are now. Thanks to all the book club participants and to everyone who has shown me support.

Last but not least, shout-out to Dr. Peter Kuhns. None of this would have been possible without you.

Tessie Castillo
It is hard to believe that a chance meeting at a Super Bowl party years ago would lead to a book with such a profound impact on so many lives. It has been an honor to collaborate with four remarkable men on Death Row as we have appraised each other's writing, weathered each other's emotional storms, and maintained friendships despite all odds.

Throughout this process, I've learned more than I ever wanted to know about the death penalty. Yet there is so much more to learn about the forgotten people on Death Row and the flawed system that puts them there.

I'd first like to thank Dr. Peter Kuhns for offering me the opportunity to volunteer inside Central Prison in Raleigh, North Carolina. His kindness and belief in the humanity of those on Death Row is legendary.

I thank my incredible team of volunteers who typed up each handwritten essay from my coauthors and whose feedback helped shape this book. I've supervised many volunteers in my life, and I don't hesitate to say this is the most sincere and dedicated group I've ever worked with. Thank you, Ian, Emma, Nancy, Elizabeth, Alaina, Simone, Georgia, Ron, Carol, Lorraine, Julie, Amelia, Angie, Mina, and Marcia. Special thanks to Michael Betts for his help with the audio recording, to Kat Bodrie for her sharp editing eye, and to Amy Trojanowski, who went above and beyond the call of duty and without whom many aspects of this book would not have been possible.

In writing the book, I am indebted to Dr. Frank Baumgartner and his coauthors for the research and painstaking attention to detail that went into publishing *Deadly Justice: A Statistical Portrait of the Death Penalty*. Their work served as an invaluable research tool to help me navigate the complex world of the capital punishment system.

Most importantly, thank you to my coauthors for their willingness to expose painful memories and secrets and for inspiring the kind of friendship that transcends all boundaries.

Lyle, thank you for your tireless advocacy for higher education and legal reform.

Alim, thank you for embodying what it means to show vulnerability and to grow as a person.

Chanton, thank you for challenging me to be a braver advocate for people in prison.

George, thank you for believing in this book and for believing in me.

Lyle C. May

This book would not have been possible without the fearlessness of Dr. Peter Kuhns, whose willingness to challenge the valuation of those who are sentenced to death brought him to us. Through Dr. Kuhns and his therapeutic programs on Death Row, we met Tessie and began this journey!

To my many mentors, teachers, and friends: your influence has been critical to my growth and maturation as a writer.

To my parents: never underestimate the importance of the lessons you provided or your successes in parenting. It may have taken a while, but they eventually became the foundation of the man I am today.

Special thanks to God, my strength in the valley of the shadow, showing me the way when despair overwhelms. Your will be done in all things.

Terry Robinson, a.k.a. Chanton

To my momma, Mary Hoskins, for her undying love and support though my best and worst of times.

To Aunt Patsy, who continuously reminds me to keep my faith in God yet be ready to fight my battles in his stead.

To Kim Carter for never letting me get down on myself and for her belief in my talent as a writer, and to Reverend Cari Willis for her patience to walk with me through this journey that came with its share of setbacks and tears.

To my family and friends, many of whom were the subject matter in my stories—without you, I am a blank page. And special thanks to Lynden Harris, Peter Kuhns, Jennifer Thompson, Jonathan Hartgrove, Ms. J. Demetral, and many others for your work on advocacy, abolition, and prison reform.

Shout-out to my co-authors for seeing this project through. Fellas, we did the damn thang.

And to Tessie Castillo, without whom none of this would be possible, thank you for believing in our shared humanity.

George T. Wilkerson

First, I want to acknowledge God for guiding us through this process, for making this book possible.

I then wish to thank my coauthors for everyone's hard work and commitment to see this through—you've all earned my utmost respect.

Finally, I wish to thank all the volunteers who have given generously of their time, energy, knowledge, and other resources to help bring the book to fruition, and also to further the mission.

About the Authors

MICHAEL J. BRAXTON, also known as ALIM, is a rapper and spiritual leader on North Carolina's Death Row. Known as RROME ALONE in the music world, he has the distinction of being the only rapper in the world to release music from Death Row. His debut album, *Mercy on my Soul*, is available through NU Revolution Entertainment. You can find him on Facebook, Youtube, and Instagram @rromealone.

TESSIE CASTILLO is an author, journalist and public speaker who specializes in stories on prison reform, drug policy, restorative justice, and racial equity. Her first book, *Crimson Letters: Voices from Death Row*, was a finalist for the 2021 Eric Hoffer award for excellence in small press publishing. Castillo has received the **Victor Hassine Memorial Scholarship at American University** for using creative work to educate the public on criminal justice issues. She lives in Durham, North Carolina with her daughter. To see more of her writings or to request a speaking engagement with her and her co-authors, visit www.tessiecastillo.com.

LYLE C. MAY is a prison journalist, abolitionist, Ohio University alum, and member of the Alpha Sigma Lambda Honor Society. While he pursues every legal avenue to overturn his wrongful conviction and death sentence, Lyle advocates for greater access to higher education in prison. His fight is that of millions, and while the opposition is strong, his desire for equal justice is stronger. His book, *Witness: An Insider's Narrative of the Carceral State*, will be published by Haymarket Books in 2023. To read more of Lyle's writing, visit scalawagmagazine.org.

TERRY ROBINSON, also known as CHANTON, is a writer who has been incarcerated on North Carolina's Death Row since 2000. He believes in the power of words and uses his writing to tear down the walls in his everyday life that are meant to restrict and deter the expression of his humanity. Chanton is a believer in faith, health, and wellness. He is family oriented and native to Wilson, North Carolina. He enjoys reading, writing, sports, and chess and is an avid role-playing member of Dungeons and Dragons. His work is featured on the blog *Walk in Those Shoes*, where he is also an active member of the nonprofit organization by the same name. He is currently working on his first solo book project, *Born to the Devil*, an urban fantasy novel, and his memoir, *Tales from the Hood: A Road Map to Death Row*. He is currently fighting a wrongful conviction and ceaselessly maintains his innocence.

GEORGE T. WILKERSON is an award-winning poet, writer, and artist on North Carolina's Death Row. His poetry has appeared in *Poetry, Bayou Magazine, Prime Number Magazine,* and elsewhere. His essays and stories have appeared in *Crimson Letters: Voices from Death Row, The Marshall Project,* the PEN anthology *The Named and the Nameless,* the anthology *Right Here, Right Now,* and elsewhere. He has won three PEN awards, has edited the anthology *You'll Be Smarter than Us,* and is editor of *Compassion,* a newsletter by and for Death Row prisoners in America. His poetry collection *Interface,* published by BleakHouse Publishing, won the 2022 Victor Hassine Memorial Scholarship and was a finalist in the 2018 Cathy Smith Bowers Chapbook Contest and the 2019 Press 53 Poetry Book Contest. His collaborative, hybrid collection *Bone Orchard,* also from BleakHouse Publishing, examines the differences between doing time with a release date and having a death sentence. To read George's writing, visit katbodrie.com/georgewilkerson.

Note from the Authors

Inside: Voices from Death Row is much more than just a book. It is a collaborative project that challenges everyone to connect and engage with people behind bars. Reading this book is a first step to overcoming the myths and stereotypes about people on Death Row, but we hope that your journey with us is only beginning.

If you'd like to meet Tessie, George, Chanton, Alim, and Lyle, we invite you to join our online book club. At each virtual meeting (hosted by Tessie), the coauthors call in from Death Row for a powerful Q&A session with the group—here is your chance to ask all those burning questions! The book club is free and open to anyone.

The coauthors are also available for speaking engagements. At each event, George, Chanton, Alim or Lyle call in from prison to engage the audience in eye-opening conversations on a range of topics, including criminal legal reform, the death penalty, restorative justice, solitary confinement, life on Death Row, and much more.

It is critically important for people impacted by the legal system to share their stories and experiences in their own words. When we see, hear, and witness the humanity of people behind bars, our assumptions and stereotypes are challenged in powerful ways.

To join the book club or inquire about speaking engagements with the coauthors, please visit tessiecastillo.com.

We can't wait to hear from you!

With gratitude,

TESSIE, GEORGE, CHANTON, ALIM, and LYLE

First printing
ISBN   978-1-7329328-6-9

PREVIOUS PUBLICATIONS. Many of the essays in this book appeared previously in *Crimson Letters*, published by Black Rose Writing. The following essays by George T. Wilkerson have previously appeared in the following publications: "Court Kings and Flight Lessons," *Visiting the Blues: 2021 Prison Writing Awards Anthology* (PEN America); "She Thought She Could Hug Me," *Interface* (BleakHouse Publishing, 2022); "The Huggy Boys," *Bone Orchard: Reflections on Life under Sentence of Death* (BleakHouse Publishing, 2022); "Limp Gray Fur," *The Named and the Nameless: 2018 Prison Writing Awards Anthology* (PEN America); "Vacant Lots and Aviaries," *Visiting the Blues: 2021 Prison Writing Awards Anthology* (PEN America).

DESIGN. Text and titles in Arno. Cover and interior design by Andrew Saulters. Scuppernong Editions colophon by Rachel York.

Scuppernong Editions offers the occasional publication of adventuresome, commercially questionable writing in all genres.

Scuppernong Editions
304 South Elm Street
Greensboro, NC 27401